ELIZABETH BARRETT

TO

MISS MITFORD

ELIZABETH BARRETT
to
MISS MITFORD

THE UNPUBLISHED LETTERS OF
ELIZABETH BARRETT BARRETT
TO MARY RUSSELL MITFORD
EDITED AND INTRODUCED BY
BETTY MILLER

LONDON
JOHN MURRAY, ALBEMARLE ST
1954

*The manuscripts of this correspondence
are in the possession of the Library of
Wellesley College, Massachusetts*

FIRST EDITION, 1954
MADE AND PRINTED IN GREAT BRITAIN
BY R. & R. CLARK, LTD., EDINBURGH, AND PUBLISHED BY
JOHN MURRAY (PUBLISHERS) LTD., LONDON

CONTENTS

*

ILLUSTRATIONS

*

* From *Mary Russell Mitford* by W. J. Roberts, *by courtesy of Andrew Melrose.*
     † *By courtesy of the British Museum.*

§ *Erratum.* The description under the illustration
should read as above.

INTRODUCTION

*

In the opinion of Mary Russell Mitford, all 'literary ladies' were ugly. 'I never met one in my life', she wrote, 'that might not have served for a scarecrow to keep the birds from the cherries.' Fourteen years later, she was to revise this opinion at her first sight of Elizabeth Barrett : a young woman, she said, 'who is so sweet and gentle, and so pretty, that one looks at her as if she were some bright flower'. This 'delightful young creature'—her immaturity proved to be no less deceptive than her air of docility—was, at the time of the encounter, a woman of thirty. Miss Mitford, unmarried ('A good-humoured ~~very likeable~~ very likeable person'), was in her fiftieth year. Although her best work was already done, her fame, established on the delightful rural sketches of *Our Village*, and, less securely, upon tragedies like *Julian* and *Rienzi*, was such that when in May 1836, she left her cottage at Three Mile Cross for a visit to London, she had to refuse over thirty invitations to dinner, and so many celebrated men and women crowded in to see her and to talk to her that a friend remarked, so she told her father, 'that he never saw any one received with such a mixture of respect and enthusiasm as I have been—not even Madame de Staël'. Elizabeth Barrett, on the other hand, an aspiring poetess whose major work was yet to come, was totally obscure. *An Essay on Mind*, published anonymously in 1826, and the *Prometheus Bound* of seven years later, attracted little attention and less enthusiasm. Country-born, she had lived almost all her life in the seclusion of the lovely Hope End estate, near Malvern ; and then, when financial reverses forced the family out of that domestic stronghold, in a no less provincial serenity beneath the mild skies and encircling hills of Sidmouth, in Devon. When she met Miss Mitford, therefore, Elizabeth was still a newcomer to the capital; for it was at the end of the previous summer, uprooting the modest intimacies lately formed at Sidmouth, that Mr. Moulton Barrett had brought a large family of sons and daughters to London, to install them, reluctant but acquiescent, in a musty furnished house in Gloucester Place, near Baker Street. Here, in the unfriendly solitude of the 'peopled town' Elizabeth saw even fewer people than at Sidmouth or at Hope End; and this seclusion might have become more rigorous still, if it had not been for the intervention of one whose influence was to prove of major importance and benefit to her throughout the rest of her life. Claiming the privileges of cousinship, of a common West Indian background, John Kenyon, a wealthy widower in his fiftieth year, a man with 'the face of a Benedictine monk, and the joyous talk of a good fellow', introduced himself to the mysteriously cloistered family of Edward Moulton Barrett. Described as 'the most admired and courted man in town', a minor poet possessed of major means, this benevolent dilettante entertained at his house in Harley Place all the outstanding literary celebrities of the day. ('He delights', wrote Crabb Robinson, 'in seeing at his hospitable table every variety of literary notabilities, and therefore has been called "a feeder of lions".') His kindly attempts, however, to draw his talented cousin into this circle met with little success, for Elizabeth's social immaturity caused her to refuse all such invitations in a state of frank and unsimulated panic. It was with the utmost difficulty that she was prevailed upon to meet the celebrated authoress of *Our Village*, and six years later (see the letter of April 1842) she was to describe, to her 'ever dearest Miss Mitford', the agonies she endured while waiting for the sound of carriage wheels drawing up outside the front door of 74 Gloucester Place. The dreaded encounter took place on the afternoon of May 27, 1836. 'Mr. Kenyon is to call for me at half past two and take me to see the Giraffes and the Diorama',[1] Miss Mitford had written to her father the previous day: and accordingly, in a hired carriage ('How strange that there are no horses!'),[2] the rubicund Miss Mitford, a complacent Mr. Kenyon, and a pale agitated Miss Barrett set off for the Regent's Park, where the Diorama, in Park Square East, was exhibiting two pictures by Le Chevalier Bouton: the *Village*

[1] MS. letter: Reading Public Library. Omitted from letter of May 26, L'Estrange, *Life of Mary Russell Mitford* (Bentley, 1870). [2] *Ibid.*

of Alagna, in Piedmont, and the *Interior of the Church of Santa Croce* at Florence. Here, amidst the unguarded ejaculations of those 'whom the restraints of *bon-ton*, or of education, have not placed under an habitual controul of the emotions',[1] they watched lights twinkling in the cottage windows of Alagna, saw real smoke ascending from its chimneys, and witnessed the total destruction of the village by an avalanche 'so admirably managed as to be almost awful'. The spectacle concluded, making their way, once more, through 'the Cimmerian darkness of the vestibule' into the bright sunlight beyond, they drove on to the Zoological Gardens, where they admired what Leigh Hunt later described as 'three ladylike and most curious giraffes', their faces expressing 'insipidity and indifference', who paraded under the care of 'M. Thibaut in his Arab dress and beard,—the Frenchman who brought them over'.[2] The protective affection of Miss Mitford appears to have inspired in Elizabeth an unwonted boldness, for, rather than miss the opportunity of seeing her again, she consented to dine at Mr. Kenyon's, where, trembling 'both in my soul and body', she met and spoke face to face with William Wordsworth and Walter Savage Landor. Thereafter, Elizabeth saw Miss Mitford 'almost every day of her week's visit to London'. On each occasion it was Mr. Kenyon who fostered, who facilitated the renewal of intimacy. His name recurs constantly in the letters Miss Mitford wrote home to her father. 'Mrs Barnes invited me to go with her to hear the Welsh Bands to-morrow— but I am better engaged, for Mr Kenyon is to come for me to take me at half past twelve to the Exhibition at Somerset House—Mr Lucas is to meet us there—and next day Mr Kenyon is to come for me again, at ½ past two to take me to see the Old Masters at the British Gallery',[3] she wrote. Two days later, on June 1, 1836, she wrote again : a letter (now at Reading) which does not appear in the *Life* : 'This is my last letter to my very dear father—and in a few hours after you receive it I shall have the happiness of embracing you. . . Today has been very agreeable—First to Mr Lucas's, whose

[1] Lady Morgan : *The Diorama*, July 1836 ; *Athenaeum*, August 13, 1836.
[2] 'A Visit to the Zoological Gardens ', *New Monthly Magazine* (August 1836).
[3] Reading Public Library. Omitted by L'Estrange from letter of May 30, 1836.

portrait of Prince George is charming and that of Talfourd a very strong but very flattering likeness. . . Then we went or rather I went with dear Mr Kenyon and sweet Miss Barrett to the British Gallery—the finest exhibition seen for years. . . I ought to have said that after leaving the British Gallery Mr Kenyon had the kindness to take me to leave a card at Lady Dacre's—How invaluable has that dear friend been! How can I ever repay him! There is no one quite like him in all London. . . To-morrow we go to Chiswick, and to Campden Hill (the Duke of Bedford's) in one way—our party is delightful and I promise myself another happy day with dear Mr Wordsworth, Mr Kenyon and Miss Barrett [1] . . . Adieu my own dear father—Tomorrow thank heaven we shall meet—Ever your M R M.'

And so ended 'these happy days'. Mary Russell Mitford returned to a beloved father, a faithful dog, a garden blazing from end to end with geraniums: while Elizabeth Barrett found herself, in Gloucester Place, restored Cinderella-wise to her former isolation. 'All these visions have passed now', she wrote to a friend. 'I see and hear nothing except my doves and the fireplace . . .' But whereas formerly her lament had been that there was no one at all 'literary in any sense' with whom she could converse, now, she had a correspondent who, 'professing to love me, and asking me to write to her', was ready to share with her an all-absorbing love of literature and literary gossip of all kinds. The letters began to fly backwards and forwards between London and Three Mile Cross, and the susceptible Miss Mitford, who had contracted an ardent admiration for the 'virtue and genius' of her new friend, was soon describing her, in letters to other friends, as 'the most remarkable woman probably that ever lived'. To Elizabeth herself she sought to explain more fully the nature of her own preoccupation. 'My love and ambition for you often seems

[1] As well as Wordsworth, Kenyon, and E B B, the party which went to visit the Duke of Devonshire's Palladian Villa at Chiswick consisted, according to other omitted extracts, of Miss Mitford's friend Mrs. Dupuy, William Ogbourn, Walter Savage Landor, and Wordsworth's friends, the Marshalls. ' I shall ask Mrs. Talfourd if she [cares ?] to go—but then she must find her own conveyance. Her dress is really disgraceful—so is her manner. . . .' (Miss Mitford complained, too, that all her money had 'gone in coach hire—for they let me pay when they go with me ! ! !')

to be more like that of a mother for a son, or a father for a daughter (the two fondest of natural emotions) than the common bonds of even a close friendship between two women of different ages and similar pursuits. I sit and think of you, and of the poems that you will write, and of that strange, brief rainbow crown called Fame, until the vision is before me as vividly as ever a mother's heart hailed the eloquence of a patriot son. Do you understand this? and do you pardon it? . . . It is a strange feeling, but one of indescribable pleasure. My pride and hopes seem altogether merged in you.'

Elizabeth's attitude was less complex. Seduced at first by the glamour of a literary reputation, it was the unbounded kindliness of Mary Russell Mitford that won her confidence and affection: and the correspondence reveals a gradual transition (too gradual, alas) from the stilted, arch, and self-conscious manner in which she presumed, at the outset, to address a celebrated woman, to the ease and authority with which, in later years, she upheld her own views and questioned those put forward by her beloved friend. There was plenty of ground for divergence: for, whereas affection could, and did, create its own unity, temperamentally, the two women belonged to opposite poles of experience. Elizabeth Barrett lived in a state of total dependence, physical as well as financial, upon the resources of others. 'Chained to the desk as the galley slave to his oar', Miss Mitford had for many years been the sole financial prop of her own household. Miss Barrett lived 'dark and pallid' in the hothouse atmosphere of a confirmed invalidism: all her colours went into her poetry: the rest of me, she said, 'is nothing but a root, fit for the ground and the dark'. The rosy, bustling Miss Mitford belonged to the garden, to the country, to the open air and the common life of men and animals. My only idea of happiness, wrote the invalid, 'lies deep in poetry and its associations': without such an object in life, she wondered how 'people find it worth while to live at all'. But Miss Mitford had always 'detested' writing: literature, she considered, was 'not a healthy occupation', and she cordially distrusted its practitioners, male and female alike. Born before the end of the eighteenth century, it was to the 'affluent and cultivated gentry of England' that she looked for 'the best class in the whole world': (it seems to me, Elizabeth once told her, that you 'care more for the respect paid to you on mere social grounds, than you care for any acknowledgement of your power as a writer').

Nor could the religious mysticism that was so strong an element in the character of Elizabeth Barrett be expected to appeal to one who had long been content to substitute 'the great precepts of justice and kindness' for 'that entire faith which, in me, *will not* be commanded'.

Deep, however, as were the differences that divided them (deeper, certainly, than Miss Mitford at first suspected), they were drawn together, not only by the force of a strong mutual affection, but by the essential peculiarities of their own domestic situation. Not only was each the daughter, and main emotional resource, of a confirmed widower, but each derived from the position an identical satisfaction: a satisfaction by no means undermined by the fact that at Wimpole Street, as at Three Mile Cross, the head of the family was 'of a temper infinitely difficult to deal with'. Mr. Moulton Barrett, it is well known, did not gladly suffer the stranger within his gate. Dr. Mitford, too, while squandering the money so laboriously accumulated by her pen, was 'constantly taunting' his daughter with those literary friends, 'not of a certain status in the county', whom he chose for that reason to treat with a frank contempt. No intemperance could alienate these devoted daughters. Miss Mitford, who admired her father in strength, was drawn to him equally in weakness: when he is ill, she confessed, 'I love him a million times better than ever, and can quite understand that love of a mother for her first-born, which this so fond dependence produces in the one looked to'. At Wimpole Street, overtly at least, the dependence was never reversed: but that which had always given Mr. Moulton Barrett, as his daughter said, 'the greatest power over my heart', the fact that 'I am of those weak women who reverence strong men', was something that Mary Russell Mitford, with her outspoken contempt for the ineffectual male, fully respected and shared. It is not altogether surprising, under the circumstances, to find in Miss Mitford an impassioned admirer of Napoleon Bonaparte; nor to see Elizabeth Barrett Browning, in later years, fervently applauding the *coup d'état*

xii

and approving the dictatorship of 'le vrai neveu de son oncle', Louis Napoleon.

Although Miss Mitford and Miss Barrett held radically different views on the subject of certain contemporary poets and novelists, affection was not impaired by this conflict of tastes. There was another subject, however, where incompatibility, going deeper, proved to be the submerged rock on which a ten years' friendship seemed likely, at one point, catastrophically to founder. Marriages, wrote Miss Mitford, 'are the most foolish things under sun'. This was not Miss Barrett's opinion, who from girlhood (' "that romantic child!" ') had regarded love and marriage as 'every woman's chief concern', and 'a happy marriage as the happiest state'. Nevertheless, in view of her friend's ill-health, of the condition of total seclusion in which for many years she had chosen to live, Miss Mitford could with reasonable confidence assume that the friendship between them would never be undermined by an interloper from the world of men. Nor could she be expected to know that the first time they took sides for and against the poetry and the personality of Robert Browning, already, many years before he was to call at Wimpole Street, they were exploring, unawares, this latent schism. As if some premonition had guided her, at her first meeting with him (it was on May 26, 1836 : the next day she met Elizabeth Barrett for the first time) Miss Mitford took a violent dislike to the young poet. The following letter makes plain the nature of that dislike.

'I saw Mr Browning once and remember thinking how exactly he resembled a girl drest in boy's clothes—and as to his poetry I have just your opinion of it—It is one heap of obscurity confusion and weakness. . . Do you know him personally? Did you ever see him? I met him once as I told you when he had long ringlets and no neckcloth—and when he seemed to me about the height and size of a boy of twelve years old—Femmelette—is a word made for him. A strange sort of person to carry such a woman as Elizabeth Barrett off her feet.' [1]

[1] February 22, 1847. Mary Russell Mitford to Charles Boner. Extract from MS. letter : Yale University Library.

Wholly unaware of what the future had in store, she sought continually in her letters not only to belittle the poetry of Robert Browning, but to keep Miss Barrett informed of all the disagreeable things she had heard about him. Miss Barrett, on her side, out of an instinctive 'fellow-feeling' for the poet, defended throughout with a singular warmth and vivacity one whom at the time she did not know, 'even', as she said, 'by correspondance'. And when at length, on January 10, 1845, such a correspondence was opened between them, when, a few months later, after his first visit to Wimpole Street, Robert Browning wrote to Elizabeth Barrett an 'intemperate' letter, making her a proposal of marriage, some instinct caused her to conceal from her closest friend both the rapid maturation of intimacy, and its culmination in an all-absorbing mutual passion. It is true that 'on pain of appearing a great hypocrite', as she explained to Browning, she was forced to tell Miss Mitford 'the bare fact of my having seen you'. But after that first, almost inadvertent confession—it is to be found amongst the present series of letters—'never from that time (you grew sacred too soon!), never again from that moment did I mention you to Miss Mitford'. Small wonder, then, that it was with a half-remorseful sense of alarm that she anticipated the moment of revelation. 'No single person will be more utterly confounded than she, when she comes to be aware of what you are to me now.'

Confounded Miss Mitford undoubtedly was. She had left her invalid friend, sofa-bound, as usual, in the secluded room on the second floor; to rediscover her, an energetic and incalculable stranger, who, having harboured all the while the enormity of this relationship (Robert Browning, of all people!), had ruptured, now, the ties of intimacy and of authority alike, and was on her way, a married woman, to a new life in a new land. Although she begged for her friend's sympathy and forgiveness, it is plain that Elizabeth Barrett expected neither. Miss Mitford, she told Browning, 'is one of the Black Stones, which, when I climb up towards my Singing Tree and Golden Water, will howl behind me and call names'.

She did her friend some injustice, perhaps. Miss Mitford's affection seems to have withstood, in the main, the shock of this desertion. (It was not, in any case, on Elizabeth that she sought to pin the blame. 'Women of genius', she later wrote, 'make great mistakes in choosing husbands.') But the friendship itself had received a jar from which it never wholly recovered. It was all very well for Elizabeth to write 'Nothing is changed between us, nothing can ever interfere with sacred confidences': Miss Mitford knew not only what it was that had changed, but who was responsible for the change; and despite the large excisions made in the text of her published letters, it is plain that she was never to succeed in subduing, wholly, her long-standing antipathy to the author of *Paracelsus*. It is difficult, in this connection, not to sympathize with her, for the loss she suffered was in fact a major one. Had she not once said of Elizabeth Barrett, 'Next to my father, she is the one I love best'? Now, Dr. Mitford was dead, and the room at Wimpole Street stood silent and forlorn. Crippled, increasingly, by rheumatism, saddened by the absence in her life of all close domestic ties, Mary Russell Mitford could not but feel, and indeed had already said, that she had no one now but 'Flush to love me, and poor Ben and K' (her servants). She made a brave attempt, nevertheless, to accept the situation and to mask her own feelings. A few months after the marriage: 'The people who know Mr Browning well seem to like him much', she wrote. 'Mr Kenyon, Mr Chorley, Mr Harness —and it is so much to my interest to think well of him, and his dear wife writes of him so magnificently, that I hope in time to forgive even his stealing her away.'

NOTE ON THE LETTERS

*

'I hear from her two or three times a week: and such letters!' wrote Miss Mitford. 'Put Madame de Sevigné and Cowper together, and you can fancy them.' If it were possible, to-day, to discern this high quality in the letters of Elizabeth Barrett, then clearly it would become a duty (not to say a pleasure) to reproduce the correspondence in its entirety. But whatever might be the result of the literary association of Madame de Sévigné with William Cowper, the offspring could bear no very close resemblance to Elizabeth Barrett, whose qualities and defects alike belong wholly to her own century; to her own individual and restrictive circumstances. Those circumstances, which cut her off from almost all contact with the outside world, served to generate in the recluse a potent psychological force; disconcertingly alive, still, in much that she has written. At the same time, the damming up of all normal social outlets led to an inundation in literary channels: when once she began to write, she admitted, it was difficult for her to stop. Ruefully, she compared herself to 'that bewitched broom in the story, which, being sent to draw water, drew bucket after bucket, until the whole house was in flood'.

In order to do justice both to Elizabeth Barrett and to the general reader, it has been found necessary to divert some of this flood, confining the residual waters within the channels of a single-volume edition. There were 430 letters to Miss Mitford in the 'large packet' sold at Sotheby's in 1913 after the death of Pen Browning: of these, 52 were published in 1897 in F. G. Kenyon's two-volume edition of *The Letters of Elizabeth Barrett Browning*. The collection, purchased by Mr. Frank Sabin, and from him by Mr. Ernest Dressel North, was later acquired by Professor George Herbert Palmer of Harvard University, who, in 1930, presented it to the library of Wellesley College, Massachusetts. Of the 381 unpublished letters, a high proportion was found to vary in length between two and four thousand words a letter. Quantity, it became evident, threatened to outweigh quality. It seemed advisable, therefore, to make a selection from the vast bulk of the letters; and, after 142 of these had been retained for use, further to prune some of the weightier or less fruitful proliferations within the selected letters themselves. This task has been carried out regretfully, and not without misgiving, by an editor fully aware that no one can presume to foretell what, from the point of view of a future biographer, may not prove to be the most unkindest cut of all. All such excisions have been indicated by the customary three dots; and the reader is asked to bear in mind that the use of *two* dots within a sentence represents a characteristic of Elizabeth Barrett's own punctuation, and not an omission from the text. Full stops have been substituted for dashes at the end of each sentence, a thicket of exclamation marks thinned out, and contracted words, *wds, cds*, etc., restored to their full proportions. Editorial interpolations are confined to square brackets. In other respects, an attempt has been made to retain, as far as possible, the spelling, alignment and punctuation of the original letters.

The years covered by these letters, 1836–46, were amongst the most significant and formative in the life of Elizabeth Barrett. They saw the growth and establishment of her literary reputation, the capital tragedy of the death of a beloved brother, the incarceration at Wimpole Street, the first meeting with Robert Browning and the whole series of events culminating in a secret marriage and the flight to Italy on September 19, 1846. No other letters introduce us so intimately to the domestic life of Wimpole street, or offer in the process so many rewarding and unexpected glimpses of the resident tyrant on the hearth. At the same time,

> moving thro' a mirror clear
> That hangs before her all the year,
> Shadows of the world appear:

from the darkness of the sick-room, the letters present a curiously bright, oblique reflection of the contemporary scene. 'I made sure of your being charmed by Mrs Browning's letters', wrote Miss Mitford in 1852. 'I have a great basket full of such, for before Mr Browning stole her from me we used to write to each other at least twice a week. . . It was really talk, fireside talk, neither better nor worse, assuming a form of permanence-gossip daguerreotyped.' What we are privileged to overhear in this gossip are the preoccupations, opinions, topics, and scandals that engaged the mind and tongue of literary London during the first nine years of the reign of Queen Victoria.

I wish to put on record my gratitude to the President and Trustees of Wellesley College who kindly gave me permission to edit this collection, and further assisted me by putting at my disposal photostat copies of the E B B letters in their possession. I am no less indebted to Sir John Murray and Mr. John Grey Murray for granting me the necessary privileges of copyright. The Graduate Department and Committee of Yale University Library have kindly given me permission to publish an extract from a letter of Miss Mitford to Charles Boner; and Mr. Stanley H. Horrocks and the Committee of Reading Public Libraries have been equally generous in allowing me to quote from letters of Miss Mitford to her father. To Mrs. Violet Altham I owe the privilege of reproducing an unusual portrait of Edward Moulton Barrett; and the Torquay Natural History Society has also kindly contributed to the illustrations in this book.

In other respects, and for services both various and valuable, my gratitude is due to Miss Hannah French, Research Librarian at Wellesley; to Miss M. Swadling, of Reading Public Library; to Mr. E. S. Murrell of the London Library; to Mr. L. B. Saunders, of Hampstead Public Library; and (once again) to Miss Eirene Skilbeck; as it is, in full measure, to Mrs. Nora Meninsky, for her unflagging interest and assistance in the long and exacting task of sorting, deciphering, re-checking, and typing the letters.

LETTERS

1836-1846

MISS MITFORD'S COTTAGE AT THREE MILE CROSS
From a lithograph, while Miss Mitford was in residence

74 Gloucester Place
Friday morning [*June 3, 1836*]

MY DEAR MISS MITFORD,

I send you the little book.[1] I have been disappointed in not being able to have it bound in time : but I wish that its worst fault were on its outside !

In ending these happy days, you must let me thank you for allowing me to join together two ideas, each of them precious in its kind . . of an admired writer . . and a dear friend—and for allowing me to call them *Miss Mitford*. I thank you for this rather than for your personal and touching kindness to me—because it is easier.

May God bless you and make you happy in your re-union to those dearest to you. You were so kind—I should not have dared to ask it—as to speak of writing to me. Will you write to me dear Miss Mitford, *before* I write to you—and will you do so as soon as you can spare a thought from the nature and affection to which you go, for the *least* important things of London ?

Your affectionate and obliged

E. B. BARRETT

[1] Miss Mitford told a friend in July 1836 that she had seen and admired Miss Barrett's *Essay on Mind* (1826), and her translation of *Prometheus Bound* (1833). (*Life of Mary Russell Mitford*, ed. A. G. L'Estrange, Vol. III, p. 56. Bentley, 1870.) One of these books was sent on this occasion : the other, on June 8, 1836.

74 Gloucester Place
June 8th 1836

It was very kind in my dear friend (I am writing so to Miss Mitford !) to suffer a thought of me to come between her and her dreams on the friday night when she must have been weary, if for nothing else except pleasure. How am I to thank her enough ? Only by loving her—and *that* is done already.

Indeed it does seem to me like a vision—and what a bright

one !—if Guido had painted it, he could not have made its
'singing robes' too gorgeous—that I should know you and be
allowed to love you and write to you and think of you as my
friend. I have had visions before of Miss Mitford. I am a
female Alnaschar for visions, and have broken more wares than
would stock the whole market of Bagdad—and have called
idealities realities all my life long. I have had visions of Miss
Mitford before now—but in *them* I saw her in the village,
loving everybody—not in London loving *me*.

Thank you for your kind sayings about my verses, and for
telling me that you had named me as a 'household word' to
your father—and for letting me *see* the garden, in your words
about it. You *used* it as a 'painter's pallette'—did you not?
You would be quite right, even if in a paroxysm of the 'enthusi-
astic vanity' you liked it *better* than Chiswick and said so. At
least I, for my own pleasure's sake, am like a bird; and would
choose the broad sky for my flight and the high mountains for
my prospe . . . and for a home, a nest just large enough to
hold me. It always seems to me that littleness in the thing
possessed is a kind of test of our really possessing it : and that
by a law of our nature the grasses we walk over, the flowers
we can almost hold in our hand, and the 'one little ewe lamb'
we ourselves feed, are more our very own than 'the flowers of
an hundred parterres', or 'the flocks upon a thousand hills'.
Or else, why when Adam had the whole earth to himself, did
he call only one nook *his own*. Now he *did*—did he not?—you
are sure that he did. And might not Lady Mary Shepherd [1]
ask some deep philosophy on the whys and the wherefores?

She was kind to me during our short intercourse years ago—
but I may confess to you in the midst of the grateful remembrance of the kindness, how she used to – – frighten me more
than any woman I ever knew. There used to be fear for me
even in the pure intellect of her eye. She has uncommon
powers of mind and conversation—and if to the energy and
force of a man's mind, she joined its clearness and compre-
hensiveness, she would be a more distinguished woman than
she is. And dear Miss Shepherd spoke kindly of me ! I know
more of her than of her mother, and not only *therefore* she
interests me more—but I thought she had forgotten all about
me long ago. She has talent, and used to have deep sensibility.

I believe I never exchanged thoughts with a human being whom I was so near loving without actually doing so—or with one, whom I would more gladly see cast at *soul's* length from the defiling dust and emptying emptiness of this London – – from the physical metaphysics of its worldly creed. You will let me scold it, will you not dear Miss Mitford—without shaking your head. And indeed you *cannot* shake your head while all the flowers of your garden are taking my part—and Dash too— who if he comes to London is 'sure to be stolen'! Yet *you* must come to London for the sake of those who are prisoners in it—and to do it justice, I do like it better than I used to like it. Wherever it is possible to think and feel, it is possible to enjoy : and it *is* possible for attaching associations to take root—even on these flagged ways.

Is not the book likely to bring you, in the course of its publication, here again? [2] I hope it may. But don't tell Mr. Mitford that I hope so, for fear he should hate me.

There is another volume of mine going with this letter to teaze you : and Mr. Kenyon [3] *will* have m. to write my contribution [4] to Miss Courtenay's album, on the n. leaf of it— which, if he had not told me to do it, I should think . most as wrong, as making that contribution at all. But he is a di. lt person to say *no* to : and has been besides so very, surprising[ly] kind to me, that every 'no' of mine would sound to me like a separate ingratitude. Yet do not think that the 'yes' was said, when he invited me to know you, because the 'no' was hard to say. Believe me, I have not the sackcloth of that recollection to put on. It was *the party* that I did not like the name of.

Dear Miss Mitford—whenever you are at leisure and inclined to write letters, do remember how much pleasure any words of yours must give to

your grateful and affectionate

E B BARRETT

[1] Lady Mary Shepherd (1777–1847), second daughter of Neil Primrose, third Earl of Rosebery, and author of *An Essay upon the Relation of Cause and Effect Controverting the Doctrine of Mr. Hume*, etc. (1827). *Essays on the Perception of an External Universe* (1827).

[2] Miss Mitford had contracted, for £700, to write a novel for Saunders and Otley. The work remained unwritten for many years.

[3] John Kenyon (1784–1856), author of *A Rhymed Plea for Tolerance* (1833) and *Poems, for the Most Part Occasional* (1838). See Introduction. He was

3

instrumental in introducing Robert Browning to Elizabeth Barrett, and left the couple £11,000 in his will.

⁴ *The Sea-Mew*. 'Affectionately inscribed' to Mary, the small daughter of the Rev. George Barrett Hunter, an Independent minister who met EBB at Sidmouth in 1832 and remained, until her marriage, a close friend, as well as a jealous and exacting admirer. The poem was reprinted in *The Seraphim, and Other Poems* (1838).

74 Gloucester Place
July 9th 1836

You have not my dear kind friend thought me unkind and thankless for not writing my gratitude to you the very moment I felt it, for your books—and for that letter having in it what is in the books and something better and dearer (to *me*!) besides. I am sure you have not. I have waited a little for Mr. Shepherd's tragedy.¹ Mr. Kenyon has promised to lend it to me. And then—or rather in the first place—I waited that I might not be thankful to you for the *one* fact of giving such a present to a person so unworthy of it, but besides for 'the spirit stirring 'neath the leaves' which I wanted time to invoke—for the gracefulness of the poetry, to understand which, it was necessary to give oneself time to read it—*only to read it*. For this I have waited. *Now* I may be grateful to you : and Mr. Shepherd's tragedy shall not make me seem the contrary another moment.

My pencil has marked Emily and Fair Rosamond and Henry Talbot The bridal Eve, The Captive and The masque of the Seasons as chief favorites of mine.² My pencil always does for me the prudent business which beans and pebbles did for the hero of childish romance : marking his footsteps in the wood. My pencil has marked for me many a green path in literature,—for me to tread and retread with a home, appropriating feeling . . as being not only fair but 'fair to *me*'. In these paths, these new paths—thank you dear Miss Mitford for letting me walk in them—I enjoy the greenness and the dew and the repose : or, to use a more defining metaphor, that gentle quiet flowing of the heart along the graceful channel made for it by the intellect, of which we scarcely know whether to say—'how beautiful',—or 'how good'. And so I have recourse to my greeks who when they said 'how beautiful' *meant* 'how good'.

4

You have done better than my greeks in one thing. Plato sent poetry away in despair out of his republic. You have not exiled her from the village. . .

If ever I write parallels in the manner of Plutarch,—and it would be wonderful if all the kindness and praising I am so thankful for and so unworthy of, should let me escape a load of '*presumption enough for anything*',—I shall write a parallel between Miss Mitford and Crabbe.[3] But no!—even if I had presumption for it, I should not have injustice. It would not be fair—would it?—with friendship and gratitude of all kinds towards the one, and . . . . .! towards the other. Not that I ever had any personal knowledge of Mr. Crabbe : but it used to be and is and ever will be an impossibility to me to call him a poet. What he wrote seems to me poetry inverted. It is a dislocation of the uses and object and essentiality of poetry. It is . . as if a portrait painter painted our skeletons. It is a depicturing of our fallen corrupted humanities without their noble self-abjurations and their yearnings after what is not self. But oh !—if after all I should be writing to an admirer of Crabbe. But she is a dear friend of *mine*, who will forgive this with graver faults and not love me less for it and them!

I remember daring to say to Sir Uvedale Price [4] that I could not like Crabbe : and I remember—how well !—his taking the 'Library' from the table and reading from it a passage to which he said his own attention had been directed by Fox, and which I could not choose but acknowledge to be fine poetry. But then—these obstinate people you know are so impossible to convince—I annexed to the acknowledgement a clause—that the passage in question was not written in Crabbe's usual style. And dear Sir Uvedale who was not obstinate, admitted at once that I was right.

If all this is very *wrong*—do forgive it! And while you are forgiving me let me try to say how deeply and truly I thank you for all your affectionateness and kindness to me. I believe I am not naturally unsusceptible to affectionateness even from those for whom I might not otherwise have cared the hum of a bee. That I should be very susceptible to *yours* is *very* natural indeed. Even if—as would have been also very natural indeed—you had past me by on the other side without a Samaritan smile, I should have gone on caring for *you* as

something much above a literary 'abstraction'; inasmuch as
—unluckily for some people—they cant have one's admiration
without taking one's affection along with it . . .

I have not seen Mr. Kenyon for some time: and so I am
sure you will not envy me the very least this burning London
sun which would have turned us into bricks, had we been the
right kind of clay for it. Perhaps after all you and we have had
only one sun between us: tho' *that* is as hard to imagine as the
absence of the morning air in the Diorama. Slant rays thro'
trees—the shadows dropping with the gleams—are so different
from pelting heat upon the pavement! And then the dire
necessity of having every window in the house open to the
ceaseless rolling of carriages, as a precursor to breathing at all.
It has been very disagreeable: and I would have given many
a night of sleep for a walk with you at the 'witching time of'
morning—five o clock! in your pretty garden . . .

Mr. Kenyon told me nearly a fortnight ago that Mrs.
Dupuy [5] would be kindly glad to see me; and it was settled
that I should pay her a visit in Welbeck Street. A few days
passed, during which I was waiting for my brother's chaperone-
ship; and then the London sun put me into prison and I could
not 'get out'. Intense heat always enervates me: and it was
quite an effort to me until this cooler today and yesterday, to
do anything morally or physically except lie on the sofa.
Yesterday I set out to Welbeck Street—and Mrs. Dupuy was
gone—not likely to return until the spring. I am very sorry—
but I cant help it, you see, now; even if Mr. Kenyon should
scold me. Do take my part if you ever hear me scolded by
anybody—even if you half think that I deserve it. I do hope
that after all it may not be quite too late, and that I shall have
the pleasure of seeing your friend in the spring.

It would be wonderful if you who can see merit everywhere,
should not see and estimate Mr. Kenyon's. You speak truly
of his *truth*. And his brilliancy of conversation is not of the
kind to dazzle our sight from us. We dont hide our eyes as
from a 'London sun'—but 'bless the useful light', and think
more of its warmth than of its rays. It is *I* who am to be
grateful to him.

I can read all your 'coptic inscriptions': and should not
object to the 'red ink' and the 'crossings crossed'. Do write

to me whenever you feel inclined to do something particularly good-natured. You who have associated London with the whirl of societies, can scarcely guess what a desert it is to me—without its silence—a solitude without the majesty of solitude. There is not a being whom I know here, except Mr. Kenyon, who ever says to me 'I care for poetry'. Yet I am contented—yet I should be more so if you would write sometimes. I have always been used to a kind of solitude tho' not this noisy kind : and should feel so disturbed if I were ever thrown out of it . . as not to tell you *how* much disturbed [words smudged] until you have known me for five years,—lest all your kindness should be unable to prevent you from thinking me affected.

Have you seen the review of Ion in the New Monthly Magazine for July? It is in the article 'Evidences of Genius for dramatic poetry',—very favorable and resistful to the 'lively critic in the Athenaeum'.[6] Towards the close of the article, a great deal of admiration is laid at the feet of Mr. Landor,—and—which amused me very much,—an extract of the finest points of his contribution to Miss Courtenay's album is given, with the most emphatic eulogy.[7] Who can have written it?

Of course I sent your enclosure to Mr. Kenyon immediately. May God bless you my dear friend! How is the novel?

Your affectionate and grateful

E. B. Barrett

Is there no hope of your coming to London in the Autumn to correct proof sheets? When you come next, you will pass our threshold will you not, and let me introduce Papa to you? We are for a little while longer in our present house, perhaps for longer than a little while : but we shall move (not I believe from *London*) before we settle . . .

[1] *The Countess of Essex.* Henry John Shepherd (1783–1855), Bencher of Lincoln's Inn, author of *Pedro of Castile, a Poem* (1838), married in 1808 Lady Mary, a daughter of the Earl of Rosebery.

[2] From *Dramatic Scenes, Sonnets, and Other Poems*, by Mary Russell Mitford (1827).

[3] George Crabbe (1754–1832). Born in humble circumstances in Aldeburgh, Suffolk, he cherished a lifelong passion for botany and for literature, applying an equal realism, in both cases, to the description and classification of his various specimens. His first poem, *The Library*, was published in 1782 ;

but he is mainly known as the author of *The Village* (1783), *The Borough* (1810), and *Tales of the Hall* (1819).

⁴ Sir Uvedale Price, Bart. (1747–1829), landscape gardener and classical scholar who lived a few miles from the Moulton Barretts in Herefordshire. Author of *An Essay on the Picturesque* (1794), *Essay on the Modern Pronunciation of Greek and Latin* (1827). 'Mr. Price's friendship', EBB wrote of her octogenarian friend, 'has given me more continual happiness than any single circumstance ever did . . .' (*Elizabeth Barrett Browning*, by Dorothy Hewlett, p. 39. Cassell, 1953.)

⁵ Mrs. J. P. Dupuy, who lived at 31 Welbeck Street, was a friend of Miss Mitford's.

⁶ *Ion*, a tragedy by Serjeant Talfourd, produced at Covent Garden on May 26, 1836. It was reviewed two days later in the *Athenaeum* by George Darley, who, having affirmed that the Drama in England was extinct, added that his own prejudices did 'not run in favour of lawyer poetry . . . the tuneful tribe can learn no very pleasing wood-notes from gaolbirds, chatterers in periwigs, and those super-annuated rooks in rusty black, croaking about the doleful purlieus of the Inns of Court'.

⁷ The extracts are from *The Death of Clytemnestra*, published in *Friendly Contributions for the Benefit of Three Infant Schools in the Parish of Kensington. Printed solely for the Right Honourable Lady Mary Fox* (1836).

74 Gloucester Place
Wednesday [*July or August 1836*]

Who was it among the French who first imagined the *horloge des fleurs*? My flowers once so fresh and beautiful and from Miss Mitford's garden, are striking their vesper hour— fading down to the stalks—defying the power of Undine's Kühleborn to keep their souls in them. They shall not quite die before I thank you for them and for the note travelling in their company. I could not thank Mr. Chorley ¹ for bringing them to me, because almost wonderfully, I was *out* when he called. It was unfortunate. I should have liked to thank him and see him not only for the sake of esteem due to him and *your* praise, but also and most (dont tell him so) for those words of dearest Miss Mitford's—'He will tell you all about us.'

I am indeed grateful to you for the kindness of your praise and the greater kindness of your criticism. The last is harder to say to *some lips*, and being less within the reach of the affectionate *exaggeratingness* (*that* is not pure English either!) of your feelings, does of course stand nearest to the verity of the case. So I shall call the criticism and praises—a 'truth

severe in airy fictions drest'; which quotation is truer in this
application than in others—seeming as it does, to uphold the
beauty of truth but to deny the *truth of beauty*. And—not to
wander into that favorite subject of mine—I am afraid I am
very apt not to speak plain when I write. Even Papa has
sometimes told me so; and in different respects my own faults
are so various in my own eyes that I can easily believe this fault
of obscurity which is of necessity less visible to the committer
than to standers by, to be an additional one. I assure you
that after the first complacency of composition, without which
no one perhaps could write at all, I never *thoroughly* like anything
of my own, and am ready to believe every kind of harm of it.
Therefore the 'terrible liberty' need not have been talked of—
unless a terrible mockery was intended. Dear friend—you
will always—will you not?—care enough for me to tell me the
truth without apology, and I will care enough for myself to try
to make a use of such truth. When the Athenaeum kindly
and unexpectedly mentioned Margret,[2] she was reproved for
mannerisms—and I puzzled, being sure that I had not written
in affectation or *out* of my own nature. But this is quite enough
about my faults—I mean, about myself—and not that the
faultiness is an exhausted subject.

A fame reached me two days ago of 'Miss Mitford's having
received a silver medal at the Reading horticultural show for'
. . for what I did not hear; perhaps—even before the publication of the novel—for *parsley*. Yet no! Mr. Kenyon says that
all the vanity lies in the *flowers*! But you will let me congratulate you on the new horticultural dignity whatever might have
been its occasion; and then I can go on with Mr. Kenyon's
name and tell you of his having given himself a great deal of
kind trouble in finding the Countess of Essex for me and of my
reading it and Paracelsus [3] besides which he also lent me. As
to the play, its talent may be both felt and seen—but felt and
seen *in parts*. It seems to me—if I dare say so—that the conception of the tragedy did not arise in the author's name [?]
as *one*, and that as a consequence the impression on the reader's
mind, when all is read, is not a settled and lasting one. Was
not the work rather constructed than created?—and is it not
observable—or is it only imaginable—that in the selection of
his scenes he *picked nature for dramatic situations* and did not

mingle the browns and greens and yellows after the manner of Nature's self and Shakespeare and Shakespeare's contemporaries? But this may be only discontent. People who can be pleased and touched as Mr. Shepherd's readers can, have scarcely a right to find fault—I mean, such people and readers as I. But have you seen Paracelsus? I am a little discontented even *there*, and would wish for more harmony and rather more clearness and compression—*concentration*—besides: but I do think and feel that the pulse of poetry is full and warm and strong in it, and that—without being likely perhaps to be a popular poem—it 'bears a charmed life'. There is a palpable power—a height and depth of thought—and sudden repressed gushings of tenderness which suggest to us a depth beyond, in the affections. I wish you would read it, and agree with me that the author is a poet in the holy sense. And I wish besides that some passages in the poem referring to the divine Being had been softened or removed. They sound to me daringly— and *that* is not the appropriate daring of genius. Poor Burns felt in his darkness one truth near to him—'an irreligious poet is a monster': and men who thank God—sometimes— when they think of it—for the dews and sunshine, should surely do it in an intense gratitude for those refreshing and bright and deathless imaginings which come from above like *them* . . .

They say, London is 'growing very thin'—which sounds to other than a Londoner, very ludicrous. There seems to *me* as much noise as ever—and for the rest I do not care. We are still unsettled as to a house, without being in the least likely to have a vision of the country this year; and instead of it Papa has given me two Barbary doves which I am sure Mr. Mitford would admire and in whose voices I seem to hear the waters and waving leaves faded by this time from their own memories and dreams. A dove's voice gives me more delight than a nightingale's—than *even* a nightingale's,—tho' I suppose I must not dare to say so to above one poet at a time. And voice and eyes and plumage go together—so beautiful and soft and calm. Is not all *calmness*, in this working grieving restless world, a solemn thing. I recognise *sublimity* in all calm moving living things, from the falling snow to the sleeping infant—notwithstanding Burke.[4]

Goodbye dear Miss Mitford. When you have a moment
to write in, do not care for opportunities and franks which are
not to be looked for from the country,—but remember how
glad and thankful I shall always be to read your writing.

Your affectionate

E. B. BARRETT

[1] Henry Fothergill Chorley (1808–72). Joined the staff of the *Athenaeum*
in 1833, and remained chief musical critic and general reviewer for over
thirty years. 'Charles Cope the artist describes him as rather bumptious
with "red hair and eyelashes, a red necktie, and reddish leather boots", and
reports that Charles Landseer said of him, "Everything about Chorley was
red but his *books*".' (*Life and Letters of George Darley*, by C. C. Abbott, p. 152.
Oxford University Press, 1928.)

[2] *The Romaunt of Margret*, published in *The New Monthly Magazine*, July
1836. 'We have not read such a ballad for many a day; and if its writer will
only remember, that in poetry *manner* is a blemish to be got rid of, and not an
ornament to be worn and cherished, he (or she) may rank very high—what
if we say, among the highest?' (*Athenaeum*, July 9, 1836.)

[3] *Paracelsus*, the first acknowledged work of Robert Browning, was published on August 15, 1835.

[4] Edmund Burke (1729–97), writer, orator, and statesman. In his
Philosophical Enquiry into the Origin of our Ideas on the Sublime and Beautiful (1756),
Burke declared that 'Whatever is fitted in any sort to excite the ideas of pain
and danger . . . is a source of the *sublime*'.

74 Gloucester Place
17th February 1837

. . . Before I read your own account I had heard of
Mr. Forrest [1] and of his intended appearance in a play of
yours; but nothing of the details; nothing of his *electing*
application to the authoress of Rienzi . . .

The opinions of Mr. Forrest's acting appear very different.
I shall like to hear from you whether he is or is not rather
melodramatic than tragic—and whether his physical does not
obtrude itself into his intellectual. You are as you always are,
very very kind in even thinking of taking me into your box on
the great occasion. If I ever went into boxes now, there should
be more than thanks in answer to that thought—but as it is—
I shall *read* Otto. By the way, according to tradition, once in
a childish fit of illhumour, I took refuge from the cruelties
of the world, in a *hat box*, and covered myself up in it. A
good deal of the sublime of misanthropy is resolvable into

such crossnesses ; and it would be much the same whether one went into a monastery or a hatbox, if the latter were equally picturesque.

I have been reading and rejoicing in your Faithful Shepherdess.[2] The general conception and plan are feeble and imperfect—do you not admit it?—but the work in detail— how prodigal it is in exquisite poetry ; and in those sweet lapses and undulations of sound coming and going without a reason—such as are not dreamt of in the iron philosophy of our days. Who is your Fletcher's Faithful Shepherdess—the mourner?—or the wronged? I daresay you will answer the first. Only faithfulness to the dead, the absent, the inoffensive, the unchanging and defenceless, is so much easier than faithfulness to the fickle and the unjust! Death has such a pleading tongue in what is called its silence . . .

And let me say 'thank you', besides, for you kind indulgence to poor Rosalind : [3] and for your advice which shall not, if I can help it, be vainly given. When it came to me I was engaged a little transcendently upon *Two Seraphim* ; [4] and I have had much to do in addition, without counting the influenza ; but I *will*, some day, write on the recommended 'probable or possible' subject, and do my possible upon it. But dearest Miss Mitford is too kind a friend to be a very good prophet.

Have you been quite well? It is almost too much to expect, considering the universal illnesses. I almost restrain my hope to the one point of neither yourself nor Dr. Mitford having suffered severely. And how is Dash? My little brother's dog, Myrtle, (a very brown ugly myrtle, looking as if it had fallen into the sere and yellow leaf) had a most *human* cough for days—and a cat died—and my poor little Doves forgot their cooing voices, and moped close to the fire, until I half despaired for them. They have since recovered their spirits : and we—that is, the Doves and I—have been very busy in making a nest—particularly I and the cock, who travelled backwards and forwards from my knee where the materials lay, to his own cage, for a whole morning at a time. The '*results*' as the Utilitarians say, were nothing better than a soft egg—but we, not being Utilitarians ('O that *profane* name !') have found it in our good pleasure to begin again.

You will doubt whether I am ever going to *end*! Do forgive all this nonsense, and remember, when you come to London
Your affectionate
E. B. BARRETT

¹ Edwin Forrest (1806–72), the American actor, once described as 'a vast animal, bewildered by a grain of genius'. 'My success in England has been very great . . .', he wrote to his friend Mr. Leggett, editor of the New York *Plain-dealer*. 'I am to reappear, at Drury Lane, in February. During that engagement, I shall bring out a New tragedy which Miss Mitford is now writing for me, under the title of *Otto of Wittelsback*. . . Miss Mitford is in high spirits, and says this play shall be a thousand times better than her *Rienzi*.' (Reprinted in the *Athenaeum*, March 25, 1837.)

² By John Fletcher (1579–1625). Of this work M R M wrote in 1817: 'What a terrible thief Milton was! All the very best and sweetest parts of "Comus" are stolen from this exquisite Pastoral, and in my mind nothing bettered by the exchange.' (*L'Estrange*, Vol. II, p. 15.)

³ A character in *The Poet's Vow*, by E B B, first printed in the *New Monthly Magazine*, October 1836.

⁴ Afterwards called *The Seraphim*, and published under that name, with other poems, in 1838.

74 Gloucester Place
May 2ᵈ 1836 [*sic*] [*1837*]

Indeed dearest Miss Mitford you never *did* write to me; for altho' you may well doubt whether you did or not, I am not in the least likely to forget having received a letter of yours. I was beginning to be very *troublesome to myself* about you—and to wonder whether I might risk being troublesome to *you* by writing again. If you knew what a builder of dungeons in the air I am—no cloud is too black to be my corner-stone—and I am sure to begin the cloudy work when I dont hear about persons for whom I care much. This is not a reproach—only a confession. You are very kind indeed to write to me even. Dont I *feel* the kindness?—and have I not to thank you for an expression of it last week?

And poor Dash is ill—or has been—for I do trust that by this time he is well again and you at ease about him. He is a mortal immortal dog—immortal in the Village, and mortal at Three Mile Cross—long may he continue *both*! It is far too soon for him to become only immortal—like Cerberus . . . And dont let the Cynics laugh at the dog-lovers—seeing that the philo-dogism (if the dog may stand as a representative of

13

all the other 'blessed living' soulless things—) is far better and higher and holier than the philosophy. Do not men dishonor their own natures in casting scorn upon the creations of their Creator? Do they not inflict injury upon their own natures in staying the flowings-out of love towards the lowest and towards the Highest? How often does their love not flow at all—not downwardly to the animal, not upwardly to the Great Spirit— but is comprehended and made stagnant within the narrow limits of their humanity . . .

As to Dash I shall certainly see *his* portrait, whenever I am able to go to the Royal Academy. I have as yet been able to see only the exhibition in Suffolk Street—in which were only Hurlstone's [1] pictures which would do to think of afterwards— or were worth wishing you away from the country to look at. His prisoner of Chillon appears to me to be a very very beautiful and touching and suggestive work. If it were not the illustra- tion of a poem, it would produce one—or might! I was haunted whole days afterwards by the silent pathos of those eyes 'as blue as Heaven', and yet sorrowful with earth—and I do wish that you would leave the 'black spring' and come and look at this shadow of the shadow of human suffering. A black spring does almost as well as a white one here—and perhaps is more appropriate, inasmuch as our Mays are associated with our chimney sweepers. Well! but the pictures. What struck me in this Suffolk St exhibition, was the want of conception and ideality—which is a serious want to people like me, who can understand and enjoy in a picture, nothing beside. But it is the defect of the age—is it not? It is terrible to be dragged cap- tive, not by a King in purple and fine linen, not by a warrior in the glittering of his arms, but by a poor paltry counting- house Utilitarianism—along a rail road instead of a Via Sacra.

. . . Do you observe that the author of Paracelsus is bringing out a tragedy at one of the theatres? [2] I admire his Paracelsus, but cannot even guess how he will be quite wide awake enough from the peculiar mystic dreaminess, to write an historical tragedy. Yes! the extracts from Mrs. Butler's play,[3] in the Athenaeum, *are* very beautiful—and so are some others which I have seen in another paper. Your observation on the plot is a true one! And yet half—at the least—of our miseries proceeds from our ignorances—and misery, as misery—

without regard to its procession—*will* have sympathy, as long as we are men.

I have not lately seen a great deal of Mr. Kenyon—but, you know, his kindness always comes where he comes at all. He must be, and is, much engaged just now with a crowd of the scientific who gather around their new magnet Mr. Crosse.[4] Mr. Crosse is staying with him. And Mr. Conybeare [5] has been staying with him—and his brother has arrived from Vienna—which would in itself be an absorption, without the insect-making from stones! Are you—or is Dr. Mitford—understanding of these things? Papa *will* have it that I hold them in scorn—which I protest against and abjure. It is quite bad enough to be known to be ignorant, without being thought to be absurd! . . .

May God bless you my dear friend. Remember me among those who love you—for I *do*. The spring is growing whiter—is it not? And oh! is it not a mockery to 'congratulate' *me* about the Spring? Which mockery is forgiven you, if you will but enjoy the sunshine and the flowers yourself. May Papa offer his regards to you?—and may *I* be forgiven this long unreasonable letter, for the sake of my being

Your affectionate

E. B. BARRETT

---

[1] '*Society of British Artists* (Suffolk St.). This exhibition, the fourteenth of the Society, seems to us to contain fewer decided failures than any of its predecessors. . . . Mr. Hurlestone stands foremost among the exhibitors, having sent no less than fourteen pictures, all of them works of pretension . . . but their artist's best work, to our thinking, is his group from *The Prisoner of Chillon* . . .' (*Athenaeum*, March 25, 1837.)

[2] On March 25, 1837, in its 'Weekly Gossip on Literature and Art', the *Athenaeum* wrote: 'From the Theatres nothing has reached us, save a very far-off whisper of a tragedy, by the Author of "Parcelsus", its subject being taken from English history'. *Strafford*, a tragedy by Robert Browning, was presented at Covent Garden on May 1, 1837.

[3] *The Star of Seville*: a drama, in five acts, by Mrs. Butler (Fanny Kemble).

[4] Andrew Crosse (1784–1855). Described after the British Association meeting in 1836, as 'an electro-chemical philosopher of eminence'. In 1837, in the course of experiments on electro-crystallization, he observed the appearance of insect life in connection with his voltaic arrangements. Upon publication of this discovery, he is said to have met with much 'virulence and abuse'.

[5] William Daniel Conybeare (1787–1857), geologist, divine, and Fellow of the Royal Society.

[*74 Gloucester Place*]
London.   July 22ᵈ [*1837*]

It is not possible for me not to thank you almost immediately my very dear friend, my dearest Miss Mitford,—for a letter overflowing with kindness. You have overflowed your banks very far in generous praises ; and have made a place very green for gratitude to walk in—and there *my* gratitude shall walk up and down with the stedfast paces of Madᵐᵉ de Genlis' Agelia ! ¹   Indeed indeed, dearest Miss Mitford,—I am touched—affected by your kindness,—and thank you for it with the heart of one who well knows the uncommoness of such ! I wish I deserved it better. . .

It is kind in you—what is there that is not kind in you ?— to say that you owe anything to Mr. Kenyon, in owing *me* to him. Certainly in this loveless world—I must say so *broadly*, tho' it holds the village—we do gain something with every heart that loves us—and certainly such a gain, have *you* made in me ! Otherwise I am not indeed, what your kindness esteems me . . .

I am sure I ought to be proud of my verses finding their way into a Belford Regis newspaper ! ² The young Queen is very interesting to me—and those tears, wept not only amidst the multitudes at the proclamation, but in the silence of the dead midnight—(we heard that she cried all night before holding her first privy council, notwithstanding the stateliness and composure with which she received her councillors) are beautiful and touching to think upon. Do you remember Lord Byron's bitter lines, said bitterly while Marie Louise leant upon the arm of Napoleon's conqueror ?—

'Enough of human ties in royal breasts !—
Why spare men's feelings while their own are jests ?'

They have never past from my memory since I read them. There is something hardening, I fear, in power—even if there is not in pomp ! and the coldnesses of state etiquette gather too nearly around the heart, not to chill it, very often. But our young Queen wears still a very tender heart—and long may its natural emotions lie warm within it—I liked to hear of her the other day, in the robing room of the House of Lords. When

MARY RUSSELL MITFORD
From a drawing by F. R. Say, 1837

the Duke of Sussex bent his knee there before her,—regardless of spectators, she threw her arms around his neck and kissed him fervently . . .

The little doves have their egg still,—and they ought to have broken the shell yesterday. But I am not at all desponding—being perfectly sure, from its appearance, that there is life within. The dear little cock persists in having it all to himself—and the gentle meek hen is satisfied with nestling by his side, with her head touching his breast, to be as near as possible to the beloved egg. I have tak[en] him away by force two or three times, and then, a little seed or biscuit quite satisfied and appeased him. Will you tell your father—with every grateful reply I dare make to his kind remembrance of me—that I should like to see the jays very much—altho' I stand [?] for the *supremacy of my doves*—and that we once, years ago, had a magpie, a very eloquent orator, who used to sit at the schoolroom window until the lessons were done without stirring a feather, and then accompany my brothers in their long country walks—flying from tree to tree, and never out of sight for miles at a time! . . . Forgive this busy [?] hurried tho' long scribble, and ever believe me

Your most affectionate and obliged

E. B. BARRETT.

[1] It is possible that E B B was introduced to the work of Madame de Genlis by Jules Janin, who, on May 6, 1837, in one of the articles of his *Athenaeum* series, 'Literature of the 19th Century, France', had described the work and personality of a woman who 'played, at Paris, the character which your Lady Hester Stanhope plays in the East'.

[2] A poem called *Victoria's Tears*, by E B B, appeared in the *Athenaeum* on July 8, 1837. It was reprinted in *The Reading Mercury, Oxford Gazette* and *Berks County Paper* on July 15, 1837.

*[74 Gloucester Place] London
Tuesday [Postmark: August 15, 1837]*

I sit down my dearest Miss Mitford before your affectionate note and beautiful flower, to try to write some sort of thanks to you—yet not very well knowing how to thank you for so unusual a compliment, paid so gracefully, that one half forgets one's unworthiness of it, in one's gratitude for it. Oughtn't I to have a 'floral telegraph' to thank you by—

> By all those token flowers that tell
> What words can never speak as well!

But where should I find flowers beautiful enough to be fit for the expression of a thought about this geranium? Unless indeed you would let me in at your garden gate.

Joanna Baillie's [1] was not so beautiful as mine! I know the reason of that—a good reason—almost as good as the kindness. *She* was immortal already and for herself: and *I* am to be *made* so by Miss Mitford's flowers—whose *smile is fame*— and therefore I certainly require the most force of beauty . . .

I have been longing to write to you ever since I heard of your being unwell, which I heard first from Mr. Kenyon: and then I was afraid of coming upon you at some busy moment, and without having a frank as an excuse. All the frankers I have access to, are wandering about out of sight and hearing— the general franker Sir William Gossett,[2] being a tracker of the Rhine and the steps of Otto. I am grieved at your having been so unwell, and of your being so in a degree, habitually. Dearest Miss Mitford, when you are out of your garden, do you *sit* a great deal? Now at night—during those long watching writing nights—against which there is no use remonstrating —do you *sit* [word smudged] them all? If you do—indeed indeed it is very bad for you. And it would be so wise if you would learn to be a *lollard* like me, and establish yourself on a sofa instead of on a chair, and study the art, not a very difficult one, of writing in a recumbent position. I can write as well or as badly when I lie down, as at a desk. I used once to suffer from a feebleness in the spine ; and even now it is exceedingly fatiguing to me, to sit bolt upright without the mediation of the back of a chair, for any length of time. But with *your* tendency, I am quite sure that a recumbent—not a merely leaning position—would be essentially useful to you. It would lessen both the actual fatigue, and the evils consequent upon sedentary habits.

This is very learned is it not?—I think I deserve a diploma.

Do you know that Mr. Wordsworth is in London? I have not seen him, but I received a message from Mr. Kenyon the other day, desiring me to envy him inasmuch as he had made the fourth, at a breakfast party of Wordsworth, Rogers and Moore! This would have seemed to me quite a dream a little time ago. I dreamed one once myself—beside the great poet—and Miss Mitford—and when she went away I heard and *felt* the brilliant but caustic Landor say . . 'She diffuses happiness wherever she goes.' There is nothing truer in all Pericles and Aspasia,[3] than *that*. May God bless you my very dear and kind friend! Remember me as

Your affectionate

E B B<small>ARRETT</small>

My compliments to Dash.

[1] Joanna Baillie (1762–1851), a niece of the celebrated doctor John Hunter. 'If you wish to speak of a real poet,' said Walter Scott, 'Joanna Baillie is now the highest genius of our country.' Author of *Plays on the Passions* (1798–1812), completed, belatedly, in the *Miscellaneous Plays* of 1836. Two of these dramas were translated into Cingalese, with the object of 'raising the minds and eradicating the vices of the natives'.

[2] Sir William Gossett, Serjeant at Arms, House of Commons (1835–48). His son was married to a first cousin of E B B's.

[3] A work by Walter Savage Landor, published in 1836.

[74 Gloucester Place]
Sepr 29th [1837]

. . . You certainly should write Dash's memoirs! My youngest brothers, to say nothing of my eldest, were delighted with the *memorabilia* I read to them out of your letter. They have an exalted opinion of dogs, and as deep a contempt for doves. There is our brown and yellow terrier called Myrtle, whose noblest qualities lie in his mind, and who can therefore be trusted to walk out by himself—and he does it with an exemplary slowness and gravity, as if revolving in his altered soul the various turns of rat to hole (oh! that Myrtle should be a confessed rat-catcher!) without any risk of being stolen. The London dog stealers are no discerners of spirits. But in the esteem of both my brothers, Myrtle is a 'first good, first perfect, and first fair'—and so they are very jealous of the doves usurping the praise and attention due to *him* . . the doves indeed! My boast of their accomplishments is always interrupted by 'Myrtle does just the same', or 'Myrtle can do much better'—but then there is a triumphant clinch for my argument in 'the doves can fly, and Myrtle can't!'—a position I half expect to be contested some day. And once, two or three years ago, I overheard a soliloquy of Octavius,[1] he sitting upon the stair case, and holding that ugliest dog of all christendom, in fast embraces—'Oh—beloved Myrtle! How I do love you!!' And so all your witnessings to Dash's genius were received—I much suspect—as an indirect homage to Myrtle— and you will easily make out the logic of it.

Do give Dr. Mitford with my kind and thankful regards, my condolence about the jays. If kindness and care do really kill, woe to my doves and me. But the little dove is quite well so far—and a thorough cockney—being known to manifest fear of only two things—first of a bottle fly—and secondly, of the wind in the leaves! He was put out into the balcony, among the flower pots—and in he came, tumbling and trembling. It is a dreadful degeneracy for a dove, is it not? But this London brings us all to a level. And in regard to it, I must not forget to tell you that Papa has concluded,—except some legal formalities attending a distinct contract,—the purchase of a house in Wimpole Street—number 50,—nearly at the top, and towards the Regent's Park. We are likely to get thro' the paint and plaster into it, before Christmas—and then we shall call ourselves *settled*—a foolish word after all, for any disposition of earthly things upon this earth of ours. One might as well talk of being settled in a parachute . . .

I shall have put out your eyes with all this writing. Do forgive me. You do not say how you are. Pray *pray* dont work yourself ill with the novel. Mr. Kenyon has not returned and was last heard of at Bridgewater. Dearest Miss Mitford's own affectionate

E B B.

[1] Octavius Butler (1824–1910). 'Occy' or 'Occyta', twelfth child, and eighth son of Edward Moulton Barrett.

74 Gloucester Place
Tuesday [*Postmark: November 29, 1837*]

From the very same sad cause my dearest Miss Mitford I have delayed and wished to write to you. It always seems to me unnatural that we should not know everything for weal or woe, about such as we much regard—and yet I *could* not give you a grief without some kind of comfort by its side. Perhaps after all you have heard, without me, of the severe illness of our dear friend Mr. Kenyon. At any rate the account yesterday was so satisfactory that I need not fear telling you of it. But it has been very severe—and not without danger—and indeed for many days I have been quite haunted by the thoughts of sad possibilities. We cannot afford—at least I cannot—to lose or to think of losing such as have been kind to us,—and sympathising—which is more than kind.[1]

He is better, I hope satisfactorily so, now. The medical men *desired* his servant to say so to all enquirers yesterday. The fever had not returned. But they will not allow any nourishment beyond tea and soda water and lemonade and bread—and this discipline has lasted for ten days, and must have much exhausted him.

It is just three weeks, or was on friday, since dear Mr. Kenyon was here . . . Very well and in very good spirits he seemed to be—and I was so glad to see him again, we on our parts being neither one nor the other—for my dear brother George had just 'stood confessed' with an attack of smallpox—and it was more than usually pleasant to us to hear a kind cheerful voice. These are the occasions on which 'troops of friends' adopt the military discipline of the Parthians—and send their good wishes behind them . . .

I had seen the Literary Gazette, and wondered why so ill-natured a critic should at all have digressed from illnature in my favor.[2] But you know, there would have been no use in a man *with a name* attacking an *initial*. It would have been like shooting a shadow. There would have been no *sport* in it. As to the blame—that 'Miss Mitford is not at home out of her green lanes'—*that* hits a shadow too! When *is* Miss Mitford out of green lanes—out of their verdure and freshness and 'sweet natural calm'? When is she? When *was* she? I never saw her out of them. Their characteristics follow in her path,—whether she walks with English rustics here, or with Italian nobles there—and so the man with the name had better forswear it! . . .

Hearing of Miss Porter [3] is like being a child again. I remember weeping and wailing over her romances, when I had nothing besides to weep and wail for. Whatever their faults may be, they have in them an elevation and an heroism which this learned age would do well to learn. Only they cant be *learnt*. Did you see Miss Pardoe? [4] Her last book is full of talent—but not quite [letter torn]. At least, I thought not.

The smallpox is quite gone—and all fear of infection with it. But dearest Miss Mitford (to return into the next paragraph) where was it, that you and I saw Miss Porter, together? [5] Dearest Miss Mitford! It is a mistake of yours! I never saw her consciously, in my life.

Do say some kind words, and grateful ones, from me to your father. May you both be quite well. I am not so myself. I caught a cold nearly two months ago which turned into a cough and has kept me to the house ever since and in a very weak state—and Dr. Chambers whom I was kindly persecuted into seeing yesterday (I have an abhorence of '*medical advice*', but my sisters were obdurate) says that I must not think of stirring into the air for weeks to come. He assures me that there is no *desease*—only an excitability, and irritability of chest, which require precaution. And nothing is much more disagreeable than *precaution*.

Have you read Ernest Maltravers? Its presence will not pass from me. It is a splendid book! If I were to tell you a heresy of mine, into which enter two names—Walter Scott—Bulwer—I should make you shudder at 'Midsummer'. And this being near Christmas, – – 'forbear'! [6]

May God bless you my ever dear friend. Do not think anxiously of dear Mr. Kenyon. I will let you hear of him soon again—and in the meanwhile you must believe that the amendment is day by day. Accept Papa's compliments and regards.

Your affectionate
E B BARRETT.

I believe that the malady is called a *bilious fever*—brought on in a measure by cold.

This is tuesday *evening*, and Papa has just come back from enquiring at Mr. Kenyon's. He is *much better*—and the medical men have allowed him to take some chicken broth. This is happy news.

¹ 'Poor dear Kenyon!' wrote Wordsworth, 'but I had foretold in my own thoughts & said also to Mrs W. that I feared it would not be long before he would have some dangerous seizure—I apprehended something of an apoplectic kind, for he is of far too full a habit—& so I rather think I told him.' (*Correspondence of H. Crabb Robinson with the Wordsworth Circle*, December 15, 1837, ed. E. J. Morley, Vol. I, p. 351. Oxford, 1927.)

² '*Finden's Tableaux*. Edited by Mary Russell Mitford. We cannot speak highly of the literary contents of this volume ; they are of a very low order. Miss Mitford does not seem at home in such very fine society ; she lacks the spirit and freshness of her own green lanes. Incomparably the best poem in the work is by an anonymous writer with the initials E. B. B.' (*Literary Gazette*, October 21, 1837.) The poem referred to is *A Romance of the Ganges*.

³ Jane Porter (1776–1850), author of *Thaddeus of Warsaw* (1803), which caused her to be made a lady of the chapter of St. Joachim by the King of Wurtemberg, and of *The Scottish Chiefs* (1810), which, translated into French, was proscribed by Napoleon.

⁴ Julia Pardoe (1806–62), a 'fairy-footed, fair-haired, laughing sunny girl', who, having visited Constantinople with her father, published in 1837 *The City of the Sultan and Domestic Manners of the Turks*. Miss Pardoe, said Sumet Effendi to Monckton Milnes in 1842, 'came here pure, went away pure and will probably always remain pure. But she is a great liar.' (*Monckton Milnes: The Years of Promise*, J. Pope-Hennessy, p. 169. Constable, 1949.)

⁵ Possibly at the Royal Academy, on May 31, 1836. 'Mrs Toy and Dr Culpeper called early this evening then came Mr Kenyon to take me to the Exhibition, where I met Miss Porter who introduced me to half a dozen lords and ladies and a tribe more of people.' (Miss Mitford to Dr. Mitford, *Tuesday night* [May 31, 1836]. Extract from MS. letter in Reading Public Library.)

⁶ E B B, whose admiration for Walter Scott was very qualified, considered Lytton Bulwer's *Ernest Maltravers* 'worth all the historical novels . . . that were ever written'.

74 Gloucester Place
Tuesday [*Winter 1837–38*]

Do write one line to me my dearest Miss Mitford, just to say how you are. I might have asked as much as this before— but felt unwilling to be in your way when so much else was there. One line—*I* must ask for now! It haunts me that you are suffering. May God grant that such a thought be one of my many vain ones—and that the amendment you spoke of be not vain at all.

This is the first day of my release from prison—for during this terrible weather which held daggers for all weak chests, I was not permitted to get up before it was *deep* in the afternoon,— and so have scarcely had a pen in my hand for a fortnight past. I was glad to be able to breakfast as usual with Papa this morning—and feel an early-rising-vain-gloriousness almost as 'thick upon me' as Mr. Boyd's [1] is upon him—when (and he always does it) he gets up at four or five o clock in the morning and looks down upon the rest of the world. You cant think how much scorn I and my half past nine o clock breakfasts have met with from him. *You* would meet with no mercy. He has intimated to me again and again, that it was both a moral and religious sin not to get up before the second cock crowing. And that Peter's repentance, besides a good deal of sackcloth, should wait upon the third. I believe I inferred the last—being logical: but the 'moral and religious sin' was just his own expression.

How high you bribe dearest Miss Mitford. *To stand alone by your side* in praising Hayley [2] and his contemporaries or in doing anything else! That *is* a bribe; and when I have read the essays on Sculpture Painting and epic poetry,—anything more than the Triumphs of Temper,—I will make a desperate effort towards admiration. I admire him now as a *man*—and as Cowper's friend. I admire Miss Seward,[3] not as a letter writer or a poet or a critic,—but as a kindly, generous hearted woman who loved poetical literature 'not wisely' but very well,—who loved her friends still better than her vanities,—and who was not frozen to her pedestal—(she had one in her day!)—as many are apt to be in all days. When Sir Walter Scott edited her poems he cancelled such praise as he had given them in his own letters to her. It was an ungenerous act. The poor poetess could no more have committed it than she could have written Waverley . . .

The poor little dove, weak for the last three weeks, perished one cold night a fortnight since. I mean the poor little cockney dove. The others, I took up to my bedroom, and kept very warm—and after some spiritless songless days, they revived and are perfectly well now. If I were to lose either of them, I should name it as a grief.

Goodbye—God bless you, dearest Miss Mitford. Do tell me that you are better. Dr. Chambers says that I shall lose my cough in the warm weather—April or May—and not before. So there is nothing for it but patience. And nothing makes me so patient, as knowing that patience is not needed for those one loves!

Your ever affectionate

E. B. BARRETT.

24

I have not yet seen Mr. Kenyon. He sent me Mr. Landor's last most exquisite book of which I have no time to speak.[4]

The kind regards of all the house—do accept them!

[1] Hugh Stuart Boyd (1781–1848), a Greek scholar, and a friend of EBB's from her early Hope End days. Blind for the last twenty years of his life, he could repeat by heart 4770 lines of Greek verse, and 3280 of Greek prose. Author of *Select Passages from the Work of St. Chrysostom, St. Gregory Nazianzen*, etc., translated (1810), *A Malvern Tale and Other Poems (1827)*, etc.

[2] William Hayley (1745–1820), of whom Southey wrote, 'Everything about that man is good except his poetry'. Friend and patron of Cowper and of Blake. The works referred to are *An Essay on Sculpture* (1800), *Epistle on Painting* (1777), *Poetical Epistle on Epic Poetry* (1782), *The Triumph of Temper* (1781).

[3] Anna Seward (1747–1809), 'the Swan', nested, majestically, in the Episcopal Palace of Lichfield, was the author of *Louisa* (1782), *Sonnets* (1799), *Elegy on the Death of Captain Cook* (1817). Her letters were published in 1811.

[4] *The Pentameron*, by Walter Savage Landor (1837).

[129 Crawford Street]
Monday [Easter 1838]

MY BELOVED FRIEND,

If I *had* heard of your being in such anxiety and distress, you would have known before now of my hearing of it. But since last Sunday week I have not seen Mr. Kenyon, and from no other except yourself could I have heard it. Into all that you must have felt I deeply enter—and thank God that this sympathy is so much too late. May you not need it for very very long again! Indeed it is not likely that from *me* you may *ever* need it. Not that I am going to die immediately you know—but that from what you tell me of the abstraction of blood and unslackened energy afterwards, I am led to muse upon differences of constitutional strength, and to count up my own years to be some fifty five *more* than those of Dr. Mitford. A few leeches, if applied oftener than once, reduce me almost to the last position suggested by the Sphinx's riddle—and drew from Dr. Chambers (notwithstanding the advantage I received from them otherwise) the oracular 'We *cannot* continue them' . . .

Mr. Kenyon's book [1] is indeed beautiful — and in all ways. I will praise 'Pretence' up to your highest wish of praising it, if you will take delight with me afterwards (as you certainly will) in 'Moonlight'. For Moonlight is vivid with

25

picture, and the manner in which the moral glides in upon the graphical (towards the end) sad, solemn, and chastened like one of its own rays—appears to me exceedingly beautiful. I have not seen the writer since he was so kind as to send me his work—but I hear of his being very well and haunted with society. Through it all, I had to thank him for bestowing a thought on me, and lending me Mr. Milnes's Poems just printed for private circulation.[2] They are of the Tennyson school, to which you know (after all the harm we grave critics are obliged to say of *schools*) only poets can belong; and very much delighted me . . .

We are no longer in Gloucester Place—nor yet in Wimpole Street. At least I and my sisters are not. The house was so unfinished, that we were obliged and glad to accept the charities of a kind friend and go to Crawford Street until the ghost of paint had been sufficiently exorcised.[3] But direct to 50 Wimpole Street—both because our stay elsewhere is very uncertain, and because our letters are brought from thence instantly.

The scratches I have sent you lately are remorseful subjects with me. These (for the most part) are made in bed: not that I am worse, but have been obliged for some time, to rest until rather late in the day. I am better—but I fear, not *very* much so. God's will be done in all things. May I have wisdom and strength to rejoice that it *must*. Dr. Chambers seems to regard the warm weather with hopefulness. In the meantime, he frowns most awfully at the snow. Nevertheless down it comes!

Do give my kindest regards to Dr. Mitford. The doves are with me here! I would not come without them.

My very dear friend's most affectionate and grateful

E B BARRETT

---

[1] *Poems, for the most Part Occasional* (1838). 'By the bye', wrote Wordsworth to Kenyon, 'Mrs. W. begs me to say that some passages of your Vol., the Moonlight especially, remind her of parts of my own Work (still in MS.) upon my early life. This is not the first instance where our wits have *jumped*, as great wits are apt to do.' (*Letters of William and Dorothy Wordsworth: The Late Years*, ed. E. de Selincourt, Vol. II, p. 951. Oxford, 1939.)

[2] *Memorials of a Residence on the Continent* and *Poems of Many Years*, by Richard Monckton Milnes, were privately printed in 1838, and published later in the same year by Moxon.

³ The rate-books of Marylebone Borough Council show No. 50 Wimpole Street as empty in 1837 and (presumably the early part of) 1838. Edward Barrett appears in the 1839 rate-book as occupier, the owner being Lady Knatchbull. Barbara McCarthy, editor of E B B's letters to H. S. Boyd, gives the number of the Crawford Street house as 129.

50 *Wimpole Street*
June 1 [*1838*]

. . . We have been moving and settling—and I have been sometimes very unwell and sometimes better (never too unwell to write to *you*—no excuse is meant by *that*!) and the proof sheets abstracted me—who am light to abstract just now—from the ballad, and I did not like to write to you late in May without being able to tell you of having even begun it. And then the book—I waited for my book—and the printers and binders were waiting I suppose for something else : but here we all are at last, letter ballad and book,¹ and you must welcome us gently for the love's sake that runs through us all.

. . . Would that the book were as your kindness would have wished it in other things. You will tell me your impression my beloved friend as openly as if you did not care for me—or rather as candidly as if you did—for if we love truth, we must surely speak truly to such as we love. For the rest I fear I know too much of the truth in this case, to be disappointed in hearing the darkest of it—and I may assure you that you could only discourage me totally, by telling me of my incapacity *ever to write better.*

In speaking of my silence I should have told you that I had heard from Mr. Kenyon of you and Dr. Mitford—that you were both better. Otherwise a conspiracy of ballads and books would not have kept me silent.

Do you know that Mr. Kenyon is going into Normandy—but not until July, and for no longer period than six weeks—with Mr. Southey and Mr. Robinson ? ² This will be very enjoyable. He is looking as well as possible—at least, *was* last week—for I have since been sorry to learn in a note from him that he has been state prisoner to a cold and swelled face. His account of Dr. Mitford and yourself dearest Miss Mitford, was pleasant to hear : but still I do want to hear more details from you than I could hear so. Are you not advised to abstain from strong medicines—such as salts? Would not an attention to your diet prove as effectual as any? Do you ever take figs —or tamarinds? . . .

For my own part, I am going on very tolerably well. A cold this week threw me back a little—but it seems to be gone, and without doing as much harm as might have been feared. The lungs are said to be affected—they did not respond as satisfactorily as heretofore to the latest application of the stethescope,—but still there are good symptoms, and Dr. Chambers insists upon my not having lost ground lately and is hopeful of my gaining some in a settled sunshine, such as I hope we *shall* have this summer. He is at once a kind and a skilful man—and my confidence in him is the greater that he has not tried to deceive me by calling things by cowardly names. Indeed he does me good, and if it pleases God, may do more still. In any case I have much to be thankful for, to God's mercy, and I wish that I could thank Him as I ought. Do not say much about my health when you write—for it is a great pleasure to Papa to read your letters (when I will *let* him—when they are not '*private*') and I would not have him fancy me worse than I am. No, nor *you*, dearest Miss Mitford. And the *real truth* is (be sure) that I am better at this time and going on to Dr. Chambers' satisfaction . . .

Here is the end of my paper—but one word notwithstanding in respect to book and ballad. Do not fancy that I shall care more for an unpleasant truth, because I happen to be not quite well. It is *just the contrary*. But indeed at any time, my caring intensely for poetry does not mean that I care intensely for my own poems : and I am not wounded easily except through my affections. In *them* I never can be wounded by *you*—and I speak plainly !—and forgive all this egotism.

Your grateful and affectionate

E B Barrett.

We like the house very much indeed. How I shall like it better still when I see you in it !

The doves and my books and I have a little slip of sitting room to ourselves ; and dearest Papa in his abundant kindness surprised me in it with a whole vision of majestic heads from Bruccani's—busts of poets and philosophers—such as he knew that I would care for. You may think how it startled and affected me to look round and know that he had found time in all his bustle and vexation of house furnishing, to remember so light a thing as my pleasure.

¹ The ballad was *The Romaunt of the Page*, written, at Miss Mitford's request, for *Finden's Tableaux*, 1839; the book, *The Seraphim, and Other Poems*, by Elizabeth B. Barrett, published at the end of May 1838.

² 'Our party consisted of my friend John Kenyon; his friend Captain Jones, R.N. . ., Robert Southey, Poet Laureate, *dignitatis causa*; his friend Mr Sennhouse, *senectutis causa* . . . Cuthbert Southey, Junr. *juventutis causa* (being a sort of hobbledehoy, and Oxford undergraduate.' (*Diary, Reminiscences, and Correspondence of H. Crabb Robinson*, ed. T. Sadler, Vol. III, p. 153. Macmillan, 1869.) Henry Crabb Robinson (1775–1867) was called to the Bar in 1813, and retired, financially independent, in 1828, free to enjoy the friendship and esteem of Lamb, Southey, Coleridge, Wordsworth, etc. Like his friend Samuel Rogers, he was renowned for his conversation, his breakfasts, and his longevity.

Wimpole Street
Tuesday [Postmark: July 5, 1838]

Your note my very dear friend 'burns the stick that whips the peg'—impels the impulse towards writing to you, which I felt before it reached me. For I wanted to tell you how Lady Dacre ¹ came here on Sunday and how I was able to see her, and what a pleasure the seeing was. Unfortunately, and most unusually our drawing room happened to be full when she called here—some old friends from the country having drawn a whole congregation of my brothers together—so that the hum of many voices made mine I fear more inaudible than it need have been and a little hindered conversation. But I could hear Lady Dacre, and delighted in hearing her and felt the full pleasure and pride of making her acquaintance at last. It was very kind and quite unexpected that she should come again after my sombre and forbidding account of myself—but she said—she thought she would give me a little time to get better and then make another attempt. I was pleased unexpectedly too in another way. Notwithstanding all that you said and all that Mr. Kenyon said, I had an idea suggested by what I had heard elsewhere—and unconfessed to either of you—that in seeing Lady Dacre I should see a *woman of the masculine gender*, with her genius very prominent in eccentricity of manner and sentiment—an idea the more admissible to my mind, as the only literary woman I ever knew—except *One* who *is One*— was Lady Mary Shepherd whose kindness and *terribleness* I equally remember. There is no terribleness in Lady Dacre, to confront her kindness—no keenness of eye or speech, or intent to dazzle by either—but as much gentleness and womanlyness as if she could be content with being loved. And that is what I like in a woman—yes, and in a man too, I like this *spirit* of it. I mean that I do *not* like in man or woman the constant carrying about of an intellect rampant, like a crest—as if thinking were a better thing than loving.

Well—but without a dissertation—how could I help being pleased with Lady Dacre, or rather *won* by her, when she said so much about *you*—when she told me how she had brought together the cleverest people to meet you, and how you were the Queen of all—and how she delighted in your frankness— and how she was indignant that Lady Morgan's ² pension should be larger than yours (when mere amusement was the end and object of *her* writings)—and how the question as to the continuance of yours was carried by acclamation, and how at the reading of your note a tear was seen to trickle even from Mr. Grote's ³ eyes! 'This' she continued 'was indeed to draw iron tears down Pluto's cheek' . . .

I saw too on Sunday, Mr. Crosse the insect-maker—who can write fervent verses besides. Nobody can be more ignorant, nor *you* more indifferent about science than I am—and yet I thanked Mr. Kenyon (in my heart) for letting me see this Talked-about by all talkers, and I think I should like him too, in defiance of acid and alkali. There is a curious contrast of quietness and energy in his deportment—perfect silence for ten minutes, and then a spasmodic outburst of speech and gesticulation, as if he could not hold any more thought . . .

I was given into the safe keeping of Digitàlis yesterday, for my *pulse* which keeps pace with the Wild Huntsman—and it is tamer today ; and Dr. Chambers goes on to think me in a better state upon the whole. If it be God's will I may emerge into health yet—and if not, I would hope from His grace that no wish of mine or of those dearest to one may cross His *other* will. The only wrong—kindest wrong !—which the living have ever done me, is in attaching me too much to life by an affection

and tenderness which were I to live very long I never could
repay . . .

Here must be room for Papa's regards and those of all of
us. How inconsiderate to crowd such a lengthy letter in among
the rest and when you have just told me of their multitude!
But we of the coronation are used to crowds, and inclined to
count being squeezed to death among the luxuries of life.
Everybody except myself and our housekeeper who cannot
walk, went out of this house to see the sight—and Sette [4] was
on his feet, Queen-devoted, for thirteen hours.

Ever dearest Miss Mitford's

affectionate E B B

[1] Barbarina Brand (1768–1854), a relative of Miss Mitford's, and the wife
of Lord Dacre. Described as 'one of the most accomplished women of her
time'. Author of *Dramas, Translations, and Occasional Poems* (1821), *Translations
from the Italian* (1836). For a more candid account of the circumstances of this
visit see letter of October 27, 1841.

[2] Sydney Owenson, later Lady Morgan (1783?–1859), was the daughter
of an Irish actor, who married the physician Sir Charles Morgan. Author of
The Wild Irish Girl (1806), *Life of Salvator Rosa* (1823), *The Princess* (1835). In
1837 she received a pension of £300. Miss Mitford's pension, granted in the
same year, was £100.

[3] George Grote (1794–1871), radical banker, M.P., author of *The History
of Greece* (1846–56). John Stuart Mill described him in 1833 as 'a man of
good, but not first-rate intellect . . . even narrower than most other Utilitarians of reading and education'. (*Letters of John Stuart Mill*, ed. Elliot,
Vol. I, p. 59. Longmans, 1910.)

[4] Septimus James (1822–70), eleventh child and seventh son of Edward
Moulton Barrett.

50 Wimpole Street
Saturday [July 1838]

. . . I am anxious to say that dear as your love is to me,
and dear therefore as every proof of it must be, it would pain
me the only way it ever could, if it led you to be displeased
with any who see me and judge me and whose office it is, to
see me and judge me, by a colder and less deceptive light. And
I wish besides to impress it upon you my very dear and generous
friend, that so far from being annoyed or even disappointed by
the review in the Athenaeum [1] I was abundantly satisfied and
gratified by it. There are more who will complain of its

praising me too much than of its blaming me at all—and I have good reason to be obliged to the critic, to Mr. Chorley, both for the actual praise he gives my poetry and for the *willingness* to praise, manifest I think in all parts of his criticism. As to the blame—certainly it is not pleasant to be called 'affected' as in the Atlas [2] (I confess to eschewing some things in that review) or even to be charged with *attitudinising* as in the more gentle Athenaeum. But you know if things appear so to critics, it is quite right and *honest* for corresponding statements to be made. *Indeed* I am not '*perverse*' as dear Mr. Kenyon calls it. I can understand what *he* means in his charge of unintelligibility, and often try tho' so often in vain, not to deserve it. But I do not understand how anyone who writes from the real natural impulse of feeling and thought,—and if I know myself, I *do*—can write affectedly, even in the manner of it. As to attitudes I never did study them. I never did take any thought as to forming a style—which formed itself by force of writing, and which (without perverseness) it will be a hard thing to form anew. But this is 'a groan' *aside*—and expressive of my misfortune and of nobody's fault. If I live I hope and believe I shall write better—not more from natural impulse—I cannot do that—I *deny that charge of affectation*—but better. But were I to do so, I would turn from the pleasure and the pride of hearing it confessed (were that also mine) to the dearer pride and pleasure of being so loved by *you*—I would indeed. You may believe it, for all this egotism.

Your note is so characteristic that it made me smile again and again. Lady Mary Shepherd *is* a kind and cordial woman—and I admire her talents and conventional eloquence. But she is 'terrible', notwithstanding, and without the *intent* of being so—and whenever I used to like to hear her talk, it was always under the proviso, that she didnt talk to *me*. And I have known gentlemen shrink away from her, from a more definite fear than mine—for fear of being examined in metaphysics! Yet I admire and like her—and the strongest remembrance I have of the short and distant period of our acquaintance is a grateful one. She once gave me sympathy when I needed it . . .

Your mentioning Mrs. Opie [3] has dovetailed an old dream. With all her feeblenesses, yes, and sillinesses sometimes, she is

ELIZABETH BARRETT
From a miniature

very moving in her best stories. Her 'Father and daughter' used to draw my childish tears—and so did 'Valentine's Eve'—and these constitute my chief impressions of her writings. The Illustrations of lying, which I read more lately, I made it a point of *concience* (very congenial) to forget immediately. If she *should* come here I shall be glad and with reason . . .

But if I write any more you will believe what I do already, that it is nearly *impossible to write a short letter to you.* I assure you I began this one with the best intentions—and you see how they end.

Give my thankful regards to Dr. Mitford. I do hope he continues tolerably well—and you yourself. I am better for the sun.

My beloved friend's grateful

E. B. BARRETT.

Mr. Kenyon we said goodbye to, on tuesday. He went on Wednesday to Cheltenham and Malvern and the Wye for ten days. On reading the Athenaeum, I sent my brother out on a vain search for Edgar Quinet [4] whom I never heard of before. A foreign bookseller told him that he had had one or two copies from Paris—'*But*' (he added ominously) 'the English wont buy poetry'.

[1] 'This is an extraordinary volume . . . but it is hardly less disappointing than extraordinary. Miss Barrett's genius is of a high order ; active, vigorous, and versatile, but unaccompanied by discriminating taste . . . her descriptions, therefore, are often shadowy and indistinct, and her language wanting in the simplicity of unaffected earnestness. She addresses herself to sacred song with a devotional ecstasy suiting rather the Sister Celestines and Angelicas of Port-Royal, than the religious poets of our sober Protestant communities . . .' (*Athenaeum*, July 7, 1838.)

[2] 'Miss Barrett is sometimes chargeable with affectation. She overworks the tints, and, if we may employ the figure, the tapestry has consequently a cumbrous appearance, here and there, from the excessive weight of the colouring.' (*The Atlas*, June 23, 1838.)

[3] 'That excellent and ridiculous person', Amelia Opie (1769–1853), novelist and poet. Over her *Father and Daughter* (1801), Sir Walter Scott is likewise reputed to have shed tears. *Illustrations of Lying, in all its branches* was published in 1825.

[4] Edgar Quinet (1803–75), author of *Ahasuerus* (1833), *Napoléon*, a poem (1836), *Prométhée*, a poem (1838). The *Athenaeum* reviewer had drawn attention to a striking similarity between Quinet's preface to *Prométhée* and EBB's preface to her long poem *The Seraphim*.

D   33

[50 Wimpole Street]
Friday [August 1838]

EVER DEAREST MISS MITFORD,

With the parcel of reviews which your kindness makes you care to see, I venture to put up a little memorial of the object of it—who although she would trust without any memorial to the pleasant likelihood of remaining unforgotten by you, yet feels that she cannot hold your memory of her (that being so precious!) by too many knotted threads!—

'And *She* must be
A *sterner* than thee,
Who would break a thread of mine'.

I am going away dearest Miss Mitford, possibly in a very few days and certainly as soon as the weather will let me, to Devonshire—to Torquay—there to remain over the winter. The plan involves a sadness of heart to me—for we cannot all go: but it is one which is to be submitted to, Dr. Chambers having used very strong language as to its necessity. Indeed he told me plainly that my recovery *depended* upon its adoption: I am therefore going—with the *cold* hope of seeing Papa *sometimes*. My aunt and uncle Hedley who have resided at Torquay for the last two or three years under Dr. Chambers's jurisdiction, on account of my uncle's being affected in some similar way to myself—are kind enough to receive me very gladly and to wish to keep me with them: but after a while and in the case of the climate agreeing tolerably with me, I shall remove to another house and to the companionship of another aunt, Miss Clarke, a dear favorite relative, who has promised to leave Gloucestershire for Devonshire just for that purpose. Here you see, is plenty of kindness. I ought not to talk of 'cold' hopes in the midst of it. But I cannot help the pang with which I think of those who must be left—altho' it would, I know all the time, be unkind to them and a wrong thing in itself, to risk my life by staying. As it is,—that is, if I go—Dr. Chambers seems to be hopeful. He believes that there is not at present, any ulceration of the lungs—only a too great fullness of the bloodvessels upon them; and he told me a fortnight ago, that he had grounds for hoping in the affected

lung's eventually recovering itself altogether. And it may
please God, that I should return next spring to rejoice in better
health and a less helpless condition—and to rejoice in seeing
you dearest Miss Mitford besides . . .

You do not say whether you are both well. I trust you
are. Offer my kindest wishes and regards to Dr. Mitford—and
accept such from Papa and all this house. *No* day is fixed for
my departure—which is to be by sea, for lack of strength for a
land journey. May God ever bless you! I shall hear from
you—shall I not?—at Torquay—whenever you can write
without adding wearily to your too many occupations? Never
tire yourself for me. May God bless you! It is foolish to feel
as if this were a farewell to *you*—but forty miles and a hundred
and seventy are so different.

Dearest Miss Mitford's

E. B. B.

. . . The wind is audible. It seems to me that I *cannot* be
on the sea until late in the next week, if then. Perhaps I *hope*
I cannot—and yet it might be as well if the business were over.
Adieu once more . . .

50 Wimpole Street
Tuesday. August 14 [*1838*]

It is not yet sure on what day I go—and they are trying to
persuade me that I *may* go to-morrow. I do not think that I
may. Everything depends upon Papa's resolve and I do not
think that he has resolved so. But even if I '*may* go tomorrow',
I *must* not go then or any day without writing a few words to
you, my beloved friend. I will write them on the strength of
that 'may', though I do not believe in it—having waited to
write them for some decision of wind and plan. Certainly I
could not go without trying to thank you for all your great
and most touching and tender kindness as expressed in the
letters lying beside me. If I did, I should sink in the sea by the
weight of my own heart—and as it must be a heavy one, any
way, I may unload it of some of its feelings of gratefulness and
affection, thus, and to you my kindest and dearest Miss Mitford.

And you would—were it not for one golden chain—may

35

God keep every link of it strong!—go to Torquay, pass the winter there, and all for me! And you *will* as it is, write to me once a week, oftener if I please (if I please!!) and love me and pray for me always. I thank you for all this surpassing kindness. But you shall not write to me as often as I please. You shall not write to me *even* once a week—never—except when you can do so without harassing yourself and tiring yourself—you who have *so* many *too* many occupations. But you shall do what I know you will—write to me when you have snatches of time in which you might talk to me—did we happen to be near enough for talking—whenever you are least likely to be tired by writing—and then I can be happy over your letters without remorse, and you can be acknowledged most worthily (in virtue of the good and cheerfulness done by those letters) a 'soeur de la charité' in opposition to us of the Port Royal.

If it be God's will to bring me here again, I shall very gladly make Mrs. Anderdon's acquaintance, and her daughter's [1]— both for the sake of what you say of them—and for a reason which might stand by itself—that they are friends of yours.

Not many more words shall be added to these; and I will keep these

[The rest of this letter is missing]

[1] Mrs. Anderdon was the wife of Oliver Anderdon, Q.C. Lucy, their daughter, Miss Mitford described as 'exquisitely fair, and modest, and graceful'.

[*50 Wimpole Street*]
Monday August 20th [*1838*]

DEAREST MISS MITFORD, you must *dree* this antique of a letter, because I cant afford to let you think it possible that I could live so long without at least *writing* a reply to some words of yours. After many uncertainties, my sister Henrietta,[1] my eldest brother [2] who boasts of having once been introduced to you, and my brother George [3] are promised to go with me— and I am going possibly, I wont say certainly, on *Wednesday* to Plymouth where we may be detained a day or two before any other vessel will take us back to Torquay. Therefore dont [write] until the day of going is a fixed one. The 'may' for tomorrow makes one feel uncomfortable and I cannot just now write about ballads or anything thereto pertaining. There shall be however as little delay as possible in returning the proof.[4] I wish that you your own self had given something *dramatic* to Finden.

The 'favorite maid'. That struck a strained string. Think of our maid—my sister's and mine—deciding just now—only two days ago,—that she would not go with me. We have been obliged to engage another, with great difficulty and haste, and she came as a stranger last night. It is another shade upon the Torquay journey! The reason given for the sudden decision was, the state of her health—and indeed she is not well, poor thing, nor does she look so. But still under the circumstances she might have decided either before or afterwards—not just at this moment—particularly as she had lived between two and three years with us, and had professed her willingness to go anywhere with me. I thanked her for saying so just three weeks ago! We have some reason for suspecting a fear of the sea-voyage to have had a little to do with the change—but I shall not mind this inconvenience much, or any other at all, if I *may* have with me one of my dear sisters. Another 'may' to make me anxious! Nothing is decided.

May God ever bless you! You shall hear from Torquay. Does Dr. Mitford, or do you, like *Devonshire cream*? Tell me whether either or both of you do?

Your attached

E B BARRETT.

[1] Henrietta (1809–60), second daughter and third child of Edward Moulton Barrett.

[2] Edward (1807–40), 'Bro', E B B's favourite brother who was drowned at Torquay in July 1840.

[3] George Goodin (1817–95), eighth child and fourth son of Edward Moulton Barrett.

[4] *The Romaunt of the Page.*

[The Braddons, Torquay]
Tuesday [September 1838]

I sit down in the ashes my beloved friend to grieve that I should have allowed you to be uneasy about me. Oh yes!—I have indeed received the three the four letters which your kindness sent, and also the separate delight from each which that kindness intended. And many many times on every day (the 'many' does not express *how* many!) I have thought of and thanked you in my heart, and felt that I truly loved you. But after all I did not write until now—and after all this silence can your affection for me make an effort and believe and understand how it was that I did not write yet did not forget you—yet did not remember you less often and affectionately than I always must? Do let it try at least!

The physician attending me here was anxious for me to have as much air as possible before the cold came—and would not allow me to keep up my late London habit (very useful in enabling an invalid to get thro' a good deal of writing without fatigue) of lying in bed until two. I was made, on coming here, to get up at ten and am always subject to a certain lassitude in the morning after little exertions—even the exertion of dressing. Then at one or two out I was sent in the chair, and seldom failed to come back quite exhausted and fit for nothing better than reading nonsense. In this way – – by these little things—I have been—not *prevented* from writing to you – – but tempted on from hour to hour and day to day into procrastination. You shall not fear of them again. To write to you is one of my best pleasures—*do* believe *that*—and to read even a little note from you is better than writing. Tell me if Mr. Serjt. Talfourd [1] is at all likely to think me a bold person in doing what you suggest. My position with regard to him, not being that of an ordinary stranger (as we *have* had a very little intercourse—by one or two notes)—nor of a personal acquaintance, makes me more scrupulous and fearful of intruding upon him than I could otherwise be. But if you really think that he would have nobody in his remembrance except *yourself*, in receiving and forwarding my letters to you, I would gladly avail myself of your suggestion.

Indeed my dearest Miss Mitford, I do believe that I am better in some respects. The stethescope was tried on Sunday for the second time since my arrival, and the report is more favorable. Dr. Barry seems to be quite sure that the respiration is clearer on the affected side—and the spitting of blood is very little,—almost [?] less than it has been at all since the first appearance of that unpleasant symptom. At the same time

the last ten days have been dreary, uncomfortable ones to me,
haunted throughout by weakness, an oppressive *sense* of
weakness, and a lowness of spirits from which I am generally
free. Such lowness of spirits, that I could have cried all day
if there were no *exertion* in crying—and feel the consciousness
of there being no cause for gloom, just as a new mortification
instead of as a comfort, the whole time ! This was the result
of taking digitalis for three weeks instead of one—and now I
am reviving, and rising again to the 'high estate' of common
sense and cheerfulness.

Dr. Barry takes Dr. Chambers's view of the case exactly—
which is satisfactory to me who trust so very much in Dr.
Chambers. The opinion given to Lady Sidmouth is quite
mine—as far as I am able to judge of 'the physicians of the
world'. But what I value in him more than even his ability,
is the combination which exists in him, of frankness and feeling.
Abernethy[2] had one without the other. Dr. Chambers never
attempts to deceive you as to your state, and yet never by a
word appears to forget . . I will not say your *feelings*, but even
your preferences and prejudices. Did you hear the cause of
his dismissal from Holland House ? He *told* Lady Holland that
she had a disease of the heart. That was the crime. I have
no Tyburn for it. Have *you* ? . . .

You are not, or have not been well my dearest Miss Mitford
—and have lost one friend by death, and are about to lose her
whom you name another, by marriage . . . Mr. Townsend[3]
too is married. My particular sofa in Wimpole St most
properly derives its genealogy from the tripod. *Dont tell him
so—now mind you dont*—but *really* a vision of his ladye love when
I knew nothing of the existence of one, did pass between my
eyes and the verses of his lady-poet ! Have you seen her ?—and
what are your thoughts ? A spirit, pleasant to meet with,
moved thro' those verses, besides the poetic *feeling* assuredly
contained in them—but they failed in *proving* to my mind the
being of the poetic faculty—and this I confessed to Mr.
Townsend, nothing daunted by the vision ! I was going to
praise him for not being angry—but I wont. Perhaps he was—
and at any rate a Tempter of his order deserves no praise. Just
the same ploughshare had I walked over twice before. First
in the case of a cousin of mine who asked me what I thought

of a gentleman whom we both knew. I said—'very amiable and of no common ability—but of a fidgetiness both in conversation and manner which spoils everything with the idea of *littleness*'. A like question—something like—came to me from a friend whom I esteemed. 'What do you think of Mr. Newnam's preaching'—and my answer was to the effect that if I were *he* I would not preach at all. In both these instances was my innocence abused—the fidget and the preacher being betrothed at the time of the questions to the questioners. Wasnt it too bad dearest Miss Mitford?—yes, and just as bad in your Mr. Townsend as in the rest! . . .

We are going from the kindness of this house next week—to 3 Beacon Terrace which is considered the warmest situation I could occupy—and there my aunt from Frocester will come to pass the winter with my sister and myself.

Dearest Miss Mitford, I send—I venture to send—a little Devonshire cream, although you wont tell me whether you and Dr. Mitford like it at all. If either of you do I shall be *so* glad.

If ignorant people are allowed to think, *I* think that Wisdom Barrett was the son of Papa's uncle. I *think* he was.

May God bless you my beloved friend. I must not write any more, though with a hundred reasons for wishing to do so. You shall not be uneasy again on account of a silence of mine! And *you*—whenever writing to me is not an unkindness to yourself do remember that there is no other way so good of being kind to your

E B B

[1] Thomas Noon Talfourd (1795–1854), lawyer, judge, Member for Reading, friend and biographer of Lamb, and an inexhaustible talker. 'It is impossible to slide in a word,' wrote M R M, 'so that Papa says he never can succeed as a counsel, for, if it should be necessary for him to examine a witness, he never will hold his tongue long enough to hear his answer.' (*L'Estrange*, Vol. II, p. 18.)

[2] John Abernethy (1764–1831), surgeon, anatomist, and physiologist, notorious for the bluntness of his bedside manner.

[3] Richard E. Townsend, whose 'pure and high-toned' contribution to *Finden's Tableaux*, 1839, was *The Coronation, or the Exile of Siberia*, in verse. 'Mr. Townsend, too is going to be married—a second marriage—he being a widower of seven and thirty—and to a poetess—a Miss Shepherd, of the neighbourhood of Frome.' (*L'Estrange*, Vol. I, p. 157.) A Miss Sheppard, of that neighbourhood, published in 1837 *Illustrations of the Scripture, the Hebrew Converts, and Other Poems*.

3 Beacon Terrace [Torquay]
Wednesday [October ?, 1838]

EVER DEAREST MISS MITFORD,

I wanted to write to you very very soon in reply to your last welcome note. I wanted to say to you very soon some words which it suggested. But I have been exceedingly unwell —confined to my bed nearly a week by a sudden return of bad symptoms and so weak since as scarcely to bear without fainting even the passive fatigue of being carried from this bed to the sofa down stairs, by all the gentleness of my brother's love for me. The prevalency of the east wind and sudden coldness of weather connected with it, are considered the causes of the attack. I was not suffered to write—and have only by mainforce written two postscripts to two of Henrietta's many letters to London—which I insisted upon doing because I knew that my writing and my *living* were ideas very closely associated in Wimpole Street. But *you*—I hope my beloved friend that another silence simply made you a *little cross* with me—and not uneasy. It is a disagreeable kind of hope—and I *indulge* in it (on the principle of a rustic friend of Papa's who always used to respond to his enquiry by—'Why Sir, I *enjoys* very bad health indeed') because almost anything is better than making you anxious, at a time too when you may be anxious enough without *me*. Henrietta proposed writing to you—I would not let her do it just to sadden you—and the physician here being very sure of my being better again, I dared making you think 'she is not worth a thought' rather than the worse risk. The pulse is quiet now, and I can *sleep*—indeed the attack itself has quite passed away. And as to the weakness it is passing. From two days to two days I can perceive an increase of strength—and if it pleases God,—He has been *so* merciful!—in two or three weeks more I may be as strong as I was previous to the last pulling down.

My sister and brother and I removed to our present residence just in time—the very day before this illness. Since it, I could not have removed—and the difference between the Braddons and Beacon Terrace is all the difference between the coldest situation in Torquay and the warmest—and my *body* was so ungrateful as to require another sun besides that of kind looks and words.

Here, we are immediately *upon* the lovely bay—a few paces dividing our door from its waves—and nothing but the 'sweet south' and congenial west wind can reach us—and *they* must first soften their footsteps upon the waters. Behind us—so close as to darken the back windows—rises an abrupt rock crowned with the slant woods of Beacon Hill—and thus though the North and East wind blow their fiercest, we are in an awful silence and only guess at their doings . . .

May God bless you. Do you write now—and what?—or are you resting from the Tableaux? Was Mr. Chorley well or tolerably well, when you heard from him?

Your always affectionate and grateful

E B BARRETT

[3 Beacon Terrace, Torquay]
March 7 [1839]

EVER DEAREST MISS MITFORD,

I must say so at the first word, though it may seem so contradictory to the long silence and neglect of which you have or surely *may* have (making every allowance for your tried kindness) judged somewhat severely. To explain it all, my beloved friend, I have been very ill—and your two last delightful letters were received by me when I was *quite* confined to my bed, and in such a state of debility as rendered writing a thing impossible. Even at this time, altho' more than a month has passed since this *laying up* began, the extent of my strength is to bear being lifted to the sofa for three hours a day—and I have not left my bedroom for six weeks. The cold weather at the end of January irritated the chest a good deal—and then most unaccountably—I never suffered from such a thing my whole life before—I had for ten days a kind of *bilious fever* which necessitated the use of stronger medicines than my state could very well bear—and then came on a terrible state of debility— the stomach out of sheer weakness, rejecting all sustenance except wine and water—and the chest, seeming to grudge the exercise of respiration. I felt oftener than once inclined to believe that the whole machine was giving way everywhere.

42

But God has not willed it so. I am much better, and stronger—and growing with my strength has been [?] the wish of assuring you – – that indeed indeed I have *not* forgotten you, I am *not* ungrateful to you. As to the fish—oh what must you have thought! But before your last letter brought me the permission of sending it, I was able to direct some to be sent to you—and the provoking fishermen or market people would not let us have any 'fresh enough' according to the doxy of our cook. Torquay thinks more of pleasure boats than fishing boats. Indeed all the fish we have, or almost all, is the produce of Brixom [*sic*]—and then the East winds set their faces against fishing anywhere. But I shall hope for better facilities henceforward—and in the meantime, if you will take the trouble of directing the empty basket back to me with '*returned basket*' written on the card, it will be ready to go to you again—and will reach me free of carriage. Thank you dearest Miss Mitford for believing that it *does* give me pleasure to do this little service. Would it were greater! . . .

I *do* feel so much for dear Lady Dacre. If you should be writing to her, and should besides feel sure that the sound of a name so little familiar to her as mine, would not be or appear an impertinent intrusion, will you say how I have felt and do feel for her. When kindness has been shown to us—and hers was shown to *me*—we are apt to be intrusive in return. But without this, and indeed apart from it altogether—poor Mrs. Sul[l]ivan [1] was herself interesting to me as a writer. Her tale of the wife with two husbands affected me very much—and appeared most striking to me from its pathos and purity of tone.

God bless you dearest Miss Mitford!

Kindest regards to Dr. Mitford. Go on to find me good news about him. I am tired with writing as you will see.

Papa and *Sett* are here again!—a good reason for my *betterness*.

Your ever attached

E B B

---

[1] Arabella, wife of Frederick Sullivan, vicar of Kimpton, the only daughter of Lady Dacre by her first marriage, had died earlier in the year. She was the author of *Recollections of a Chaperon* (1831), *Tales of the Peerage and Peasantry* (1835), both edited by her mother.

[3 Beacon Terrace, Torquay]
April 10th [1839]

MY BELOVED FRIEND,

The east wind is here instead of the fish—and it seems that we must wait longer for the latter than one of us can, to reply to the dear interesting letter you sent me. I like the tour plan so much—so very much—and I am so very anxious to know your decision as soon as it is made, with regard to the book . . .

With reference to my own self my dearest Miss Mitford, you know very well that I am a slave to the genius of your lamp—if the title be not too high for me always. In the present case I am afraid it is most surely so—although I thank you for the proud pleasure suggested to me by the very *idea* of being associated with you in your undertaking.[1] There never was a more empty-headed body than I am, as to antiquities or local traditions—a more *wonderfully* empty-headed body, considering my delight from childhood until now in unbelievable irrational things – – in all such wild stories as are most apt to stride down to us by tradition. But as to localising or caring for the localities of any, just there is my deficiency—and here is a proof . . that, living for years and years a three miles distance from Ledbury, I never had an opportunity of believing in St. Catharine until Wordsworth gave me one.[2] Would that I were at least so far fit for localizing as to be *loco-motive*—and do something for you in the way of local tradition-hunting in books! Dear Sir Uvedale Price used to say that I was a very good ferret—and so I am – – an indoor ferret. But what can I do bound hand and foot in this wilderness, in the way of book-ferreting—with a physician who groans in the spirit whenever he sees within my reach any book larger and graver looking than 'the last new octavo neatly bound'? Luckily my Plato looks as good as a novel on the outside—but you tempted me with Bishop Andrews,[3] and the Bishop is in folio, and I was in an obstinate fit—and I *did* read – – and *was* scolded—and 'all for the love of you'—and for Mr. Cary's[4] praise of the Bishop . . .

Is Alfred Tennyson among your personal acquaintances? I heard of him the other day as having an unduly large head, handsome features, and a fathoming eye—and that they had

44

all settled into a cottage in Devonshire where he smoked and composed poems all day, suffering many of the latter to escape him for lack of industry to write them down—and separating from his family *because they distracted him*. This was told to my brother by a friend of Mr. Tennyson's, but may be very gossip after all . . .

They carried me down stairs into the drawing room for two weary hours about ten days ago—but the weather has since kept me upstairs. I have had no new attack from this east wind—but feel very oppressed and uncomfortable. Dr. Barry considers that upon a change of temperature I shall certainly come to the surface again—and it is satisfactory to be sure that I have gained strength surprisingly during the last two months, or rather six weeks. For weeks before I was reduced to all but the harmlessness of babyhood—lifting a spoon to my own lips being the only point on which I could claim precedence. Even now I am sure I could not stand a moment alone—but here is summer, *coming* tho' not in sight— and she sends a sort of mental sunshine *before*. It is wonderful that I should have rallied at all from the last attacks—and I cant help feeling very often that I *am* to rally from everything and fulfil some of those affectionate prayers of yours for which, in reference to all results I do most tenderly thank you . . .

Oh!—they were *so* delighted (in Wimpole St.) with the seeds—and Arabel's [5] pleasure in hearing from you (such kind words she said they were!) was worth a garland full-blown. You would laugh to see the primroses in this room—and the branch of yellow heath which I like better than all the rest, because it seems to me a token more directly from Nature's own heart. And yet it is a shame to bring them into the dark, to die,—and I could, if I tried, get up a very pretty tragedy of remorse about it . . .

Here must be the end, dearest Miss Mitford.

I am ever and ever

Your gratefully attached

E B BARRETT.

---

[1] Miss Mitford's proposed tour was to be 'written up', with 'room for traditions and descriptions and antiquarian references of all sorts'.

² Wordsworth's poem, *St. Catharine of Ledbury*, was published in 1835. The poet visited E B B's friend, Sir Uvedale Price, at Foxley Park in 1827.

³ Lancelot Andrewes (1555–1626), Bishop of Winchester. Ninety-six of his sermons were published under the editorship of Laud and Buckeridge in 1628. In 1648 Richard Drake gave to the world the *Manual of Private Devotions*, the *Manual of Directions for the Sick*, and *Prayers for the Holy Communion*, all translated from the Greek and Latin manuscripts of Andrewes.

⁴ Henry Francis Cary (1772–1844), who published in 1812 his translation of Dante's *Divine Comedy*, was 'the mildest and most amiable of men. The extreme gentleness of his face almost hurt its intelligence.' (B. W. Procter, *Autobiography*, etc. p. 207. Bell, 1877.)

⁵ Arabella (1813–68), sixth child, and fourth daughter of Edward Moulton Barrett. (A third daughter, Mary, died in infancy in 1814.) Arabel, wrote E B B of her favourite sister, 'is the least wanted in the house here'. (*Letters of Robert Browning and Elizabeth Barrett Barrett*, Vol. I, p. 193. John Murray, 1946. Afterwards referred to as *Love Letters*.)

[*3 Beacon Terrace*] *Torquay*
Tuesday [*April, 1839*]

EVER DEAREST MISS MITFORD,

I have been a little anxious about your muteness as well as about the 'mute fishes'—wondering whether I had any right to imagine you and Dr. Mitford tolerably well. Do, when it does not too much cross your convenience, let me hear! It seems so long since I heard last, and there are so many disagreeable and painful things in the world notwithstanding all these spring flowers, and I have such a knack of imagining them, that I would gladly be sure of none of them having touched you. Dont fancy me forgetful of the fishbasket. But our servant seems to be a nervous person as to the qualifications of travelling fish—and I told you before that fish in this market, when worth anything, is not very often fish directly from the sea. Did you look into Blackwood this month—and (à propos to fish) perceive how Christopher's 'Oystereater' ¹ congenially with Tait's Opium Eater,² apostrophizes the 'charming and adorable Mary Russell Mitford'? You see no sort of diet will expel the admirations due to you—and the imaginative with their opium, and the literal with their oysters come to the same point at last. Nay—the very oysters are infected, if it be true that ' *The worlds an oyster*' . . .

How right you are not to give away your time to languages. So is everybody who can do anything better.

'And Hebrew roots grow best on barren ground.' The grammar and dictionary drudgery are past bearing, as soon as we have learnt to think. Faust's incantation threw me upon German a year or two ago, but could not keep me in a very exemplary humour notwithstanding. Yet there is a use for all things—for thistles and Babel too : and at painful times, when composition is impossible and reading not *enough*, grammars and dictionaries are excellent for *distraction*. Just at such a time . . when we were leaving Herefordshire . . I pinned myself down to Hebrew, took Parkhurst and Professor Lee [3] for my familiars, and went through the Hebrew Bible from Genesis to Malachi, Syriac and all, as if I were studying for a professorship,—and never once halting for breath. But I do hope and trust to learn no more new languages. There is no mental exertion, per se so little beneficial to the mind.

I covet your familiarity with all sorts of French literature . . a little : but not painfully. French poetry, so called by courtesy, always comes to me cold as prose—and this indisposition of mine has conveyed itself to the prose perhaps scarcely consciously. I believe Pascal stirs me more than any other French writer—at least strikes me as less French – – and as endued with a sort of intellect that reaches deeper down to the feelings . . as deep intellectuality will always do . . than that of the national multitude. I am very backward as to the *Memoirs*—and a hundred miles behind everybody as to French literature of the present day—knowing scarcely anything except of Lamartine and Victor Hugo—and Edgar Quinct, by grace of the Athenaeum,—and the Athenaeum's own Rhapsodist in criticism (Jules Janin) [4] who in his proper particular practice you know, adopted the Siamese twins idealised, as heroines of romance. Peace to the souls of the heroines ! They had two pairs of eyes . . black and blue . . hadn't they?—and only one heart—which was scarcely fair, and turned out to be very unfortunate . . .

What exquisite weather. They have carried me down to the drawing room—twice in the light of it—and I am very tolerably comfortable and well—longing to get back to London, longing to be with them all once more, in Wimpole Street.

But moving is out of the question for me just now . . and must be, before quite the end of May or the first days of June—and even then, there is no plan fixed for me. I *must* be with them this summer—I *must indeed*. I keep saying *that* day after day . . .

Once more God bless you.

Most affectionately your

ELIZABETH B B

Cheveley or the man of honor.

Lady Cheveley or the woman of honor.[5]

Have you observed the latter advertisement? I have seen neither book, but am arrived at two conclusions. The first is, that however infamous Sir Lytton's conduct as a husband may have been—heaping it with every imaginable infamy—Lady Lytton deserves the whole of it. The second—that when a husband lives in London and his wife at Bath, there is no excuse for either, upon any disturbance of their *domestic harmony*. A hundred miles between, really ought to secure some degree of connubial felicity as the world wags—but unfortunately it *wages*. Seriously, how could a woman if ever so unwomanly achieve such a unwomanlyness? The flippancy too of some of the extracts which is irreconciliable with the only excuse for her . . a good earnest downright fury of a passion . . is inexpressibly disgusting to me.

[1] 'Our village! I thought of the charming, the adorable Mary Russell Mitford. Our village!—there was nature, kindliness, and simple-hearted tenderness in the very sound . . .' ('Some Account of himself', by the Irish Oyster Eater. *Blackwoods*, April 1839.)

[2] '. . . Miss Wordsworth was as thoroughly deficient (some would say painfully deficient—I say charmingly deficient) in ordinary female accomplishments, as *Cousin Mary* in Miss Mitford's delightful sketch . . . We all know with how womanly and serene a temper literature has been pursued by Joanna Baillie, by Miss Mitford, and other women of admirable genius . . .' ('Lake Reminiscences from 1807–1830. No. 3, William Wordsworth', by the English Opium Eater. *Tait's Edinburgh Magazine*, April 1839.)

[3] John Parkhurst (1728–97), author of *An Hebrew and English Lexicon* (1762). Samuel Lee (1783–1852), appointed Professor of Hebrew at Cambridge in 1831, wrote *Grammar of the Hebrew Language* (1827).

[4] Jules Janin (1804–74), journalist and dramatic critic; translator of Richardson and discoverer of Rachel. Author of *L'Ane mort et la femme guillotinée* (1829), *Barnave* (1831), *Les Catacombes* (1839), etc.

EDWARD MOULTON BARRETT
From a painting by H. W. Pickersgill, R.A.

⁵ *Chevely, or the Man of Honour*, by Lady Lytton Bulwer, was reviewed in the *Athenaeum* on March 30, 1839. On April 27, 1839, the *Athenaeum's* List of New Books announced *Lady Chevely, or the Woman of Honour*, a rhyming brochure published at 2s. 6d.

[3 Beacon Terrace] Torquay
Thursday [May 1839]

I write in the utmost haste dearest Miss Mitford—that the fish may not go to you in their native silence. May you both be quite well when this reaches you! Give my regards to Dr. Mitford.

I heard the other day a story which amused me. Mr. Garrow¹ in writing to Mr. Landor said (of course in jest) that from the numerous Latin quotations in Chevely he was generally supposed to have assisted in the composition. To which Mr. Landor replied in great indignation and a very seriously crossed letter, that the report was quite untrue and he was much astonished at its having gone abroad—not that he cared so much about the book and its tendencies—but he was excessively annoyed at being considered a dealer in quotations—he, all the time, hating quotations, and feeling perfectly able to *walk without crutches*! How characteristic this is in all ways—and very true—for my brother heard Mr. Garrow talk of it only a few days since.

I am heartily glad to see in the Athenaeum Sir Lytton Bulwer's denial of the brochure attributed to him.² In the meanwhile the 'wife of Bath' so far from wearing sackcloth, is heard of (since the infamous publication) at the Bath masquerade in a *Pompadour costume*!

Ever your most affectionate,
hurried ELIZABETH B B

¹ Joseph Garrow, father of Theodosia Garrow, the poetess. His correspondent, Walter Savage Landor (1775–1864), author of *Count Julian* (1812), *Imaginary Conversations* (1824–29), etc., had recently returned from Italy to live at Bath.

² 'Our Weekly Gossip' quoted a letter to the publisher of *Lady Chevely, or the Woman of Honour*, which expressed concern at the announcement of the work. 'Whatever the views and objects of the writer may be . . . Sir Lytton Bulwer is compelled, for the sake of his children, and in their name, to enter his most earnest protest against any attempt to prolong or widen the notoriety of a recent publication, which carries its own answer and its own condemnation.' (*Athenaeum*, May 18, 1839.)

[3 Beacon Terrace] Torquay
August 11th. 1839

. . . Thank you again and again for your delightful letter
about Mr. Webster [1]—so nobly toned from your own heart—I
do like to read such letters—but I cannot say more, in my haste
today, of yours, than that if I were to confess my ignorance
until very lately, about him of the American Senate, you would
be sure to despise me very much. The first orator in the world,
I think you call him—'except another Daniel'. *Do* you mean
Mr. O'Connell ? [2] Oh surely if he is a great orator, he must
be the height of the sky above Mr. O'Connell. Do you seriously
consider Mr. O'Connell to be a great orator ? Try to forgive
a little astonishment. I disarm you by confessing my ignorance.
I never heard him speak and seldom read his speeches—and
when I do, my doxy is that Mr. Shiel [3] is a greater orator than
Mr. O'Connell, and that strictly speaking nothing oratorically
great belongs to either of them. . .

The coteries must be very close offensive menageries, and
I am glad that I have none of their dust to shake from my feet.
But oh, dearest Miss Mitford if you were to shrive me and find
out what a strong heart I have for making pilgrimages to
certain shrines, and what impulses to lionising hang about me,
you would be ashamed of me—you would indeed. When I
was between child and woman I prayed and teazed a dear old
friend of ours into taking a long hot disagreeable walk in
London (I happened to be there for a short time) just to look
at Campbell's [4] house – – and I did just see the red curtains in
the dining room, and with full contentment of heart – – while
my companion half amused and half annoyed declared over
and over again that I was '*such* a child'—as if that was all to
be said for me. And really I am just 'such a child' at this
moment. Mr. Kenyon would not believe that I cared about
the autographs he brought me—he was sure that I was taking
him in, and wanted them for a blaze [?]. But the religion of
genius or you will say the *superstition*, is over me still. My
organ of veneration is as large as a Welsh mountain. I could
kiss the footsteps of a great man—or woman either—and feel
higher for the stooping. Now make allowances for me. I
was never in literary society, and have not learnt the difference

between books and the men who made them—or the distinctive signs by which you know a genius from an angel—I suppose there are some . . .

God bless and keep you my ever dearest and kindest Miss Mitford!—and all dearest to *you*!

Your attached and grateful

ELIZABETH B BARRETT.

Between my physician and my maid I did what is called *walking* (by courtesy) a few days ago—about three yards of it—and I am better.

Arabel is not come.

¹ Daniel Webster (1782–1852). Described by Miss Mitford, when he visited her in 1839, as 'the first lawyer, orator, and statesman of America' and 'the man who more completely realizes my idea of a truly great man than any one whom I have ever seen'.

² Daniel O'Connell (1775–1847), the Irish 'liberator', orator and politician, who, as M.P. for Dublin and founder of the Repeal Association, held 'Monster meetings' all over the country.

³ Richard Lalor Shiel (1791–1851), dramatist and politician. Returned for Co. Tipperary to the first reformed Parliament of 1833. His ambition, despite a defect of speech, was to be a great orator.

⁴ Thomas Campbell (1777–1844), 'such a pretty, little, delicate, ladylike, finical, gentleman!'. (*L'Estrange*, Vol. II, p. 119.) Author of *The Pleasures of Hope* (1799), *Gertrude of Wyoming* (1809), *Theodoric* (1824), and *The Pilgrim of Glencoe* (1842).

[3 Beacon Terrace, Torquay]
Saturday [September 1839]

MY BELOVED FRIEND,

. . . Poor Dr. Barry my able and most kind physician who for above a year has attended me almost every day—and at my best estate never left me longer than a day,—is seriously ill with rheumatic and nervous fever, has been confined to his bed for ten days and was yesterday in much danger. The crisis and danger are now said to be past—but I still feel anxious and saddened—and not the less so of course, from hearing of the continued solicitude he is expressing about me,—begging me to call in another physician . . which I cant and wont do. May God grant that the improvement in his state may be lasting. He has one dear little girl scarcely past her babyhood,

—and his wife is about to become a mother again : and from his talents and rising reputation, and undeviating attention and kindness towards his patients his loss would be greatly felt in this place, in a professional point of view as in many others. May God spare him to his family and friends! I am very anxious.

Has Mr. Talfourd written for you? I hope so. Mr. Shepherd did not send me his poem, nor have I read it—but I shall try to do so, since your opinion of it is so high. My acquaintance is confined to Lady Mary and her daughter—and even in their case seems to have come to an end—and Mr. Shepherd I never saw in my life. It was when they were staying at Malvern and we were residing at Hope End, that I had my only inter-course with Lady Mary : but two years afterwards Miss Shepherd visited the former place with the Chief Baron of Scotland,[1] and then she came over and spent a week with me—and we parted as friends. I never was so near loving anybody very much whom I did *not* love very much! She might be . . or at least *have been* . . anything! Rapid intelligence and fancy—strong natural sensibility . . rendered peculiar . . at once interesting and repulsive to me . . by the very *naivetè of worldliness*. To explain what I mean, I need only tell you that she used words of this sort in talking to me – – 'I cannot be distinguished by either great beauty, great genius, or high rank. Nothing is left to me but to be faultless in high breeding—an *elegante par excellence*'. Words to that effect . . I am not accurate as to syllables. And in order to confess an object so inglorious i.e. this distinction par Almacks—she spoke openly of the necessity she was under of sacrificing friendship to surtouts,—and how friends in vulgar waistcoats and question-able situations never could be visible objects to her eyes, however dear to her heart. She is *all* vulgar—vulgar—vulgar! more vulgar than any waistcoat or locality—the vulgarity on all sides of us every day in one form or another! But her open-ness in telling it, and the kind of principle upon which she based the profession struck and amused me,—and contrasted so blackly and whitely with much besides which I observed and estimated and admired in her, that I could have wept real tears and loved her through them all, to hear those shackles rattle 'abhorred music' as she cast them off . . .

When my Prometheus came out, I directed the publisher
to send a copy to Lady Mary as from the author—which
remains unacknowledged : and when we went to London and
had ascertained that she knew of our being there, I did not
like to be the first to break the silence and renew the acquaintance. I dont know much about etiquettes. Perhaps I should
have sent a card. But under the silence and the circumstances,
and the remembrance of dear Miss Shepherd's old theories, I
did not like to do it. Suppose I had been convicted of a vulgar
waistcoat ? . . .

Do let your next account of yourself be a better one. I
am anxious about you my beloved friend. For my own part I
have not been very well for some days—suffering from oppres-
sion on the chest and old symptoms consequent upon the
changeable moist heavy state of the atmosphere. The fearful
winter is at hand again ! On the first of October we remove,
or intend doing so now, to a new house, *1* Beacon Terrace,—
which is promised to be a warmer residence than our present
one . . .

> Believe how very truly you are loved by your
> Elizabeth B Barrett—

. . . My sister—Henrietta has made the acquaintance of
the Miss Goldings, neighbours of yours, and *nightingales*, I
understand. They have left Torquay? Are they your
acquaintances or your friends? I would rather have heard
them talk of you—than sing !

---

¹ Sir Samuel Shepherd, Miss Shepherd's grandfather.

> [*3 Beacon Terrace*] *Torquay*
> *Sept. 27th 1839*

Thank you again and again my beloved friend for your
kindest solicitude. Since I wrote to you last I have been much
grieved and very anxious. Poor Dr. Barry's illness could not
have been simple rheumatic fever. At any rate, a few hours
after Mrs. Barry had written to beg that I would write to him
most particularly about myself as he was much better and

very anxious on my account, a relapse came, and for a night and a day his medical attendants had little or no hope of him . . . I do thank God—everything is going right now, and there is no room for fear. I do thank God. Had the worst happened, I should have scarcely borne to stay here—and I could not ever have shaken from my mind, in any case, that I must have been the involuntary cause of some of the evil,—poor Dr. Barry having risen from his bed two days before he was quite confined to it, for the purpose of coming thro' an atmosphere saturated with rain, to see me between nine and ten at night. I said at the time 'Oh how ill you do look! How could you come out in such weather!' little thinking what was impending. Well—I thank God that all is bright or brighter now. And as to my sending for a substitute my dearest Miss Mitford, if you know how I shrink from a *stranger* in the shape of a physician, you would not ask it . . .

Lady Mary [Shepherd] *is* a singular woman. I think gratefully of her from some passages of kindness which passed from her to me, when I wanted kindness most, and the saddest of domestic losses was nearer than I thought or *would* think.[1] I believe her to be a *kind woman*—a better if not a higher name than a great metaphysician . . . Her daughter at once admired and *feared* her—feared her very much—and nobody else in the world. She seemed to love—in the clear meaning of love - - her father—with no fear in *that* love. There was love too in abundance, I am sure, between the metaphysician and the dramatist—and Lady Mary used to say jestingly—'We are *very* much in love with each other'. Notwithstanding which, he used by her own account to take up his hat and walk out whenever she began to dissert (she *does* dissert you know) upon primary and secondary qualities in matter—and she on the other hand was the *authority* in all domestic matters and wouldn't suffer any interference. 'What can *he* know about children? Why he was only a boy *when I married him*'! Just those words! I am certain this time about the syllables. They are unforgettable.

Now you see what a gossip you have made of me. Dont tell it all again to Sir Samuel.

She used to keep Miss Shepherd up to three or four in the morning after a conclave of waltzers to hear (she being 'sole auditor') vocal dissertations upon spirit and matter and such high arguments—then suddenly check herself with – – 'My dear!—how *can* you stand with your left foot before your *right*'! . . .

Poor poor Lady Flora Hastings![2] Sir James Clark has *hallucinated* considerably from the high sphere in which you place his profession. The *ignorance* was the least of the injury. It appears to have been combined with coldness and coarseness of feeling. I would give much to rescue the young queen from any such imputation. *Can it be done?* I heard gladly of the tears she shed when tears were vain—but still the circumstances can scarcely be effaced by tears—and perhaps the most ineffaceable of all, was her cold long silence to the poor victim whose innocence was proved,—*in consequence of her uncle's publication of facts.* That the queen could have been provoked by any publication, by any insult which that publication was *not*, by any injury which that publication was *not*, to give *more* pain to a heart so pained by herself, is an atrocity I would fain hear explained away.

So much for human ties in royal breasts—
Why spare men's feelings when their own are jests?

But surely surely the young Queen with her fair happy-looking face, and her warm ready childish tears for the departure from office of her political friends, cannot be a mere Queen Stone, co-regnant with King Log. I would fain hear differently. Have you heard anything? . . . Do give my love to Dr. Mitford. We go to number one on this Terrace, on Monday or tuesday—and there wont be much risk for me in the removal for so short a distance. My brother means to fold me up in a cloak and carry me.

May God ever bless you! Pray dont throw away more anxious thoughts upon me. If I had any really *bad* symptoms, I would call in another physician. As it is do let me enjoy the luxury of being obstinate and perverse as Mr. Kenyon calls it.

Your obstinately affectionate

E B B

---

[1] E B B's mother, after some years of ill-health, died at Cheltenham Spa in October 1828.
[2] Lady Flora Hastings, a lady-in-waiting to the Duchess of Kent, was

accused by Sir James Clark, the Court physician, of being pregnant. With the Queen's approval, Lady Flora Hastings was medically examined, and Sir James found that he was in error. The incident made the Queen very unpopular, and when, later in the year, the unfortunate lady-in-waiting died of an internal tumour, the carriage the Queen sent to the funeral procession was stoned on its way to the cemetery.

[*1 Beacon Terrace*
Postmark : *Torquay, October 30, 1839*]

I am afraid ever dearest Miss Mitford, to think what you may think of me with all these days nay, weeks between your last interesting letter and my acknowledgement of it. But I have been much grieved—and too unwell to *stir* to seek for your sympathy. Dear kind Dr. Barry is no more. A second relapse followed fast upon the first, and you could scarcely have read what I wrote in hope and gladness before all lay reversed, and by a startling decree of God, the physician was taken and the patient *left*—and left of course deeply affected and shaken. He was a young man—full of energy—with a countenance seeming to look *towards life*—devoted to his profession and rising rapidly into professional eminence—a young man with a young wife and child, and baby unborn – – and in such circumstances there should not be room for *me* to feel my own loss in his unslackening kindness and interest—yet I made room for my selfishness !—have deeply felt it. To the very last his kindness did not slacken – – but I need not bear down upon you with all this sadness. God's will be done . . be the close of all.

You did your part in waging war against my obstinacy, beloved friend—but you see I *would* until dear Dr. Barry was *gone* . . struggle on without medical advice—and the effect was a great deal of irritation superinduced into the system—so that upon my removal to this house and the agitation of mind instantly succeeding, I was ill, and had my old attack of fever and imperviousness to sleep, and have not indeed left my bed for a longer period than three quarters of an hour, these three weeks or more. They called in the senior physician of the place, Dr. Scully,—who is considered clever and safe—and his verdict upon the pulse this morning appears much more favorable. But you will understand that I have not been neglecting you through too much prosperity—and forgive a silence so sadly and heavily passed by me. And if you *do*, prove the clemency by the writing. I want to hear of you so very much, and besides of dear Dr. Mitford!

Oct. 29th The above was written some days ago. Would that it had been finished and sent then, because in such a case, I might be watching for a letter from you during this *now*. However, the delay allows me to tell you of my being better,— and able to get to the sofa for an hour every day, notwithstanding the terrible east wind . . Papa being here to counteract it with the 'sweet south' of his presence. And he looks so well that everybody who loves him as I do, must begin to look well too . . .

Miss Anderdon has written. And do when you see her, express my thanks for the kindness which she did write, inclusive of her wish to begin our acquaintanceship to come, next summer. I am sure I cannot know her too soon—but our meeting then *at Torquay* depends on two great uncertainties, and one of them, the last, is most unpleasant for me to think of—viz the continuance of my life—and of my residence at this place. I *long* to go away. How we drag our weary wills after God's will . . reluctantly sadly heavily . . as if we did not recognise in *it* the chief wisdom. '*We*' is written and it should be '*I*'—'*I*' being the most inconsistent of all disquieted waters. God keep me and make me better and meeker and lower beneath His feet!

Dearest dearest Miss Mitford, I liked the Athenaeum note about your garden and the King of Prussia's policy![1] I wish I could see it and you—and love both of you at a distance.

Your attached

E B B

The new house is warm and in all ways or *most*, superior to the last.

---

[1] H. F. Chorley, on a visit to Berlin, described the English garden of the Pfauen-Insel, and added in a footnote: 'There is a greater variety of plants in one patch the size of a table, in Miss Mitford's flower garden, than in the whole open-air "policy" of the King of Prussia.' (*Athenaeum*, October 26, 1839.)

[*1 Beacon Terrace*] *Torquay*
Jan. 3rd. 1840

EVER DEAREST MISS MITFORD,

I long to hear about you. May I? I am gathering strength (stick by stick) myself—but the movement to the sofa from the bed for the first time last sunday produced such fainting and exhaustion that it is not to be repeated immediately. Still the strength comes—*however* slowly—and I am able to write and read pretty much as usual—and Papa is here still—so that there is nothing to repine about. Dreaming of going to London which is my dream, whenever my spirits rise into sight, in relation to myself, is a dream unpartaken I fear by my physician. I do long, naturally and fervently to be at home—but he says there are two reasons against it—one being that I couldn't go, and the other, that Dr. Chambers would send me back again if I could. Well—I dream.

And my dreams involve much of you my beloved friend and dear Dr. Mitford. Oh do let me hear of you. It seems lately as if the mountains and rivers between us had grown higher and broader. Whose fault is this! I dont feel as if it possibly could be *mine*. How are you? How is he? How are the *letters*?—in the press? How is the garden?—and Flush? And what summer plans have you all taken up?

Thank you for the beautiful geranium which held its colors fast, and let me look at them entire. So that is *I*! Bearing my name, its bloom put me to shame—in my thinness and ghastliness! The contrast suggested a very 'pretty moral'—only I chose rather to think of the graceful compliment implying the dear kindness.

Have you given up the idea of ever seeing Mr. Darley's [1] book again? It chaperons or is chaperoned by some Devonshire cream – – but I beg you to remember that the stains upon its back came to me as they go, and proceeded from neither cream nor me. The chronicle is very clever and spirited—picturesque and racy—and the character of Becket appears to me developped with no ordinary power. At the same time I confess myself disappointed in the absence of tragic passion and concentration, and in the boldness as to poetry generally. Is it a work of talent merely—or of genius? Of high talent, I should say – – if I might. The want of imagination rather than its exuberance is manifest in Dwerge who is simply *nasty*. I should like to lift her out of the book with a pair of tongs! Not without them—notwithstanding my earnest wish for the triumphant speeding of Mr. Darley's indubitable powers.

Oh yes! I have often attended religious branch meetings, in country towns, whose *roots* are in Exeter Hall. I never was at a meeting in *Exeter Hall*, on account of the crowds—and never read the book you speak of. The book may be vulgar enough—but surely there is nothing vulgar in that gathering of mighty sympathies in order to a mighty end—God's end as well as man's—which we find embodied in our Bible society and the various missionary societies. Dont let anybody prejudice you, dearest dearest Miss Mitford. Some of those exposition books whether in relation to religious views in the abstract or habits founded upon such, often do the very greatest harm with the very best intentions. Save me from friends of that class.

Have you seen Mr. Horne's [2] Gregory? It is a work of surprising power—altho' it does not, to my mind, reach the tragic heights of his Cosmo.

Love to dear Dr. Mitford. Forgive my abruptnesses. I have written myself quite tired.

Your ever attached
E B B

[1] George Darley (1795–1846), poet and mathematician. Author of *Sylvia, or the May Queen* (1827), *Nepenthe* (1839), *Thomas à Becket* (1840), *Ethelstan* (1841). 'He is a remarkable person,' wrote Miss Mitford, 'son of an alderman of Dublin, and disinherited because he would be a poet . . . He keeps aloof from the whole world, in consequence of stammering to a degree which is most painful to himself and others . . . He calls Miss Barrett mediocre. He cannot think so.' (*L'Estrange*, Vol. I, p. 278.)

[2] Richard Henry (later Hengist) Horne (1803–84), a picturesque character, and a prolific writer, who at this time initiated a correspondence with E B B. It is evident that E B B derived a certain emotional satisfaction from the relationship, which preceded her introduction to Robert Browning. Horne's chief works were *Cosmo de Medici* and the *Death of Marlowe* (both 1837), *Gregory VII*, a tragedy (1840), and *Orion, an Epic Poem* (1843).

[1 Beacon Terrace. Torquay
January 1840]

. . . Can anything grow anywhere or anyway with this terrible wind? The temperature of my bedroom is kept up day and night to 65 and I am not suffered to be moved from the bed even for its making—and yet the noxious character of the air makes me very uncomfortable and sleepless. I took two draughts of opium last night—but even the second failed to bring sleep. 'It *is* a blessed thing!'—that sleep!—one of my worst sufferings being the want of it. Opium—opium—night after night—! and some nights, during east winds, even opium wont do, you see! . . .

[1 Beacon Terrace. Torquay]
Jany. 15th 1840

DEAREST DEAREST MISS MITFORD,

Shame on me to have let you write again, without any words of mine, in grief and sympathy for your illness, coming in between! It seemed to me when I received your letter just now that I deserved much less than usual of all your affectionateness and dear Dr. Mitford's too! And yet if loving you very much and thinking very much of you make the silence excusable, I am safe. You said you were a good deal better again—and I on my own part was wrestling with the east wind or rather prostrated by it, and waiting for its going away, to get up again and write to you—the getting up being altogether metaphorical, inasmuch as there appears no hope of leaving my bed until the warm months begin . . .

The spitting of blood has never intermitted from last March twelvemonth, and my voice has never been able to lift itself above a whisper since October. There has been by Dr. Scully's desire, a consultation lately with a physician high in authority in Exeter whom I was ensnared into seeing, and they agreed that after all I was likely with care to get through the winter safely, and to be better in the warmer season. I made an enquiry whether it was considered medically possible for me to be *ever* quite well—and the answer modified my 'quite well' into a tolerably well – – such a degree of health as would admit of my creeping about again with some comfort and independance; and this is considered both possible and probable. I heard it thankfully . . .

How is your godchild? Do tell me. The Bishop of Exeter's [1] dealing damnation round the church on Christmas day, is no romance. The curate was I suppose a soft-hearted man and tried to escape the Athanasian creed, when 'Whereas' prompted the episcopal voice from the episcopal pew, and 'whereas' said the curate by constraint. And then again at the sacrament, he, in his benignity substituted the word 'con-demnation', . . 'damnation' cried the bishop, holding up the book of Common prayer as if it were a *missile*. And then once again—for 'thrice the brindled cat has mewed'—he cried out 'That bread is not consecrated!'—which really, taking one demonstration with another, was enough to tempt any person into responding 'That bishop is not consecrated'. He is the very parody of what a minister of peace should be—and this is the consequence of crowning pamphleteers with mitres. Isn't it enough to provoke many thinking and feeling people into dissent—or at least to beguile all thinking and feeling people into forgiving that offence?

I know you of old in your theory of names my dearest Miss Mitford (which parentheses began itself by breaking through a reverie upon *Philpots*) but I thought then and think now that you stand upon terrible vantage ground in holding it. Mary Russell Mitford is simple and noble at once—but what are we of the commonalty to do—and others of the more decided snobocracy and cacology? What are they to do? Would you for instance sweep away all the multitudinous Smiths on the predestination of this new nominalism—all the Thomsons and Simpsons and Browns without the e? As to my first name, you have made me like it—but

> 'One name is Elizabeth
> Th' others let them sleep in death'

Elizabeth Barrett Barrett . . so that I never never could by the shining of any connubial star, have put away both Barretts . . and have nothing as it is, for consolation except etymology, Barrett Barrett, meaning in the Saxon tongue helmet upon helmet—and even *that* is indicative of some unheroic liking for a superfluity of defence . . .

My beloved friend, good night. I am so tired. *Can* you make out this intolerable writing? May God bless and keep you and dear Dr. Mitford.

Your ever attached

ELIZABETH BARRETT BARRETT.

¹ Henry Phillpotts (1778–1869), author of the *Canning Letters* (1827), a pamphlet defending the settlement under the Poor Law, and another defending the Peterloo massacre. Created Bishop of Exeter in 1830, his action in voting against the Reform Bill led to a mob attack on his palace. A high churchman who was reputed to have changed his opinions to win preferment, he was also a pugnacious man who spent over £20,000 on law suits. This strict disciplinarian was the father of fifteen children.

[1 Beacon Terrace] Torquay
Thursday [February 1840]

. . . Now do my dearest Miss Mitford, write and tell me all about yourself and dear Dr. Mitford! It would revive me like an inward spring, to hear a great deal of good about you. Is it to be heard? God grant *that*. I have asked all I have access to about the maid, and cannot hear of a place for her,— and I do hope that by this time your success has been greater. My own maid and my sisters' is faultless in kindness and attention to me—or—had there been a vacancy near myself—I should have very much liked to fill it with anybody *consecrated by association with you*! Papa has not come yet :—so that I am not as silly as Dr. Scully fancied, when he found me with tears running down my cheeks because of 'a fortnight's absence',— and sate down in a kind of despair at my bedside, with his 'Well Miss Barrett—there is no *reasoning* on such subjects!' But I know very well how these 'fortnights' are apt to grow. *That* was a fortnight before Christmas! Dearest Papa has so much occupation, and so many to care about and discipline in London, that it is very difficult for him to go two hundred miles away from it—though Styx be 'nine times round him' with promises.

I am tolerably well—but there is an east wind, and I feel it—and I feel too, by way of accessory *in* the way of inconvenience, this perpetual blister . . which is to do me good perhaps, and which in the meantime keeps me very quiet and *un*comfortable !

Thank you for all your amusing *Mitfordiana*. I will tell you as a secret, that a Mr. Henry Mitford (in the navy, I think he is) behaved nearly as ill to Mr. Boyd's daughter as his uncle did to the Greeks.[1] (Forgive me—but I am sure you dont admire that *h*istory (pro *m*ystery) of iniquity !—) She is married now . . but she did at one time feel the cruelty very deeply—at least as deeply as a woman of rather quick than profound feelings could be supposed to do. They met at Malvern—she, a singularly pretty girl and very young—and a guitar between them and a great deal of flirtation . . causing them to separate under a tacit sort of engagement and with exchanged locks of hair. She received back a few days afterwards her ringlet wrapt up in an old newspaper, and without a word ! So I say '*cruelty*'. They met again after years and years, and he told a long tale about a plot against them both . . how he was persuaded that she had married, . . and was married himself in a kind of trance . . an absolute state of unconsciousness, he maintained it was ! Altogether the explanation sounded to me rather worse than the thing supposed to be explained—but *she believed it*, poor thing, *of course*. That a woman should fancy herself beloved, and be mistaken, . . would always seem to *her* a stranger thing, than that a man should be married in a trance,—or any other miracle ! . . .

Mr. Horne since I named him last to you, has sent me his *Marlowe*—and moreover written in the very kindest way to propose amusing me to the end of the cold weather by sending anything amusable that might pass thro' his hands and thoughts —a proposition arising from his having heard something of the closeness of my imprisonment, through a mutual friend. The whole manner of it was most abundantly kind—most singularly so considering that we are strangers to each other. I am in a fit of gratitude—and believe more than ever in my edition of the Tales of the Genii. Your ordinary ladies and gentlemen would never think of doing such things. In the first place they couldnt make their way so close to a stranger as to make their kind feelings audible—they couldnt for conventionalisms—for the rustling of their petticoats and the creaking of their shoes.

Mr. Horne has told me too of what I never dreamt - – that

I am named in Leigh Hunts 'Feast of the Violets' . . published two years ago—and very kindly named.[2] Some lines he extracted . . but *not* those in relation to *you*, altho' he refers to *them* besides. Did you ever see the poem—a pendant to the Feast of the Poets? And have you seen the new tragedy—this *Legend of Florence*? To judge from very scanty extracts it seems to have deep pathos and poetry—but rather, I should fancy, an ultra laxity of versification. Where is Otto? Are you arranging anything?[3] Do tell me all—and with my love to dear Dr. Mitford, believe me ever and ever gratefully yours, in true affection

E B B

Do mention your health *very* particularly!

[1] The uncle, having 'philandered with three young ladies', became engaged to a granddaughter of William Mitford, author of the *History of Greece*, but 'put off the marriage for fifteen years, under the plea of illness, hunting every open day all the while'. Ann Henrietta Boyd, the only daughter of Hugh Stuart Boyd, married Henry William Hayes at Marylebone Church on August 1, 1837.

[2]
      A young lady then, whom to miss were a *caret*
      In any verse-history, named, I think, Barrett,
      (I took her at first for a sister of Tennyson)
      Knelt, and receiv'd the god's kindliest benison.
      —'Truly', said he, 'dost thou share the blest power
      Poetic, the fragrance as well as the flower;
      The gift of conveying impressions unseen,
      And making the vaguest thoughts know what they mean.
      Only pray have a care, nor let Alfred beguile
      Admiration too far into manner and style;
      Nor divide with the printer your claim to be read
      By directing our faculties when to say *ed*.
      Such anxieties do both your Geniuses wrong;
      Tend to make things too verbal, the mind not so strong;
      And besides, my dear, who has not read an old song?'

(*Blue Stocking Revels, or the Feast of the Violets*, by Leigh Hunt. *Monthly Repository*, July 1837.) *A Legend of Florence* was produced at Covent Garden on February 17, 1840.

[3] There was some talk, at this time, of putting on Miss Mitford's unacted tragedy at Drury Lane. Once more the scheme failed to materialize.

[*1 Beacon Terrace, Torquay*]
May 17 [?] *1840*

My beloved friend, I must try to write a few lines to you today, lest you should in your kindness turn my long silence

3 Mile + May 10th 1839
J. Mitford

DOCTOR MITFORD
From a painting by John Lucas, 1839

into sad thoughts for yourself. There have been many many [?] for me—worse than sad—lately. Dearest Miss Mitford I have been very unhappy—and very ill besides or you should have heard before. Dreadful news came from the West Indies five weeks ago—and I have lost one of my beloved brothers [1] – – lost him whilst I was thinking of him as being in health. Gone [?] and with a long earthly futurity before him yet [?] God's will be done—but it has worked of course much bitter suffering to all of us—worked it *in love* – – I would not forget *that*. But I was weak you see, and was struck down instantaneously as by a bodily blow. I have been very ill with fever—passing from delirium at nights to such extreme exhaustion by day that I never thought to write to you any more. It would have been very melancholy for poor Papa if he had lost two children by one stroke—would it not?

But I am much better now, and have been able to read for these ten day's past—and for a whole month my dear dear Papa has been with me—I ought to be better . . with *him*. We are all better now. I am sure you will feel for us, my beloved friend . . .

[1] This was Samuel (1812–40), the second of Edward Moulton Barrett's eight sons. He died of yellow fever on February 17, 1840, at Cinnamon Hill Great House, in Jamaica. (*The Family of the Barrett: A Colonial Romance*, by Jeanette Marks. New York, 1938.)

[*1 Beacon Terrace, Torquay*]
Monday [*Autumn 1840*] [1]

MY BELOVED FRIEND,

You have not thought me ill or—worse [?] still—unkind for not writing. I feel bound more than I ever remember having felt, in chains, heavy and cold enough to be iron—and which have indeed entered into the soul. But I do love you still—and am rather better than worse—likely, I do suppose to live on. In the meantime, thank you thank you for your letter, and *both* of you dear Dr. Mitford, and my beloved friend, for your affectionate sympathy. Months roll over months. I know it is for good—but *very hard to bear*. And now—at least a week ago—my kind physician, after having held out hope from time to time, for the sake I do suspect now of drawing me onward, brought me his ultimatum—that he cannot sanction my attempting to leave this dreadful place before the spring. He told me he had wished and prayed it might be otherwise, but he was convinced now that in the case of my removing even to another house *here* much less to London, the consequences would be fatal.

After all, I suffer so in staying that I would dare it and go. But my saying this is quite vain, with Papa and my sisters looking on. They wont hear of it. So I stay. They are well I thank God . . .

May God bless you always. My sisters love to you—and mine to Dr. Mitford. *Can* you read?

Your unchangingly affectionate

E B B

Notwithstanding this trembling hand I am better and stronger—and more tranquil as to my thoughts. I suffered from what was called *congestion of the heart*—and was [?] in so singular and frightful a state of weakness as not to be able to sleep for five minutes together without *fainting*. For weeks they watched me in their kindness night after night—only ascertaining the transition by a sigh, or the sudden coldness of cheek and forehead. And now I can sleep for an hour or more at a time—and the faintings are almost quite gone. Dearest Miss Mitford—I do truly love you. Love me a little. You understand so well—and will—besides—that I want them all to go and leave me here with my maid for the winter. I should be far easier and happier if they would—*far easier* but I fear they wont go,—dear things! . . .

---

¹ In the interval between this letter and the preceding one, tragedy had once again struck at the Moulton Barrett family. On July 11, 1840, three months after the news had reached England of the death of Samuel in Jamaica, Edward, the eldest son, was drowned while yachting with a friend in Babbicombe Bay. Against his father's wish, he had prolonged his stay at Torquay in order to be near his invalid sister; by the malice of circumstances, she had parted from him on that day 'with a pettish word'. This loss of one whom she had loved more than any other human being, was to mark EBB for the rest of her life. Although she never again pronounced his name aloud, to the end of her days, she continued secretly to mourn his loss, and to reproach herself for being the indirect cause of his death.

[*1 Beacon Terrace, Torquay*
October 1840]

MY EVER BELOVED FRIEND,

I never once thought of your thanking for such a thing—
nor could any of us—although it seems to me that no hand can
so rightly express this as the one which trembles so in doing it.
You are always among the most affectionate and disinterested.
I supposed it to be a duty on my part to give up the trust into
your hand.

I am better you see—and thankful for being so, on *one*
account (as far as concerns myself) for it gives me hope that
they will soon let me *go* away from this dreadful dreadful place.
The physician said I should die in going, if they took me—but
nearly three months anguish here has been the worse killing.
Oh my beloved friend! These walls—and the sound of what
is very fearful a few yards from them—that perpetual dashing
sound, have preyed on me. I have been crushed, trodden
down. God's will is terrible!

But they are well—those who are *left*. I thank God. I
pray for you beloved friend and yours—loving you truly and
to the *end*.

Your E B B

I am very much better. Arabel's affectionate [?] thanks.
Write to me.

[*1 Beacon Terrace, Torquay*]
Decr 10th 1840

. . . You cant guess what my business has been lately.
Chaucer? No!—not Chaucer.[1] Chaucer was done with
some time since, and I received him the evening before last,
with a vernally green back like 'A sweet new poem'. No—my
business has been—retracing my steps in the Village, your
village,—step by step, up and down, and never feeling tired.
You cannot realise,—you the writer—cannot,—the peculiar
effect of that delightful book, upon one in a prison like me,
shut up from air and light, and to whom even the captive of
Chillon's bird does not come to sing. It is not sadness—it is
not regret. On the contrary. It frees me at once, for the

moment—shows me the flowers and the grass they grow by, and pours into my face the sweetness and freshness and refreshment of the whole summer in a breath.

Oh do tell me whatever more may be decided in respect to *Otto*. I care so much.

You were in London! When I read *that* I began to dream what joy your going would have been to me if I had been in London too! But perhaps my turn may come to take joy in your being in London. Perhaps. If such a word as joy is ever to come to my lips again—with a meaning in it—for indeed the three letters in that word, seemed to mock me as I wrote them. And yet, I have thanked God tonight for a deeply-felt mercy— for the safe arrival of my beloved brother Charles John from the West Indies. I thank God for His abundant mercies. Abundant, past my deserts, they are always. Only hearts in a manner broken, do not hold the right and full sense of them—I fear, not . . .

---

[1] The *Poems of Geoffrey Chaucer Modernised* (1841). At the suggestion of Wordsworth's friend, Thomas Powell, and with the assistance of Wordsworth himself, a group of contemporary poets was invited to co-operate in the task of translating Chaucer into modern English. The book was edited by R. H. Horne. EBB's share in what Landor called the breaking of Chaucer's 'dull but richly-painted glass, to put in (if clearer) much thinner panes' was the modernization of *Queen Annelida and False Arcite* and *The Complaint of Annelida*.

[1 Beacon Terrace, Torquay
December 1840]

EVER EVER DEAREST MISS MITFORD AND DEAR DR. MITFORD,

May I say so? May I thank both of you for letting me and liking me to have Flush the second? I do, you see—if I may or not. I must. No dog in the world could please me so—and if really and truly I dare accept him, that is if you are quite unrepentant of your kind proposal, why there is nothing to be done but to be ready to receive him at the earliest moment, and to love him at all moments, for your sake, until we reach the 'inherent merit', the loveability for his own.

But dearest Miss Mitford, we have considered, and enquiries have been made for me at the Hotel here,—and it is matter of assurance that there is no room for fear, if you send him directly hither through Basingstoke. Send him by the railroad to Basingstoke, with a direction on the card . . 'to be forwarded by the first Exeter coach'—and the coachman both there and at Exeter shall be commissioned to feed him and see to his comfort generally. There is no danger Mr. Webb assured my councillor—that is, if he is packed carefully in a *hamper*.

But then comes my dread. Is it not a robbery?—or rather shall you not miss him? Will Dr. Mitford miss him? Will Flush (the first) miss him? Now I trust to you not to *grieve* me by suffering such things to be.

And if the kindness says '*no*', will you

[The rest of this letter is missing.]

[*1 Beacon Terrace, Torquay*]
Dec. 28th. 40

MY EVER DEAREST MISS MITFORD,

When you first 'thrust [?] the honor' of your little Flush upon me, I clasped it by the first impulse, as I think I told you, 'with both hands'. But now I stand perplexed—(oh, dont wonder at me!) and lose my hold.

Because you see, my beloved friend, with all my thankfulness to you and dear Dr. Mitford for wishing me the space of a minute, to have your Flush, I could not be comfortable in going farther than the thankfulness, into an acceptance. Oh no! *Let* me say 'oh no' without building up a character for capriciousness! I keep the thankfulness—I thank you both cordially—but I let little Flush go.

In the first place, the dog is of far too great value; which objection I never thought of at first—knowing, you see, so little about dogs! The price *I* set upon him, was his having been near *you*: the inherent value was overlooked. And indeed a very small quiet little dog was the limit of my dog's ambition— and a larger one, a valuable one, and fit *for sporting* purposes would be thrown away upon me, and exposed to a martyrdom, whether in this room, or hereafter, in London. You will understand how it is dearest kindest Miss Mitford! You will understand how foolish, almost cruel, I should be, to introduce a sporting valuable spaniel into the London streets prison, for

69

ever and ever. Dr. Mitford will agree with me, that it wouldn't do at all. But I thank you—both of you—none the less—and shall hope, to greet the paternal Flush some day at Three Mile Cross, in lieu of the earlier greeting of his son!

And perhaps no dog would quite suit me, with my present habits, except a certain Mayfair one of which I once heard – – given, whenever exposed to the cold air, to faint away and be revived with hartshorn. Until I meet with its counterpart, I must try to do 'without a velvet gown or a little dog or a gentleman usher, or anything befitting a lady' . . .

[The rest of this letter is missing.]

[*1 Beacon Terrace*] *Torquay*
Jany. 2 [*1841*]

'You are invincible'—you, my beloved friend, and your kindness,—dear Dr. Mitford and his—and I have not a word to say about Flush, except grateful ones—thanks upon thanks. Yet for obstinacy's sake, *my* obstinacy's, or rather my *perversity* (*that's* dear Mr. Kenyon's word for me!—) I must go on being sure that the dog is too good, too caninely noble, for some of my base purposes. But I shall make it up to him, at least something of it, in love and care. I must love him, coming from *you*—pretty or not—ears or not. The love is a certainty whatever the beauty may be—and if I am to see in his eyes, as you say, your affectionate feelings towards me, why the beauty must be a certainty too.

Well—dearest Miss Mitford. So I open my arms to your Flush—and shall give notice to the coachmen, that he may suffer no cruelty on his Wednesday and Thursday's journies. And pray do be sure that I did not struggle against your kindness, as if it could be a burden to be obliged to *you*. Oh no. It was not *that* . . .

My dear dear brother Charles John, from the East Indies, and my youngest brother Octavius came yesterday. They came against my will. I would rather, for love's sake, they had stayed at home. But since they wished to come and *would* come, dear things,—and since the *meeting* is over—(more full of anguish than any parting—) we shall have the comfort, if not the enjoyment of those who love each other and are together—and I cannot *say* to them, looking on their dear faces 'I wish you had not come'. Indeed looking *there*, I can scarcely go on wishing it to myself.

But my headache, carried from yesterday, is very bad, and makes this note stupid to some intensity. I conjecture so—not having clear-headiness enough to be sure even of *that*.

My sense in writing, is simply to welcome *Flush*. With my most affectionate and earnest wishes for all happiness to you and yours my beloved friend—and my thanks upon thanks for all your kindness, ever believe me

your E B B

[1 Beacon Terrace, Torquay]
Monday [May, ?, 1841]

. . . *You* have been ill my beloved Miss Mitford—and are not well, I fear, even now. That sickness!—I know how distressing it is,—having suffered myself from it dreadfully—in consequence of no stomachic affection, but mere debility. All the latter part of last year, . . indeed until very lately the simplest causes . . even *speaking* a little too much, provoked the most violent vomiting which of course increased the weakness *in* which it originated. So I can feel for you—know fully what you suffer. You *suffer*—ah—may that be a wrong word now . . a wrong tense for the word. Mind you tell me exactly, when you write my dearest friend. I say, you see '*when* you write', not daring to say 'write'.

In the long letter, you mentioned friends of yours who had suffered deep affliction. Tell me how they are.

Then the little puppies, Flush's puppies, whom you and Ben [1] were nursing. Dont forget about the puppies.

And tell Master Ben . . will you?—with my thanks for his kind message to me that I hope he may see my Flush some day and judge with his own judgement as to whether he was thrown away upon me, in the matter of being cared for and educated and *spoilt properly*. For voices north and south cry out 'Flush is spoilt'! 'Flush wont eat mutton—he objects to it! Flush wont be left in the room by himself—he cant bear it!

And worse than all, if somebody isn't ready to play with Flush just when he likes, he thinks himself ill-used and begins to cry with that inward moaning cry which exacts the attentions he desires. Very affectionate he is ! But tell Ben that as to 'going through fire and water' under any possible circumstances or for any possible body, such heroic self-devotion is quite out of Flush's *line*. Flush is, in fact, the prince of cowards—if he does not wear the crown—shudders all over at his own shadow in a looking-glass, runs away from the least of little dogs in his path, and in the case of a coal cracking in the fire, leaps upon the bed to me to be taken care of. In fact Flush is a proverb for cowardice in this household. There never was such a coward— not even his mistress ! And with that bond of sympathy added to other still faster bonds, he and I are very near and dear. The first person who comes to wake me in the morning is Flush—to wake me and remind me of *you*. There he comes, all in the dark . . before the shutters are open . . pushes through the bedcurtains and leaps into the nearest place by me and bites each of my hands very gently after the manner of his customary salems. Every morning he does this—and once when I *wouldnt* see him and kept my eyes fast shut, Flush began to moan, quite despairingly.

So you see what friends we are ! But it is not only he and *I* who are friends. Everybody likes Flush—everybody in the house. Even after he has done all the mischief possible, torn their letters, spoilt their books, bitten their shoes into holes (these favorites, these Buckinghams are always full of mischief) everybody likes Flush, and nobody refuses his pretty paw when he holds it out apologetically 'to shake hands and make friends'.

I have written myself tired, my dearest Miss Mitford. May God bless and keep you and yours.

I should like much to hear something of the tragedy— whether any suggestion would be quite too late now.[2] I wring my useless hands for being so useless to you !

Give my love to dear Dr. Mitford. May he and you be both quite well—and happy . . as far as that can be here.

Your E B B

[1] Ben Kirby, Miss Mitford's manservant.
[2] Miss Mitford, having been asked to write a tragedy for Charles Kean, had begged her friend to supply her with a suitable subject.

[1 Beacon Terrace, Torquay]
June 14, 1841

Thank you my beloved friend for your kindness in writing and wishing to have me within teazing distance. Ah!—I hope you wouldn't have reason to repent it if I were to go!—I should be on my guard, and never say 'Do come', and *look* it as seldom as possible.

I have told Papa about the house, but have urged nothing,— because under the circumstances and in the state of feeling natural to me at this time, my only full contentment can be in his doing his own full pleasure. I want to be with him and in a situation which would least threaten a future separation—a want which involved the objection to Clifton, I could not keep concealed. But if his wish remain fixed upon Clifton, even to Clifton I must go. And in any other case, the reason is strengthened for my suspending every form of interference.

I came here, you see, not indeed against his desire, but against the bias of his desire. I was persuaded—he was entreated. On his side, it was at last a mere yielding to a majority.

Well—and what has been the end? The place - - no! I will not say that it was accursed to me . . but the bitterness suffered in it has been bitter, (in regard to present endurance as any curse. All the sorrows of my life besides, and that life not free from sorrow, showed without sting or agony in comparison with the deep deep woe of last year. It was the sharpest laceration of the tenderest affection—an affection never agitated till then except with its own delight. Oh my beloved friend— there was no harsh word, no unkind look—never from my babyhood till I stood alone. A leaf never shook till the tree fell. The shade was over me softly till it fell. And although what I cannot help feeling as an unnatural tenacity to life prevented my following my beloved, quietly quietly as I thought I should—and although I have learnt even to be calm and to talk lightly sometimes, yet the heavy sense of loss weighs at my heart day and night, and *will*, till my last night or day.

There is much much to love, left to me, close to me always. But there is no one close to me always, to whom I can say 'Is this which I have written good? Is it worth anything?' and be sure of the just answer. The nearest sympathy, the natural love which was friendship too, is not close to me now.

I have thrown down my paper and taken it up again. It was wrong, very wrong, to write so. It has pained your kindness, and done no good to me—except indeed for the pleasure's sake of speaking out a pain. Take no notice of it dearest friend!—ever kindest and dearest you are! I know that the stroke fell in blessing and not in cursing, and that when we see each other's smiles again in the light of God's throne, not one will be fainter for the tears shed here. Blessed be God in Christ Jesus, who consummates grief in glory.

But you will understand from all, that my poor most beloved Papa's *biases* are sacred to me, and that I would not stir them with a breath. Yet he says to me 'Decide'. He is so kind, so tender. No love of mine can echo back his, as far as the demonstration goes—I love him inwardly, I was going to say better than my life . . but that is worthless, was so always, and is now so most of all.

I shall like you to know Papa—ah, you smile at my saying *Papa*—I am too old for such a baby-word I know—but he likes to be called so, and therefore I dont like to call him otherwise even in thought—I heard him say once 'If they leave off calling me "Papa", I shall think they have left off loving me'. I shall like you to know him. You will certainly like and estimate him. Mr. Kenyon does thoroughly. Mr. Horne, who has seen him once, has begun to do it already. He is not poetical, or literary even in the strict sense—but he has strong and clear natural faculties and is full of all sorts of general information. I have consoled myself sometimes when you were abusing the professional literati with the thought that you would be sure to like 'Papa'. You like, you know, sensible men who dont make a trade of their sense,—reading country gentlemen who dont write books. I have hopes of you.

Well—and thus then it remains. I have put him in possession of your report about the pretty house—but have received no notice of his decision, or of any sort of decision about any place. Thank you, thank you, for thinking of me in reference to the Chiswick show.

[The rest of this letter is missing.]

[*1 Beacon Terrace, Torquay*]
June 23, 1841

I cannot delay my beloved friend expressing to yourself
the thrilling thankful sense of escape with which I read your
letter.[1] May God bless you and keep you among those who
love you and look to *you* for love, as long as they live to do so!

But do *do* tell me – – how are you now? How is the spine,
the jarring of which I liked least of all to hear of? Do you
lie down rightly and prudently, and remain quiet in every way
until the system recovers itself? Because, *indeed* you should—
indeed dearest Miss Mitford, you *must*. Leave the garden to
the wind and the dew, and trust the strawberry-gathering to
. . K![2] That is the only letter you ever told me of your
maid's name, and I guess it stands for her name! Tell me if
you do everything right, and nothing wrong . . and whether
the swelling upon the spine has passed away. I dont like
hearing of that, indeed!

For the rest of your dear delightful letter whence are the
words to come which should thank you!—for what you say
of Papa—for what you say of me—for your wish that I were
near you—without one word or fear about the teasing! How
kind you are! How grateful I am to you! How I love you
out of a heart which *can* love though it has not loved many!
How I count your love for me among the blessings left to me,
to be remembered among the tears left too. May God bless
you and return it to you, my beloved friend!

I have heard from Papa and he has heard (so he tells me)
from you. You who speak pearls and diamonds without any
fairy but yourself, must be used to hear of the pleasure conferred
by your words. *He* seems to [be] pleased and over-pleased—
for he is inspired into an impertinence wonderful in a country
gentleman—and scarcely tolerable in a poet. Shall I tell you
what it is? Will you be angry? He isn't a poet I do assure
you—so dont think very ill of him. Nevertheless he had the
impertinence to say (to *me*, mind) that the writer of such kind
words as some which somebody wrote, 'should be kissed *by all
of us*' in answer.

Ah!—I wish I were near enough to do my part in the
kissing! But dearest friend there is no settlement yet of the

grand question,—and in what direction I am to remove remains less certain than the removal. To be patient during the long process of deciding, or rather of being decided for, is hard : and I who thought, not many months ago, that I never could care more about anything earthly relating to myself, am detected in the very act of caring a good deal, . . more than I ought, more than you would think or do think I ought !— about this simple turning to the left or right. I dread so another separation—or isolation—such as it would be at Clifton. No !— my physician does not recommend the place. He would rather, I believe, that I went straight to London, and shut myself up in a large airy room, and took counsel and quietness with Dr. Chambers. But he fears the *journey*—a journey anywhere— and has tried hard and vainly to frighten me out of the thoughts of it. I on the other hand, hold fast—and *wont* be frightened— simply because the moral terrors which rise up with the prospect of remaining here, are more terrible to me. . .

[1] While Miss Mitford was being shown over a half-built house, the owner of it fell through the rafters, dragging her with him, and severely bruising her spine in the process.

[2] Miss Mitford's maid was called Kerenhappuch.

[*1 Beacon Terrace, Torquay*
Postmark : *July 16, 1841*]

[The beginning of this letter is missing.]

. . . be repeated nowhere. But is it not abominable cant to cry out as people do in behalf of domestic delicacy, whenever a great man is spoken of abstractedly from his works, and as a man ? Isn't it folly besides cant ?—or rather, wouldnt it be, if all cant were not folly. For my own part, I do feel strongly that when a man has either by great deeds or noble writings, passed into the heart of the world, he gives that world the *right of love* to sit at his fireside and hear him speak face to face and with a friend's voice. The man being ours to love, is ours to look at as our familiar—and if he be a man who can love as he is loved, his countenance will gather more brightness from our 'curious eyes' than from the sense of his own dignified privacy. Dont you think so ? Dont you laugh to scorn Monsieur Necker's [1] complaint of the wrong done to men of genius by calling them out of their titles? As if Shakespeare, our Shakespeare, were not better than Master Shakespeare, or for the matter of that, than Monsieur Necker? As if love were not the best dignity! And after all, to return to my position which of us wouldnt like to know how Shakespeare came down stairs one Wednesday morning with his hose ungartered? Wouldnt you climb your ladder ten times, to catch the colour of them—garters? I know how you agree with me—and how, admitting my principle, you give your gracious forgiveness to Miss Sedgewick [*sic*] for that graceful characteristic sketch of your own self in the midst of the geraniums. The words too—the very words full of you and true to you—'I love my geraniums next to my father'— why shouldnt we every one hear those words? Well done, Miss Sedgewick! And you my beloved friend, will guess that I have been reading all this in the Athenaeum . . feeling a smile upon my own lips almost as if I saw *you*. . .[2]

Poor wretched L E L[3]—I grieve for her. But I hold stedfastly—perversely perhaps you think—(yet dont!) that her faults were not *of* her poetry but *against* it.

To speak generally, there are errors which make a blaze and a noise, more than some of a worse kind, and which are peculiar to quick irritable excitable temperaments—such as go commonly with vivid imaginations. Sin is sin—but it often happens, and did happen in the case of poor Lord Byron, that we do not deal tenderly and pitifully enough with the sinner. We are apt to judge the man of genius by his own ideal —and to apportion our severity by his eminence. This would be cruel if it were not ungrateful. By the pleasure he has brought us, we measure back our stripes.

The end of it all is, that *I do not believe there is or was or ever will be a 'good for nothing' poet in the world.*

There is a doxy for you!

But poor poor L E L—I feel all you say of the material unworked. She might indeed have achieved a greatness which her fondest admirers can scarcely consider achieved now. And do you know (ah—*I* know that you wont agree with me!) I have sometimes thought to myself that if I had those two powers to choose from—Mrs. Hemans's[4] and Miss Landon's—I mean the *raw* bare powers—I would choose Miss Landon's. I surmise that it was more elastic, more various, of a stronger web. I fancy it would have worked out better—had it *been* worked out—with the right moral and intellectual influences in application. As it is, Mrs. Hemans has left the finer poems. Of that there can be no question. But perhaps . . and indeed I do say it very diffidently—there is a sense of sameness which goes with the sense of excellence, while we read her poems—satiety with the satisfaction together with a feeling 'this writer has written her best', or 'It is very well—but it never can be better'. It is the flat smooth ground at the top of a hill—table-ground they call it—and many hills in Devonshire are shaped so—a little to their loss in picturesqueness. If she had lived longer would she have been greater? '*I trow not.*'

I have read the Bells and Pomegranates![5] 'Pippa passes' . . comprehension, I was going to say! Think of me living in my glass house and throwing pebbles out of the windows!! But really 'Pippa passes', I must say, Mr. Browning's ordinary measure of mystery. Now laugh at me. Laugh, as you please. I like, I do like the 'heart of a mystery' when it beats moderate time. I like a twilight of mysticism—when the sun and moon both shine together. Yes—and I like 'Pippa' too. There are fine things in it—and the presence of genius, never to be denied! At the same time it is hard . . *to understand*—isn't it? Too hard? I think so! And the fault of Paracelsus,—the defect in harmony, is here too. After all, Browning is a true poet—and there are not many such poets—and if any critics *have*, as your critical friend wrote to you, 'flattered him into a wilderness and left him' they left him alone with his *genius*,—and where those two are, despair cannot be. The wilderness will blossom soon, with a brighter rose than '*Pippa*'. In the meanwhile what do you think of *her*? Was there any need for so much coarseness? Surely not. But the genius—the genius—it is undeniable—isn't it? . . .

God bless you my dearest friend. Love me as long and as much as you can! I love you [obliterated by seal] as I cant . . help it!

Ever your E B B

---

[1] Jacques Necker (1732–1804), French statesman, banker, and Finance Minister to Louis XVI. He was the father of Madame de Staël, who in 1804 published the *Manuscrits de M. Necker.*

² Catherine Sedgwick, the American novelist, after a visit to the Mitfords, published a description of the ménage at Three Mile Cross in *Letters from Abroad to Kindred at Home*. An extract from the account of the visit appeared in the *Athenaeum* on July 10, 1841, and in the *Literary Gazette* on the same date. This latter was described by Miss Mitford as 'grossly vulgar'. The *Athenaeum* objected to the manner in which Miss Sedgwick had 'carried her researches into the parlours, nay, into the very pantries of private individuals'; and Wordsworth wrote that 'such productions add to my dislike of Literary Ladies—indeed make me almost detest the name'. (Selincourt, p. 1091.)

³ Letitia Elizabeth Landon (1802–38), author of the *Vow of the Peacock* (1835), *Traits and Trials of Early Life* (1836), *Ethel Churchill* (1837), etc., and a posthumous volume, *The Zenana and other Poems* (1839). Described by Disraeli as the 'snub-nosed Brompton Sappho', she was reputed to have 'associated with a very undesirable literary set', and as a result of scandal, her engagement to John Forster was broken off. In June 1838 she married George Maclean, governor of the Gold Coast; and two months after her arrival there, died, in mysterious circumstances, of an overdose of prussic acid.

⁴ Felicia Dorothea Hemans (1793–1835), author of *The Domestic Affections* (1812), *Records of Women* (1828), *Songs of the Affections* (1830). After reading her first book, Shelley asked her to correspond with him, and persisted in writing until Felicia's mother, in alarm, put a stop to the correspondence. Her style, said Scott, presented 'too many flowers for the fruit'.

⁵ *Pippa Passes*, the first of Robert Browning's 'Bells and Pomegranates' series, was published in April 1841.

[1 Beacon Terrace, Torquay]
July 17, 1841

. . . I have been beating my brains to remember exactly what the nonsense of my last letter was. I beat them—and the chaff flies up in my eyes and blinding me leaves me my obscurity. But you will do me the justice (this is my hope) of inferring from the very nonsense, that I could have seen only the corrected Athenaeum and was altogether unaware of the want of delicacy and respect towards you, demonstrated in the work itself. The little vision of you made me feel glad . . something as if I really had seen you. There seemed to me nothing in it which was not true to your nature, and therefore pleasant and good for other natures to contemplate. And I was pleased—as I always am when you are brought closer to me by thought or word—and in the crisis of my good humour, achieved every sort of benediction for all sorts of literary gossipers. Well!—I do like them after all. And if I didn't, the generations after me, would—now, wouldn't they? Oh yes—I do like, . . with the strong eager earnest liking of an enthusiast in books, shut up a life-long among books *only*, . . to look at the book's motive-power and externity! *You* do not feel this so strongly—just because you have 'seen, touched, and handled'. *You* cant imagine how happy I felt once, to know—nay, to have beheld with my eyes, that the poet Campbell had red stuff curtains in his dining room. But push back the clock—and think. Push it back to Shakespeare's day! The colour of his hose—or wasn't it of his garters—didn't I say his garters?—*their* colour is a case in point. Think of the 'Shakespeare *garters*'! . . .

After all, was it so very bad of me to like that vision of you, given in the Athenaeum? Read it over again, and think! Now was it? My only word against it at the moment, was to my sister who happened to stand at my bedside. And what do you guess it was? . . 'Why there is one peculiarity in her face without a notice. The eyes—and *not* the forehead! Oh something should have been said of her forehead.'

Is it very very wrong of me? But you have, you know, a peculiar, massive forehead. Coleridge was

'The creature of the godlike forehead'—

and Mr. Kenyon once said to me (There—now *I* am the gossiper!) Mr. Kenyon once said to me, 'I never saw any forehead like Coleridge's, except Miss Mitford's' . . .

Thank you, thank you for Browning's poem. My thought of it escaped your question about my thought, Mr. Kenyon having kindly sent me *his* copy ten days since. But I must tell you besides that I read it three times—in correspondance with Mr. Chorley's four—and in testimony both to the genius and the obscurity. Nobody should complain of being forced to read it three or four or ten times. Only they would do it more gratefully if they were not forced. I who am used to mysteries, caught the light at my second reading—but the full glory, not until the third. The conception of the whole is fine, very fine—and there are noble, beautiful things everywhere to be broken up and looked at. That great tragic scene, which you call 'exquisite'—and which pants again with its own power! Did it strike you that there was an occasional *manner*, in the portions

BEACON TERRACE, TORQUAY
From a lithograph by George Rowe

most strictly dramatic, like Landor's, in Landor's dramas, when Landor writes best. Now read—

> —'How these tall
> Naked geraniums straggle! Push the lattice—
> Behind that frame.—Nay, do I bid you?—Sebald,
> It shakes the dust down on me! Why of course
> The slide-bolt catches. Well—are you content.
> Or must I find you something else to spoil?—
> Kiss and be friends, my Sebald!'

Isn't that Landor? Isn't it his very trick of phrase? Yet Mr. Browning is no imitator. He asserts *himself* in his writings, with a strong and deep individuality: and if he does it in Chaldee, why he makes it worth our while to get out our dictionaries! Oh most excellent critic 'in the glass house'.

After all, what I miss most in Mr. Browning, is *music*. There is a want of harmony, particularly when he is lyrical—and *that* struck me with a hard hand, while I was in my admiration over his Paracelsus.

This is for *you—I do not know him*. Ten o'clock—and not a word of the last subject—the last dread subject! I will write tomorrow. But I must say before my eyes shut tonight, that I thank you most gratefully and fondly, beloved kindest friend, for the frankness of your words. Oh advise me always—tell me always what I ought to do—or oughtn't! It is so, that I feel sure of your loving me.

I will write tomorrow—but do not wait until then to be in true grateful attachment

Your E B B

Can you read? My hand shakes, . . goes east and west . . today—and it is *tonight* now.

I have sent for the *Literary Gazette*.

[1 Beacon Terrace, Torquay]
August 25, 1841

. . . I confess to a love and reverence for Goëthe above any to which Schiller could move me. Goëthe was surely the greater genius—and he did not, as you admit, neglect the humanities, in their strict human sense. It was Shelley that high, and yet too low, elemental poet, who froze in cold glory between Heaven and earth, neither dealing with man's heart, beneath, nor aspiring to communion with the supernal Humanity, the heart of the God-Man. Therefore his poetry glitters and is cold—and it is only by momentary stirrings that we can discern the power of sweet human love and deep pathos which was in *him* and should have been in *it*. . .

[*1 Beacon Terrace, Torquay*]
Saturday. August [*1841*]

MY DEAREST FRIEND,

I read your letter just after sending my own to you, with a sympathy as true and full as the love it came from. . . Life is dreary indeed without love—the sand were not worth the footsteps. And love is nearer to us than even the more sanguine of us reckon upon—over us, in the Heavens—and *with* us perpetually, whatever we may lose, in what is called lost. 'He will not come to me—I shall go to him.' The connection, the meeting, the embrace, remain as sure in the case of death as life—the change being simply in the action . . in the going instead of the coming, . . and in the person acting . . '*I* shall go', instead of 'he shall come'. It is well for us perhaps—not to live without love—and not to die, because we have not love—but to have love on each side the grave. . .

Mr. Kenyon arrived the day before yesterday,—and as that day went down, he had your letter. Yesterday morning before my sofa-hour, he kindly came to see my sisters, and promised to be here again today—which promise he is perjured in. So I haven't seen him! But I may still. He looks, my sisters say, most excellently well and is in his usual spirits—those you know, being holiday ones. Was there ever anyone who made such a holiday of life as this dear friend of ours? Is there anyone under twelve years old?—or ten perhaps?—or six?—to ante-date the latin grammer! I know of nobody.

He is here, he says, for a week,—'with two ladies'—and as they feared the noises of an hotel, has taken a house for their common use. 'Two ladies', he said—naming no name. One house, one carriage, 'two ladies' (introduced namelessly) and Mr. Kenyon! [1] Can you pluck the heart out of the mystery? Isn't it a mystery? Isn't *there a heart*? I assure you I am pondering it gravely. And then the broken vow about coming here today! And another vow, which he mentioned besides, not broken yet and strange upon *his* lips—to abstain from the society of the place—during his stay!! They were a week too at Sidmouth,—and from hence cross to the north of Devonshire! Dear, dear, Mr. Kenyon, what can you be about?

He *is* very fond of Miss Garrow [2]—and so is Mr. Bezzi, [3] and so is Mr. Landor. But how am I to answer your question in regard to my sisters? I open my heart to you always,—and I have wondered sometimes whether you ever wondered at my saying so very little about her, when everybody else of better judgment, said so much. Well—my sisters do *not* very much admire Miss Garrow—and now the *inness* is *out*. I may trust you. I *do* trust you—for I should be very averse to any word of mine on this subject being repeated to anybody in the world. *I do trust you solely.* My sisters—I should say, my sister Henrietta —since Arabel has seen so little of her—my sister Henrietta then, does not admire her, for manners or simplicity, or any other quality than her superior musical accomplishments. A musical talent goes a great way with Henrietta, and she can appreciate it more fully than literary attainment—but with all this appreciation of and admiration for Miss Garrow's remarkable proficiency in her own favorite art, she does not . . to speak plainly . . she does *not* admire the musician. And it is not merely Henrietta. There is a great lack of popularity here I understand—and (which I think of more gravely) there have been those, whose general charity and particular sensitiveness to certain graces of character failed to include them among her admirers. The charges are—affectation—at least want of naturalness—and a leaning to light flirty manners . . .

Oh my dearest Miss Mitford, the carriage is come! We are going! We shall probably go on tuesday or wednesday. There is much to bear—much to dread. The physical danger almost passes from my mind. How I shall thank God, if He *do* reserve to me the comfort of being at home again. Poor Papa is too frightened to come, and will meet us, he says, somewhere on the road—while Dr. Scully, repeating 'If a lady *must*, she *must*' is obviously drawing philosophical inferences upon the indomitable obstinacy of womanhood generally. How can I help it? *I cant stay.*

God bless you—dearest and kindest! I am leaving a place where in the midst of unspeakable anguish I have known when I could know anything the truest kindness—the soothingest ceaseless touch of yours. I thank you, thank you for it all.

While I live, I am

Your attached

E B B

¹ Mr. Kenyon, who had been twice married, was a very eligible widower. The possibility of his taking a third wife was one that continued for many years to enthral both Miss Mitford and E B B.

² Theodosia Garrow (1825–65). A precocious musician and poetess, whose early poems were printed in Lady Blessington's *Book of Beauty.* 'Wonderful creature!' wrote Landor, 'pity that Byron did not live long enough to profit by her refined taste.' (*Literary Life and Correspondence of the Countess of Blessington,* by R. Madden, Vol. II, p. 393. Newby, 1855.)

³ Mr. Bezzi, a friend of Kenyon's, and a Torquay resident, was exiled from his native Italy 'on account of his connexion with the Silvio Pellico plot'. He was instrumental, according to Kenyon, in causing the rediscovery of a portrait of Dante, hidden for two centuries beneath the whitewash of a painting in one of the prisons of Florence.

50 Wimpole Street
Monday. Sept. 13th [1841]

MY EVER BELOVED FRIEND,

The first line written by my hand in this dear home is, as it should be, written to you. I arrived on saturday just after post time—and yesterday being sunday there were no means, you know, of passing a letter upon it. I could only read over and over *your* letters, and thank and bless you for them!

I write only a line. I am tired of course, with a sense of being thoroughly *beaten*,—but bad symptoms have not occurred —at least the spitting of blood increased *very* little in proportion to what might have been expected—and the whole amount of God's mercy to me is told in the fact of my being *here*. 'How great is the sum of it'! Here—with Papa—in the midst of all left! No more partings—nor meetings which were worse— almost *much* worse, sometimes. I thank God for the undeserved mercy.

For the rest, there was of course much to remember and suffer both in leaving Torquay and coming *here*. But my weakness helped to spare me—and now, I try to be alive only, or most, to the sense of blessing.

Thank you thank you for your too much kindness! The precious ringlet! It might serve, as far as the preciousness goes, to hold a city by—only being cut off, it is precious still. The fable ends there—and the truth begins. And isn't it truth that I love the least part of you?

You say too much—far too much. Its all too much kindness. Give my love to dear Mr. Mitford. How close we are now—and how I would say a hundred other things which I cant.

Goodbye—God bless you! . . .

Ever your
E. B. B.

[50 Wimpole Street]
Sept. 21, 1841

Dearest dearest Miss Mitford, the note I wrote yesterday had scarcely passed from my hands when the flowers came! I have looked at them and seen you in them, and borne for your sake that some of them should be put into a vase in my room. It is the first time since the time I cannot speak of, that I have borne to look at flowers so nearly as to have them in my room. They *used* to find free entrance there, and the people at Torquay were kind in sending me bouquets—but *after that time* I grew changed you know altogether and shrank from the things I liked best—and the colour and the smell of these beautiful creations became terrible to me, as if they were noisome instead of beautiful. Since that time, there have been no more flowers in my room until now—and here are yours. . . Yet I do praise and admire them—do today and did yesterday—and can look at them without crying, for your sake. Dont take any notice of all this weakness. But I felt impelled to explain how I owe a new spring to you—among the rest of the debts—among *all* the rest, my beloved and kindest friend.

All the rest indeed! For how could I thank you first for

85

flowers, when you promise me the gift of yourself. Is it possible?
Come to see *me*, such a long long way! Oh—how can I
thank you enough for even the thought of it? And will you
do it? Ought I to let you?—I, who am so spent and worn
of the little good-for-companionship that ever was in me?
Ought I to *let* you?

There is a question for a debating society of starch con-
sciences—but mine, I fear, wont make a very long speech
about it. It will '*let* you', I see from the beginning.

But not just yet—do not come just yet, my beloved friend.
I must *quite* take breath before that joy, and have time for a
dream of it. In the meantime—when you come, must you go
back the same day?—must you? We are full here, I am sorry
to say—but still, I do think with a little more thought, we
might conjure up a bedroom for you. I feel myself smiling at
the very thought of it. *Will* you come—or is it too much
pleasure for me? I was confessing the other day that I felt
myself (now that I had come *home*) growing credulous of joy,
again! The credulity seems to roll on like a bowl. What if I
should set up again for a castle builder!

When you come, you wont see any 'little brothers'—and
when *I* came, I looked for them in vain! Not a brother to be
seen out of a long-tailed coat—and even Set (Septimus—you
must learn our names!) sidling away from Papa's morning kiss,
because he's too old! . . .

'Poor little Flush'. You may well say so. He didn't like
London at all at first—not through rural preferences so much,
as through fear of the crowds of strangers which presented
terrors to him on all sides. The journey, Mr. Flush enjoyed no
less than any other classical traveller inclusive of Eustace. He
wouldnt sleep in the carriage, but sate at the window upon
Arabel's knee or Crow's,[1] with his two paws on the sill, and his
glittering ears dancing up and down over his nose—the eyes
dilating with the prospect. Through all my exhaustion, I
couldn't help now and then smiling at Flush. No student of
the picturesque ever gazed more intently upon hill and valley—
only he had a decided preference for animated nature. A flight
of crows—for instance—drew him half out of the window—a
flock of sheep produced a wag of the tail—a man on horseback,
of the whole body – – and, best of all, from this 'high sphere'

he had the honor of barking at many a large dog who, if both had been on equal ground, would have gobbled him up. At the inns too, Mr. Flush took his pleasure. My bed used to be drawn out of the carriage like a drawer from a table and was carried by men, with a shawl over the face of the occupant, up stairs to a bedroom. Well!—Flush thought himself bound in duty to pay every attention to this process. He walked and stood and paused and gazed, just as others did—and when I was laid down safely, the first living thing I used to see was Flush standing on his hind legs to reach up and kiss me. Then he established himself on my bed until he was taken down to dinner, always returning, finding out my bedroom door in the strange houses, with as little delay as possible, and most absolute in his resolve of passing the night with me. And every morning, he watched all the preparations for setting out again, evidently rejoicing in all and the first to spring into the carriage and take his usual seat. I am by no means sure that Flush wont bring out as good a two volumes of 'Travels' some day—of notes and documents—as anybody from the new world.

Well, but—when he came here—it was different. He liked my room very much indeed,—but my brothers he altogether disapproved of—and, what was rather worse, he thought it necessary (being a moralist and a traveller) to express his disapprobation most loudly and tumultuously—starting up, whether by night or day, everytime he heard a footstep, throwing himself upon my shoulder and barking like a pack of hounds in one. My quiet Flush—whom I always praised for quietness—was there ever such a beginning! I was in despair— not so much for myself as for Papa who is not perhaps very particularly fond of dogs and most particularly, of silence. Papa said Flush made him nervous, and that he must not sleep in my bedroom until he was reformed altogether. So Crow took him for a night—and everybody paid court to him— and in a little time, his terrors passed away and he permitted himself to be walked near and talked to and even patted. Oh— he is quite contented now—quite friends with the whole world. Poor dear little Flush! And he likes London 'pretty well, thank you'. He has had two long runs the Hampstead way, and runs out in the Parks, and thinks it pleasant enough.

Oh the post, the post—I shall be too late—and mustnt and wont. . .

Thank you for thinking of Arabel in regard to the studios. Over-kind you are! All their love to you—and mine to dear Dr. Mitford. Tell me if the tamarinds relieve the thirst. God bless you. I *do love you indeed*

Your own E B B

¹ The lady's maid who had accompanied E B B to Torquay.

[*50 Wimpole Street*] *London*
Sept. 25, 1841

The pause of a day brings me another dear letter for which to be glad and grateful. Thank you my beloved friend—and thank you above all for what you say of the coming. I am sure I am in fairyland all at once—I must be! Only think of how I was a few weeks ago—shut up in a dark room with its associations tugging at my heartstrings—everything I could see, everything I could hear, to the very footsteps on the stairs, giving me pain—and just beneath the window (for our house was the lowest down of all upon the shore) that dreadful perpetual sound! When I think of it, it makes me shudder and wonder how I could live on there so long! But we dont know what we can bear—and only a few weeks since it was so. And now—to be at home again—to see the dear faces—no more thought of goodbyes—everybody smiling as if grief were not in the world—and this dream of seeing *you*, set as a crown upon the general gladness. No wonder that I should wonder! Thank you and dear Dr. Mitford for being glad for me. It is a renewing of life to me. Not that the deep grief is not here still—like the clay beneath the grass. That must be: but I could not without sullenness be insensible to the full pleasantness of the sweet dewy verdure, which has sprung up so suddenly after a long desolation. 'Shall we receive *evil* from the Lord's hand, and not *good*?' May His goodness forbid that evil! . . .

Thank you for the delightful chronicle of Flush. *He* must come too, you know! I long I long to see him. And pray dont forget to thank K. and Ben for their kindness about putting up the basket so beautifully. How fully and truly and utterly

I agree with you in all you say about the luxury or rather necessary of having people round you who love you, yes, and whom you love again. The Edgeworth [1] doctrine (not peculiar to that rational cold school) in regard to domestics, was always abhorrent to me. To teach children 'not to talk to servants'! And a bible in your room—and God above you—and the quick sense of universal brotherhood at your heart! It is an atrocity both in morals and instincts.

I must not let you fancy that Papa does not like Flush, because Flush for a day or two made Papa nervous. No indeed—I prophesy that Mr. Flush will, in time, climb into favoritism. He is admired already.

My brothers Charles John (Stormie we call him) and Henry have two splendid dogs chained up in the yard—one of them a bloodhound and the other an Alpine mastiff, Catiline and Resolute—and Flush who violently objected to them at first, admits them now occasionally into his society—that is, he has condescended to walk out with them once or twice.

God bless you my ever beloved friend! Thank you for all your kindness—but to the geranium extravagance I say 'Oh no, no indeed! That is too much.

But ever and ever yours
E B BARRETT.

[1] Maria Edgeworth (1767–1849), author of the *Parents' Assistant* (1796), *Early Lessons* (1801), *Castle Rackrent* (1800), etc. ; described by Lockhart as 'a little, dark, bearded, sharp, withered, active, laughing, talking, impudent, outspoken, honest, Whiggish, unchristian, good-tempered, kindly, ultra-Irish body'. (*Sir Walter Scott, Bart.*, by Sir Herbert Grierson, p. 214. Constable, 1938.)

Oct. 9th 1841
50 Wimpole Street

. . . Scandal about Mr. Kenyon! Why who could dream of such a thing? Nobody, that I ever heard. Whatever I gossipped about the fair double mystery he carried with him, was for joke's sake! There might as well be scandal about your double dahlias! Very elderly intelligent women I understand they were—one of them, the Miss Baillie,[1] but no relation to 'Queen Joanna', said to be, said by Mr. Kenyon to Papa to be, the deepest thinker for a woman, he ever met with! There is no marrying or giving in marriage in question any more than in heaven—neither marrying nor gossiping my dearest friend !

The scandal referred to other parties altogether—and I am sorry almost I referred to *it*. Some of it is *so bad* that I reject the belief of it on the ground of the badness. I should not like to write down the least odious of it—but when we meet, I will give you a shadow by which to measure the pyramid ! . . .

Dearest, dearest Miss Mitford, I am punished for my not writing to you by not hearing ! When shall I hear you best,—face to face?—when ? You are to listen to all the voices in Wimpole Street, Papa's loudest, through the voice of this letter,—and all saying 'Come'—but all saying besides, my dearest friend, that we cant and wont have you (except by an effort and with a lessening of pleasure) unless you will condescend and consent to one night's rest at least, under this roof. . . I told you once, we had a full house. Nevertheless I deny myself now. There is full room for you—there is indeed ! *Full room!* Papa's only fear is, our quietness—'How will she be amused?' You know, you celebrated authors pass over our heads in such an awful roll of thunder, that we are afraid sometimes to look up. How afraid I was to see you the first time ! And I observe that gentlemen are not the less afraid when the celebrities are feminine, but the more. . .

I have not heard from Mr. Horne since he wrote to me of Martinuzzi.[2] A friend of mine, Mrs. Orme (who lived once with us as my governess and my sisters',) promised to procure for me from Dr. Stone a copy of *Martinuzzi* which he had marked the margin of, with 'great laughter', 'peals of laughter', as the spectator's laughed where they ought to have cried. This copy I should like to show you as well as myself. It was a transcript of the impressions of the first night. Now the English Opera House is, I hear, no longer the authors' theatre—the 'good floundering beginning' having floundered to a bad end. I was quite sure that you would like the canadian workman in his tarpaulin hat; and liking him so much as *you* do, I doubt as little that Mr. Horne himself *heros* his tale. He has resolute energies in all things—and what is rare, can suffer bravely as well as act. On the first night of the 'floundering', when the audience was in fits (of laughter) and a friend of his, a lady, sent a message to him praying his presence to conversation then and supper afterwards, his reply was that he could not

stir or speak the whole night long,—and there he sate side by
side with the poor author, they two together in a conspicuous
box, the only two in the theatre, with grave faces. . .

Say how you both are. Give my love to Dr. Mitford and beg
him not to begin to hate me because I want to steal you away.

Ever your E B B

¹ Sarah Bayley (?–1868), a woman 'enviably free from the weaknesses
of her sex', remained the close friend and companion of John Kenyon to the
end of his life. At his death he left her £5000. Miss Bayley died on July 27,
1868 : and Robert Browning, recalling 'a mild little doubt of mine, once' as
to one Lloyd 'being the "adopted son" of Miss Bayley', asked : 'did he prove
so, and duly inherit, I wonder?' (*Dearest Isa : Robert Browning's Letters to Isa
Blagden*, ed. McAleer, p. 326. Texas, 1851.) In her will Miss Bayley left
£500 to Watkin William Lloyd, Esq. : two years before she died she revoked
this, leaving him only £100.

² *Martinuzzi or the Hungarian Daughter*, by George Stevens (1800–51), was
produced at the English Opera House on August 26, 1841, with Samuel
Phelps and Mrs. Warner in the chief rôles. R. H. Horne had some financial
interest, at the time, in the English Opera House (originally the Lyceum),
which was rebuilt in 1834 by an architect who forgot to supply stairs leading
to the gallery. In 1842 the theatre was renamed the American Amphitheatre
and housed a wild beast show.

*[50 Wimpole Street]
Monday Oct. 25, 1841*

MY BELOVED FRIEND,

I am in a straight—and know not what to do or say. You
are coming on thursday, and I must be glad—overjoyed—that
is certain. But you will know what it is that I dont know what
to say about ! There's an 'about and about' for you ! I suffer
under one terror—*that* being lest I may have expressed myself
coldly or awkwardly or mysteriously in relation to the room
in this house which awaits your acceptance, or, worse than all,
to the will of this house's inhabitants to make it available.
Dearest dearest Miss Mitford—my ever beloved friend—if I
have been so guilty, or say rather so unfortunate, I do entreat
you by that dear loving heart of yours to forgive my misfortune.
There *is* a room—without disturbing any separate bandbox
belonging to any individual petticoat or long coat. There *is*
a desire on everybody's part (petticoated or longcoated) to
have you here. We all feel the honor of it and desire the
gladness of it ! If I spoke obscurely at first, it was through my

ignorance, and because the subject had not been talked over with Papa. Will you believe this; however you determine? And will you be sure that in the case of your coming, it should be our ambition to give you an 'at home' feeling—that you should dine at luncheon time, and go in and out to your friends or receive them here just as you pleased? We have not a carriage at present— altho' Papa talks of getting horses—but if you dont mind the lack of 'purple pall and array' there is the carriage which our people use when they want one, and which looks 'respectable', they say although falling short of 'an equipage'. If you condescend to it, my sisters will be too glad to take you anywhere and everywhere, and leave you with your friends, calling again for you—and this they would too gladly do, in the case of your sleeping here or elsewhere, should it be the slightest convenience. . . Decide exactly as you think best. I quite see some reasons leaning to the Chapel Street plan. Your friend may claim a promise—and she may help to lighten your evenings—while I (luckless wretch!) am shut up myself between eight and nine . . soon after sunset! Altogether I leave it to you—promising to be contented with your finality-measure. I do promise. And now I shall turn my face to the full light, and think of nothing but the great great joy which I am sure to have on thursday. Thank you a thousand times, my beloved friend! 'Ready to see you?' Yes, to be sure. Ready and eager. And as to your tiring me—oh never think of it. I wish there were time to be tired in! I shall throw away all pruderies of costume and place—, and not mind intruding myself upon you before I get up. I wish there were time for etiquettes—but being on the sofa only for two hours, I cant afford to waste all the rest—can I?

Talking of pruderies,—I agree with you my beloved friend altogether upon that particular matter. Your expression 'Such are exactly they who would not go to *balls*' is pregnant—and we may look to it for the precise restriction between mercy and licentiousness. For my own part I do think somewhat differently from many on this very subject. The censure '*with a difference*' extended by our gracious world to male and female offenders—the crushing into dust for the woman—and the 'oh you naughty man' ism for the betrayer—appears to me an injustice which cries upwards from the earth. Fair wives of honorable husbands who shrink from breathing the same air with a betrayed woman, yet bend their graceful heads and sit in quiet

[The rest of this letter is missing.]

[50 Wimpole Street]
Tuesday [Postmark : *October 27, 1841*]

. . . Much of the verse of the day, rather poetic than poetry, rather tuneful than music, stands in the same relation to poems of endurant construction, as the soft sweet moanings of the Aeolion harp do to the works of Handel or Beethoven.

Keats—yes—Keats—*he was* a poet. That Jove is recognised by his Thunder. A true true poet, from his first words to his last, when he said he 'felt the daisies growing over him'. Poor Keats! Do you know, did I ever tell you, that Mr. Horne was at school with him and that they were intimate friends? 'The divine Keats'—he says of him—and will not hear the common tale, which I for one thought deteriorative to the dead poet's memory, that he suffered himself to be slain outright and ingloriously by the Quarterly reviewer's tomahawk. No, said Mr. Horne to me once—'He was already bending over his grave in sweet and solemn contemplation, when the satyrs *hoofed* him into it'.

I am going to confess to you my dearest friend, and when you come you must advise me—for I have a weary conscience about a person whom I heartily admire—Lady Dacre. Three years ago, after the passing between us of a few notes which left me her debtor for much graceful and gracious kindness, she called upon me. It was a strange sort of visit. Oh I do believe she thought me in a strange sort of situation, if not strange myself. She was announced one sunday, when we were all together in the drawing room, and I, very unwell and helpless, had'nt time to crawl into another room and receive her as I should have done. There was a crowd in the drawing room. Two of my cousins, the Mr. Clarkes of Kinnersley castle were there—and in addition to our ordinary household helped to produce the effect of a crowd of young men—besides two lady-neighbours of ours when we lived in the country, country neighbours of Irish extractions who had come to town 'to see the lions'—the sort of people who look quite out of place in town,—very kind, very warm-hearted, very broad Irish, anything but very refined,—what is worse than all, very præternaturally smart,—looking as if they had just emerged from a bog into a rainbow! Well—Lady Dacre found us just so. And I, proud and pleased to see her, yet a little vexed at the combination, and very vexed with myself at my own half consciousness of being ashamed of my friends—(and really I couldn't help being the very least in the world ashamed of the blues and pinks and lilacs) had not half the pleasure from her visit which under ordinary circumstances I should have had. Well—but, here proceeds the confession. You know how unwell I was—and how distressed to be forced away from home. I was not able to return Lady Dacre's visit, but I might have sent a card, and *I didn't*. Never from that day to this hour has her visit been returned or acknowledged. What should I do? Nothing, I suppose. I cant go now—that is sure—and as to sending a card, it would be out of time and tune now. She would finish thinking me out of my wits. Haven't I disgraced you? . . .

God bless you, my beloved friend. My love to dear kind Dr. Mitford. How I *do* thank him! But it seems like the dream of a dream—, this thought of seeing you on thursday. I return your suggestion of High-Priestess-ship and thank Mr. Haydon for his kindness to a friend of *yours*. That is a prouder name [two words obliterated by seal] *priestess'* for your attached

E B B.

[*50 Wimpole Street*]
Nov. 8, 1841

I hasten to return Mr. Haydon's [1] letter,—altho' I shall be driven to write hurried lines in the process. Of course it can only be felt as an honor that he should take any care about coming here—and he may like to see two or three of the pictures whatever else he may not. . .

But now you want to hear something of dear Mr. Kenyon, who must have reached London as you say about the beginning

of last week, absolutely in time to be too late! He came, we
never hearing a word of it—he living at I wont count the precise
number of paces from where we live. He might have sent us
a word—an 'all hail'—mightn't he? But he didn't—he didn't.
Henrietta and Septimus came into collision with him in the
street on *saturday*—and though no lives and tempers were lost,
he looked a little remorseful, and I, if I had been there, should
have looked a little ruffled. He had had a cold, however, since
his arrival, and he was coming to us, and would come the next
day at two oclock and see me. I wish he had, for the sake of
what I might tell you of him, and also for the sake of seeing
him—dear Mr. Kenyon—my own self. But he didn't come,
because Papa, in ignorance of the arrangement, went to his
house instead, and I have not seen him or had a line from
him up to this moment. Papa says he is to remain in town a
very short time—perhaps a very few days—that he has been
journeying through Herefordshire, to Malvern . . 'tramp
tramp across the land' with his fairer demon—and is now
about to return . . to Torquay! He goes to spend a fortnight
with Mr. Bezzi. Dearest dearest Miss Mitford, may God bless
you . . . Give my love to dear Dr. Mitford, if I really may say
so. Flush is quite well—and siezing upon Mr. Haydon's letter,
left his autograph. The letter was barely rescued. Naughty
Flush! As mischevous as a magpie, Crow says he grows—
more and more mischevous.

Ever your own

E B B

[1] Benjamin Robert Haydon (1786–1846), the painter,—friend of Wordsworth, Keats, Shelley, Lamb, Hunt,—was introduced to the Moulton Barrett
family by Miss Mitford. He corresponded with E B B, but they never met.

[50 Wimpole Street]
Novr. 12, 1841

. . . No—I have not seen dear Mr. Kenyon. I *ebb and flow*
about him. I think if I were encouraged, I *could* work myself
up into a wrath. Scarcely had I written a note to escort the
parcel left in my care, when he came—called—stayed one
minute in the drawing room. Arabel said—'I will run up

stairs and see if Ba is ready'. Oh no—he wouldnt hear of it. He had come just for a moment, and couldnt wait to see me—but *would* come another day on purpose. There it remains! To be sure he *may* come! I sent your book and letters to him that night.

During the moment he was here, he told them he had changed his mind about going to Torquay immediately. He found his home so pleasant that he couldnt part with it immediately. But, that he actually offered a sum of money (in vain) for a certain house there, we have heard from himself—and that he is likely to be persuaded or tempted into the purchase of an uncertain one, we may derive from the circumstances. He admires the scenery passionately—and then that is not all. As to seclusion—it is not *that*, believe me. There is not such a dancing, fiddling card playing gossipping place in all the rest of England as Torquay is—there is not such a dissipated place, in the strongest sense. And its a ghastly merriment. Almost every family has a member either threatened with illness or ill. Whoever is merry, is so in a hospital. They carry away the dead, to take in benches for the company.

I do not say this from a soreness of individual feeling, which perhaps you may suspect—because long before my own miserable associations with that miserable place, I had a strong apprehension of the ghastliness of the collision there between life and death, merriment and wailing. It has made my flesh creep sometimes—

'Wretches hang that jurymen may dine' being a fainter antithesis than is suggested on everyside. Think of a grand ball being given, where Moses stood—between the dead and the living?—no!—between the dead and the dying. A woman in the last agony in one house—a corpse laid out in another—and the whole of surviving Torquay dancing intermediately! . . .

And now, in reply to your question, my beloved kindest sympathising friend - -*yes*. Yes—*you did*—and you were estimated aright and fully.[1]

There, went a high soul to God!—high talents—only not distinguished among men, because the heart was too tender for energy. Only God who is love, knew how tender to *me*.

I cannot write of those things—you see I cannot—I cannot

write nor speak. I never have spoken—not one word—not to Papa—never named that name anymore. He was *and is* the dearest in the world to me—the first dear and dearest—and because he loved me too well to leave me I am—thus—and he is thus—earth's sorrows and God's angels between us. The great Will be done. I am weak and ignorant, and cannot speak of the doing of it.

Thank you for saying it *was not I*—and for your tender tears. It was not I in a sense. I would have lain down this worthless life ten times, and thanked God—but the sacrifice was unacceptable. On the contrary, I was used, I and my love were used as the wretched ever miserable instruments of crushing ourselves in another.

I beseech you to say no more. I love you more dearly for what you have said—but do not say any more. My head turns to write. I never knew *despair* before those days—never. And the grief I had felt before so lately—nay, all my former griefs and I have had many, were bruised out of my heart by one.

'Let us praise God in Christ for the hereafter—*His* hereafter—the place of meeting and ever lasting union.

Your own [?] attached
E B B

¹ The reference here is to the death of Edward at Torquay. As always when E B B is alluding to this event, the handwriting becomes markedly tremulous and agitated.

[*50 Wimpole Street*
Postmark : *December 23, 1841*]

. . . Now I will tell you my story of Mrs. Jameson,¹ which Mr. Kenyon said something to confirm the other morning. Mr. Jameson proposed to her and was rejected—upon which, goaded by vanity into hatred, he vowed to win her and be avenged. By the apparent devotion of years the first object became attainable. They were married—when, at two steps from the altar, he broke upon the echo of his own oath to love, by words of this kind . . 'I have overcome—I am avenged. Farewell for ever ' !

This is *my* story—close, you see, upon Lord Lyttelton's, but not, perhaps, less true for the resemblance—it may be true *twice* : and it goes on to describe how the lady, cast out so abruptly and cruelly from the sphere of her conjugal duties, devoted herself with a brave and high tho' sad heart to the discharge of all filial and sisterly ones, . . and in possession of an independent income sufficing for social enjoyment among her chosen friends in Germany, sacrificed taste and comparative luxury in order to inhabit and brighten a poor lodging at Notting Hill which is the home of her family. There, her father lies bedridden, and her sister keeps a little school,—and she supplies a necessary in one place and a comfort in another by her literary industry—reserving one morning (thursday) in every week for the reception of those friends who crowd in to her society with emulous respect and admiration. . .

[1] Anna Brownell Murphy Jameson (1794–1860), author of the *Diary of an Ennuyée* (1826), *Characteristics of Shakespeare's Women* (1832), *Sacred and Legendary Art* (1848–52). A prolific writer, the friend of Lady Byron and Ottilie von Goethe, and, in later years, of both the Brownings, whom she met in Paris after their marriage, and escorted to Italy.

[50 Wimpole Street]
Jany. 11, 1842

. . . Thank you my dearest friend, for the *Key*.[1] I used it with the eagerness of Blue Beard's wife—and am satisfied, thank you, to the uttermost of the curiosity of my malice—or of the malice of my curiosity . . whichever it should be philosophically. I had guessed a good many of the names—but, from the want of personal knowledge, was quite at a loss for many—for instance I stared myself blind at Lady Dort, Lady Pasten, Bradley ! I did not guess *Contrarius*, either the least— and mistook Rolfe for Roscoe instead of Mathias ! . . .

You cannot think how your letter has amused me. *One* of the portraits of Miss Pardoe, engraved and attached to her work upon Hungary, suggests certainly *twice eighteen*.[2] And so she would take Mr. Henry Chorley in lieu of the Sultan ! You know how *he* turned a longing lingering look upon her in the streets of Constantinople . . with a view probably to the scraglio ! And she would catch Mr. Chorley's handkerchief after *that* . . and settle down into the armchair of an English matron—as if she had never touched a Turkish cushion or seen a Dervish spin! Allah Kerim! It is astonishing indeed.

She has talent—she can even be eloquent occasionally—and word-painting is an art with her. And her last book (it *is* the last—isn't it? the *Hungary*?) has far less wordiness and affectation—a less smell of the theatre. As she *grows older*, my dearest friend, she may be worthier and truer, and more secure of your esteem. I hope she may. Not that I wish her ever to marry your friend unless you desire it!

Mrs. Trollope's book *is* clever, do you not admit?

And Bradley is Edwin Landseer! Well!—I have heard only just now, only today a dreadful story relating to him. Do you know that he is insane—has a keeper now, while I write? The story is terrible! That he had been subject to cruel agitations through an attachment to the Duchess of Bedford—that they were secretly married—that after the murder of Lord William Russell, he was employed to paint a portrait of the dead . . to which effect he, and *the Duchess only*, were shut up with the murdered man—that the picture was never finished . . that the artist overcome by a dreadful complexity of feeling and emotion went mad at his task and has never recovered his mind from that dreary day to this. Tell me, if you can, that there isn't a word of truth in it. It makes me shudder while I write it. The *fact* is that no picture of his has been exhibited since,—and the rest I do hope, rose up armed out of somebody's tragic head. . .

---

[1] To *The Blue Belles of England*, a novel by Mrs. Trollope (1778–1863), mother of Anthony, and author of over 100 books. 'The Blue Belles of Mayfair', wrote the *Spectator*, 'is the proper title for this satire of the lionizing coteries in the fashionable world.'

[2] Julia Pardoe's *The Hungarian Castle* was published in 1842. Miss Pardoe is reputed to have sought in later years to retain the qualities of youth, and to have striven, at fifty, 'to be as vivacious as at eighteen'.

[*50 Wimpole Street*]
Jany. 12, 1842

. . . If Moore be not a better poet than Willis, he is surely a better artist.[1] As a versifier to a particular tune, with a fancy singing through it, there never was or will be or can be, I should think, an equal to Moore! 'Born, with a nightingale

singing in his ear'—as somebody said of him. *And* quite truly.
A tame nightingale, and in the place of Nature's universal
harmonies! Still he is excellent in his department—an
accomplished artist; the very snuff-box musician of poetry.
And such, Mr. Willis is not—or *is he*?

Mr. Kenyon has told me something to the effect of what
you have told me as to Trans-atlanticism. It is surprising that
the Americans who hold in their hands the same talisman of
literature with ourselves, should not be preserved by it from
such corruptions of speech. The cultivated man or woman
here, however cut off from society and the acquisition through
society of colloquial elegance, does not become *provincial* in the
loss of it. Why should it be otherwise with them? I do not
understand.

Still they are a noble people, speak how they may. I love
America for its brotherhood with us—and venerate it for its
separated brotherhood—and look on to the day when, as its chief
glory still lies in our literature, our increased glory may be
reflected from its own. The day has not dawned yet—but the
red light is in the sky.

No. The beloved relative who loved me and whom I
loved and love on so tenderly, was *not* the Speaker of the House
of Assembly. The Speaker was a cousin of ours, between whom
and us there was *no* love [2] . . a man of talent and violence and
some malice, who did what he could, at one time, to trample
poor Papa down . . did trample him at one moment when
he felt him under his feet . . but when the moment passed
and the Law gave the triumph to other hands, and the Speaker
died . . to the astonishment of everybody his will testified, by
a particular mention of Papa in which the sentiment only was
of importance, – – that he bore to his old victim much esteem
and a tendency to friendship. I remember seeing him, when I
was a child—and he gave me a subject for a poem about a
run away negro which I still have somewhere, in his handwriting.[3] He *was* a handsome man . . after a fashion—good
features and the short upper lip, full, in his case, of expression.
Still it was a face, that I, as a child, did not care to look upon.
The perpetual scowl spoilt it—and the smile was worse. It
was a face, not for a bandit . . oh no—but *perhaps* (altho'
I really should not speak so of my cousin, an old enemy too;

and no more!) *perhaps*, . . between us two, . . of an 'honest honest Iago'! But it was good natured of him to write out 'a subject' for me; and I thought so even then.

My beloved uncle, the only one of my uncles I really loved, and so I may say emphatically, as it would be tenderly and gratefully in any case, *my beloved uncle* . . was for many years a member of the English House of Commons, a dear and affectionate friend of Lord Grey's and Lord Durham's, and at one time himself a man of large fortune. He might have lived like a Duke—he *would* live like a Prince. Jamaica failed. Then, he was *talked into* the new South sea bubbles of some years ago—it was his defect to be easily talked over and into. The great failures came—and he found himself responsible for companies to whom he had simply given his name. It was a situation full of perplexity and distress . . and he was not made, like Papa, for battling with adversity. He left it and went to the West—and so ended all!

Oh to look back and think! What he might have been! What he was even! For the talents of general society, I do not know his rival. For playful brilliant *persiflage* . ., Mr. Kenyon, the most brilliant talker I can think of, was nought to him. And then, that high and delicate sense of honor, agonized by an unpropitious situation till it helped to drive him to the wilderness! A bright, gifted being! His letters worthy of his faculty. His affections—for that memory clings the closest— so tender and strong—passionate yet something wayward. All gone down, like so much else! How awful it is to love. . .

Your E B B

---

[1] Thomas Moore (1779–1852), friend and biographer of Byron, author of *Irish Melodies* (1807), *Lalla Rookh* (1817), etc. Nathaniel Parker Willis (1806–1867) was an American, author of *Melanie and Other Poems* (1835), *Bianca Visconti* (1839), who described himself as 'steeped to the lips in London society, going to everything, from Devonshire House to a publisher's dinner in Paternoster Row'. Willis, according to Wendell Holmes, was 'something between a remembrance of Count d'Orsay and an anticipation of Oscar Wilde'.

[2] Richard Barrett (1789–1839), first cousin of Edward Moulton Barrett, an influential Jamaican landowner, three times Speaker of the House of Assembly, who died in mysterious circumstances on May 8, 1839.

[3] A poem by EBB, *The Runaway Slave at Pilgrim's Point*, was first printed in *The Liberty Bell*, by Friends of Freedom (Boston, Mass., 1848). Reprinted as a pamphlet in 1849, it was later included in the *Poems* of 1850.

[50 Wimpole Street]
Jany. 20th 1842

. . . I have been wishing so to write to you day after day
these three or four days; but other letters pressed in . . letters
necessary to be written—not that it isn't necessary my beloved
friend, to write to *you*. That is a heart-want. But I couldn't
do it all at once—and then these Greek poets and the Athenaeum have been pulling at me, more than I supposed they
would.[1] One is forced to be accurate in print, and absolute
accuracy one cant or oughtn't to be content to go to the
memory for—and I wanted books out of my reach, and have
been beating against my cage till my wings are tired. After all,
not a line is written yet.

You are right and wrong too in all the advice you give me
and the superfluity of kindness you add to it. I have grown
large O my dearest friend, in the mist of your great affectionateness which I prize, believe me, more for the thing it is, than the
praise it brings. You overvalue me in all things but in love.
Nevertheless you are quite right in telling me not to give up
poetry for magazine-writing, or for prose of a higher character.
You will be satisfied when you hear me say that I couldn't if I
tried. Whatever degree of faculty I have, lies in poetry—still
more of my personal happiness lies in it—still more of my love.
I cannot remember the time when I did not love it—with a
lying-awake sort of passion at nine years old, and with a more
powerful feeling since, which even all my griefs, such as have
shaken life, have failed to shake. At this moment I love it
more than ever—and am more bent than ever, if possible, to
work into light . . not into popularity but into expression . .
whatever faculty I have. This is the object of the intellectual
part of me—and if I live it shall be done. There will be no
bitterness in the process whatever the labour . . because it is
not for the sake of popularity, no, nor of a higher kind of fame,
but for poetry's own sake—rather, to speak more humbly and
accurately, for the sake of my love of it. Love is the safest and
most unwearied moving principle in all things—it is an heroic
worker.

Perhaps we may differ a little upon what is called religious
poetry . . though not at all upon the specimens extant. My

fixed opinion is, if I might express it with the deference due to your views of literature, . . my fixed opinion is, that the experiment has scarcely been tried . . and that a nobler 'Genie du Christianisme' than has been contemplated by Chateaubriand, will yet be developped in poetical glory and light. The failure of religious poets turns less upon their being religious, than on their not being poets. Christ's religion is essentially poetry—poetry glorified. And agreeing with you that human interest is necessary to poetical interest, I would yet assume that religious interest is necessary to perfect the human—as the great and ever-influencing prospect and crown of universal humanity. . .

In the meantime, here is the Athenaeum. Oh, but for a time, my dearest friend—but for a time. Mr. Dilke does not even wish for me for long. And who knows, but what I may break down at the first three paces? Well. Even *I* cant know anything about it, without trying. Only one thing is sure—that I shant be *cold upon poetry*. Another thing, too, is sure, that the Athenaeum has been so! You are quite right—I skipped the science and took patience—but I couldn't take it and keep it, when I found them all so deeply interested in American Indians and English travellers, and every sort of savage and steam-engine and musical instrument, . . and all at once, struck cold, indifferent, nay, a little malicious, with a manifest curling of the upper lip (none the better for being Mr. Darley's who ought to *know* better) when a true poet or tragedian endeavoured to articulate those great thoughts which he inherited of nature. It was—it is, dispiriting and mortifying. For there *are* true poets, even as literature is now. Mr. Browning deserved better than that light, half jocose, pitifully jocose, downward accent of critical rallying—'Forsooth they are almost tired of him! and yet he has some good stuff—but they have almost lost their sublime critical patience!!'[2] Why what if he did mouth in his speaking,—was there nothing worth reverence in his speech?—worth a critic's reverence—or a world's! I would not speak so of Mr. Browning in a whisper —I would not dare—even to myself. And then Mr. Horne! Where is the excuse for the blank silence, or the still worse word! The Athenaeum provokes me. . .

E B B

¹ Earlier in the year, C. W. Dilke had arranged for E B B to write a series of articles for the *Athenaeum*. 'Some Account of the Greek Christian Poets' appeared in that journal from February 26 to March 19, 1842.

² 'ANTHOLOGY FOR 1841 :—

'*Pippa Passes*, by Robert Browning.—Mr. Browning is one of those authors, whom, for the sake of an air of originality, and an apparent disposition to *think*, as a motive for writing,—we have taken more than common pains to understand, or than it may perhaps turn out that he is worth. Our faith in him, however, is not yet extinct,—but our patience *is*.' (*Athenaeum*, December 11, 1841.)

[50 Wimpole Street]
Jany. 20, 1842

Oh my dearest friend how you frightened me with the inscription on the back of your letter 'The opium has failed— and now there is no hope'! Thank God it is not as I fancied! But indeed you electrified the handle of your letter . . and I could scarcely get it open.

Well—but how did you try this opium. I quite agree in the wisdom and propriety of giving it a fair trial, and I venture to suggest another attempt by way of *morphine*. The muriate of morphine is what I take—what I call my elixir, and I take it in combination with aether and something else. Aether is highly antispasmodic. I suggest a mixture of the morphine with the aether—only of course you wouldnt think of giving either without a direction as to quantities from your medical adviser. Do speak about it—do try it, if it is not advised against. My elixir has a sort of ubiquitous influence upon all parts of my system—quiets my mind, calms my pulse—warms my feet—spirits away any stray headache—gives me an appetite— relieves my chest—to say nothing of the bestowment of those sudden pleasant feelings belonging by right to better health and extreme youth—to say nothing of causing me to grow all at once, as young at least . . as Miss Pardoe!! Now I recommend my elixir . . you know I never tried it upon cramp—but I believe in its ubiquitous infallability, and recommend it. I chalk it up upon your walls, wherever there's a blank one from creepers, at your village of Three Mile Cross! —as MY ELIXIR! . . .

Do you really think that Aeschylus or Chaucer or your Fletcher ever did 'adapt their writings to the public taste? I doubt—nay, I disbelieve. *Did Milton?* Did Coleridge? Did Wordsworth? Did not the public go to all of them? It seems to me that the poet has to do, has to think of doing, rather with humanity which is grand world-wide and time-wide, rather than with the limited changeful capricious thing, called a public—and subject to all the base uses of a self made fashion...

But do not fancy that I am over-worked by the Athenaeum. Oh no—I am pretty well supplied with the books I wanted,— and the actual writing is the least thing—and I think now that I shall not go into chronological and historical detail quite as much as I proposed. It will be best to keep cl [rest of word obliterated] the poetry. And really the *body* of the poetry of the first centuries, is not worth a great deal.

My love to dear Dr. Mitford. He *is* a little better—and *I* am so glad!

Papa has just sent up the new Athenaeum number by Mr. Flush! He ran up stairs, struck his fore paws against my door, sprang dancing with triumph upon the bed, and gave it into my hands with a kiss! He is quite well—and vivid in spirits and affection—but *not* fat like your Flush, the paternal!

Wimpole Street
Feb. 4, 1842

My dearest friend—do let me see Dryden. Oh yes—I shall certainly like it! I like anything of that sort—anything that brings nearer, or seems to do so, to the *Immortals*. I am capable of all sorts of foolishnesses (which Mr. Kenyon thinks so degrading that he does me the honor of not believing a word of them—at least *he says so*) about autographs and such like *niaiseries*. I might, if I were tempted, be caught in the overt act of gathering a thistle because Wordsworth had trodden it down .. of gathering it eagerly like his own ass! ..

'the duck
Which Samuel Johnson trod on' [1]

being left for you, of course! So you dont 'think anything' (as people say) of Samuel Johnson! How Boswell would distrust, in his magnanimous 'hero-worship', your compliment which brushes by Johnson! And after all, he *was* a fine show giant—a memorable Gargantua. He was a 'man'—as Carlyle boasts of him—and a specimen-man; and if he does 'say things three times over,' he says things sometimes which are worth the repetition. Take notice, this is all in the spirit of contradiction, for I haven't the least bit of real love for this great lumbering bookcase of a man. Oh I quite agree with you in my inner woman. Think how he treated our poets! Even I, who care almost less for Gray than for him, shrink away from the sight of his injustices in the life of Gray.[2] Still, there were some fine things about Johnson—and what with them and what with Boswell, one is worked up into an attitude of respect to him from which there is no quite relaxing. I observe that the imitators of his style, are for the most part superficial—they catch his mechanical trick,—but the intellectual atonement for it, the thought which causes us to pardon the reiterated emphasis, is passed over altogether.

Yes—Wordsworth is wordy sometimes—in his blank verse he is. But he is—Wordsworth—a great poet and true!

As to Dryden . . why perhaps . . nay, certainly, he doesn't lie as near to my heart as yours. And yet how true is every word that you say of him—every word except— The truth is I never could believe him capable of being a true dramatist under any possible combination of favorable circumstances. I do not believe it, simply because I believe that his defect as a poet is, still more than his verbosity, a defect of sensibility and consequent power over the feelings. Dryden always makes me think of Lucan, who was called by the Roman critic, an *orator* rather than a poet. He roars magnificently to be sure! 'Yes'—to the *letter*, my dearest friend! Yes, frankly!

I am impatient to read Madme D'Arblay [3]—I like diaries and letters and all that sort of gossip so much! Have *you* Jephson's *plays*? [4] I never read one of them—and should like to glance thro' them, in à propos to the times! Think of him and Hannah More [5] dividing the stage between them!

Ever your attached

E B B

. . . As to Flush . . I did hear once of his condescending to stoop his head over the dripping pan—and I will speak to

Crow about it. She is gone out to see the show of the Queen and the Prussian King, and not being at home at one oclock, as usual nothing could persuade Flushie to go down stairs to his own dinner. He wouldnt stir. So the housemaid brought his plate up to my bedside! . . . What do you think Papa said to me a few days ago? 'It is my opinion that you love Flush better than anyone else in the world'! . . .

1   Here lies poor duck
                   That Samuel Johnson trod on ;
                   If it had liv'd it had been good luck
                   For it would have been an odd one.

(Johnson's epitaph upon the duck he killed by treading on it at five years old.)

2 Thomas Gray (1716–71), author of *Elegy in a Country Churchyard* (1750), *The Progress of Poesy* (1758), etc. Gray, said Dr. Johnson, 'was dull in company, dull in his closet, dull everywhere. He was dull in a new way, and that made many people think him great.'

3 Frances Burney (1752–1840), daughter of Dr. Burney, and author of *Evelina* (1778). Her *Diaries and Letters* were published in 1842.

4 Robert Jephson (1736–1803), author of *Braganza*, a tragedy (1775), *The Count of Narbonne* (1781), *Julia, or the Italian Lover* (1787), etc. Horace Walpole was an admirer of Jephson's plays.

5 Hannah More (1745–1833), disrespectfully known as 'the old Bishop in petticoats'. A practical philanthropist, and an influential writer on the social, political, and ethical topics of the day. Author of *Percy* (1777), produced by Garrick at Drury Lane, *Sacred Dramas* (1782), *Coelebs in Search of a Wife* (1809), etc.

[50 Wimpole Street] London
Feb. 31, 1842.

I struggle from under a heap of proof sheets, my dearest friend—just because I must say one word to you before the week closes. If it had not been for writing, writing, . . and such reading of heavy books as makes ones arms ache long before one's head, (my head is quite secondary!) you would have heard from me some days ago, nay, day by day. So trace up the silence to the source. In the meanwhile, I think of you, dream of you, love you, read your letters three times over and leap up as high as I can when I catch the first ray of them as their orient appears in Crow's hands. . .

Well—then! there's the autobiography! 1 I will tell you how it was with *me*. For a long time, I thought Hayley was scarcely put-up-able-with! So powdered and pigtailed—so primly elaborate as to diction—so anointed with fine words and fine phrases—there was no coming between the wind and his nobility—so conscious of his bardship, in the length and breadth of every sentence—so be*bard*ing his readers till they would nearly as soon be bombarded!—so determined on being very good, and very delicate and very generous and very magnanimous—oh—so magnanimous!—and praeter-determined that nobody should miss seeing the full extent and degree of said goodness, delicacy generosity and magnanimity – – that I all up [*sic*] but threw up the book—or threw it down,—as one for whom the 'Halleyan periods' to use his own speech, were full too much! I all but did it—but I did not actually. I, another 'pitiable Eliza',[2] read on, on the contrary—and by degrees, by slow degrees, and sure I suppose,—the extreme overcoming sense of self-occupation seemed to wear away—I liked the 'poet' better and his phraseology better—at last I almost loved him for his lovingness to his friends—to his son. His tenderness to his son and his grief at that parting won my heart! It is touching and beautiful as love always is. . .

Still the expression of sentiment is occasionally most strange. The funeral sermon he wrote for 'his pitiable Eliza' . . a copy of which he sent to his son 'to recite' to his friends the Flaxmans in London, while the mournful ceremony was performed at Eartham!! The poetical 'recitations' which he prepared on the birthdays of his dying son, wherein his dire estate as a cripple is set forth rather according to the 'bardship' than the father-hood – – with so little of the shrinking delicacy of love! It is strange. Tell me 'your thought'. The book is interesting after all! . . .

You cant care a great deal more for biography than I do. My thirst for it is not quelled though I sit by a fountain. . .

I send the Athenaeum, my first Athenaeum! Try to read it to the end—though I fear it wont be called very readable by the most of those who do try.

Your
E B B.

---

[1] *Memoirs of the Life and Writings of William Hayley, Esq., the Friend and Biographer of Cowper, written by himself* (1823).

[2] The temperamental Eliza Hayley, believed by her husband to be mentally afflicted, is thus solicitously described throughout his memoirs.

[*50 Wimpole Street*]
16th March 1842

MY EVER DEAREST MISS MITFORD,

You will laugh at me for my important profession of business! which could possibly stand in the way of the expression of that going out of my heart to you the reality of which nothing interrupts. Yet for these two, three, four, days past, most particularly for two of them, I really have seemed to myself much like a hare tearing away before the huntsman sweeping over the most fragrant of thyme without the power of pausing to crop the least head of it. Two books were wanting for my last paper—so I waited and waited till Mr. Dilke sent for it 'at my earliest convenience' whereupon I had to scurry rather than write .. scurry, hand and eyes and pulses—the last, Papa declared was past the hundred, and well it might be—and only finished last evening at seven! Quite finished though! What a triumph as Lady Mary Shepherd used to say, 'to be just in time'—what a triumph to throw one's weight off, not from despondency but completion! What a gladness to get back to one's leisure, and *you* my own beloved friend,—to one's leisure which may be one's idleness if one pleases,—and to *you* who must be one's happiness besides. I am so glad, the papers are done!—quite *glad*! Writing to the clock is against my nature. . .

And here am I writing about wishes and painting brushes, as if I were not to be swallowed up by before twelve of the clock on this present Wednesday night!¹ I should instead be sending you my solemn benediction, and no sort of good wishes except the last! But you see what a tittle tattle Humanity is, even on the edge of an earthquake! Make a little philosophy out of us my dearest friend, I bequeath it to you—and although all your publishing business is over for ever and ever in London,—Bath, or Liverpool may inherit our printing presses with our metropolitanism, and you may bring out somewhere else a new book of the 'Last days of London', with a vein of the melancholy Jaques crossing your own in the marble!

You know of course,—I am not writing to anyone 'ignorant of the knowledge dearest chuck' . . you know of course how it is with us in the eye of the prophetic and with the cognizance of all almanachs? Of course you know, that London is to be swallowed up bodily to say nothing of a circumference of fifteen miles of country, within these present four and twenty hours . . probably, people say, 'in two minutes time', at a gulp! The sensation excited among the lower classes, in station and education, yes, and the sensation fluctuating and rising up into the bewildered wits of better-informed persons, is more than you would be prepared for. Crowds of the poor Irish have been pressing away out of their holes and corners— householders removing their furniture to Hampstead and Highgate . . clerks throwing up their offices – – the panic active in absurd gesticulation. Mrs. Orme who was mine and my sisters governess for two or three years—quite a woman of the world, agreeable and clever in a certain way, . . said to me seriously the other day—'Are you frightened?'—'No—are *you*?' 'Why really it is as likely to happen as not—but I wouldnt leave London on any account! All I care for are here, and I prefer sharing their fate'! Quite in earnest really!—in sober wonderful earnest. I have plenty of credulity and super-stition myself—but I stand bravely this earthquake shock— which is far more than might be expected of me. . .

Your own attached E B B.

No Mr. Kenyon! He does not come—we do not hear a word of him. Perhaps some particular earthquake is engaged upon him . . aside! . . .

---

[1] '*The Earthquake.* The prophecy of this event has not only been very popular, and held in much repute at the east end of London, but has obtained influence at the west. . . The origin of the prophecy cannot be traced to any authority more authentic than that London would be destroyed within a certain period when it had no king.' (*Annual Register*, March 1842.)

[50 Wimpole Street]
March 24, 1842

I write to you my beloved friend in the full gladness of receiving your letter—beyond hope—this morning. Is my beloved friend such a sceptic as one question seems to say? 'Do you really care for my gossipping letters'! Care for your letters!—what,—*I*? What am I then?—(there's the elemen-

tary question in philosophy to meet yours) what am I, that I
should not care for your letters!

If I do not empty my heart out with a great splash on the
paper, everytime I have a letter from you, and *speak* my gladness and thankfulness, it is lest I should weary you of thanks-
givings! For no other reason, be sure! Your letters have
been my palm trees in the desert, my nosegays from the garden,
my 'sweet south' and singing nightingales, since the first day
they came to me. Even Crow's face shines with affection from
my face when she gives them to me—and if Flush is the bearer,
as he very often is, it seems to me that he wags his tail and
shakes his ears ten times for once under another burden. Your
letters—do you know what they are worth, that you should
ask me such a question! Why if they were not yours—but
that is an impossible hypothesis—why if I did not love you—
but that is another—take the letters up in a pair of tongs as an
abstraction and hold them in the air, . . what spirit in the
world would not leap high to catch them? Do you not *know*
their price and delightfulness – – as bare letters? Surely you
must guess a little at their value! You who care for Hayley's,
must divine the higher light. Still—if they were dross, I
should care to have them because I love you—and if you were
naught to me, I should care to have them because they are so
far from dross. . .

Richardson's correspondence has charmed me—'charming'
being the right word: since I verily and indeed believed
myself wrapt up close in the domestic brocades of the Harlowe
family, all the time I spent in reading it.[1] His own letters are
letters out of his romances to the very crossing of the ts—and
they seem capable of eliciting a Miss Howe out of any sprightly
correspondent he may be pleased to magnetize with the waving
of his pen. Lady Bradleigh is delightful—I dont wonder that
he tired himself with pacing up and down Hyde Park in his
desire to catch a glimpse of her! That he didn't fall in love
with her in all gravity, I wonder at more. . .

What I grumble at—if I hadn't something to grumble at,
this world of ours wouldnt be *grumbledom*—, is that Mrs. Barbauld
should have thought it necessary to cut down the MSS to
fit her particular box. Why the materials might have filled
twelve volumes instead of six. Oh those sensible editors!—

what harm they do in the world! If they should treat your letters so! . . .

I like the waste of the public money upon bishops of New Zealand!! and of Jerusalem!! as little as you do, and have ventured to be open with Mr. Townsend and tell him as much. The utter absurdity (to say nothing at all of money) of forcing out the forms and ceremonies of this Parliament church, out among the savages, I could even cry over in utter vexation. Think of the lawn sleeves and the mitre, beautifying a 'spiritual lord' under circumstances of such utter incongruity. A bishop of New Zealand! No—let them send missionaries, simple men with simple words—and I would not grudge them the monies from Glasgow or elsewhere. Spiritual wants are crying wants—more touching perhaps to such as know the price of spiritual comfort than any cry of the bare body; and particularly, when we recollect that to such as do *not* know *that*, the physical cry is moving. But let those who are sent, be *missionaries*. The bishops are impotent, have been *found* to be impotent, in all situations of the kind—and as I ventured to tell Mr. Townsend, the martyr soul of poor Williams [2] was the true Bishop-Soul for the South seas. . .

Half way in this letter—dear Mr. Kenyon came suddenly again!—beyond hope and expectation as I had seen him four and twenty hours before : and his coming prevented the going of all this writing to you. He has dined with Lady Morgan, and seems to be almost under a vow, never to dine with her again. Dont tell anybody. It was whispered to me—and I whisper it back to you—a confidence in both relations : but he was disgusted, heart-startled at the hardness and worldliness of the talk at dinner. Clever, he said it was—very clever—but of the cleverness which comes by speaking one's soul out 'without regard to any social or moral restraint'—the subject, during dinner, the poor people who were to come afterwards— and who, coming, were all welcomed with extended hands, as very dear friends, whom it had been a pleasure to cut up (*not* 'into little stars') in their absence. Lady Morgan said to him—'Oh—you have shut your house to us!—you wont let us in at all now'—to which he answered that he used to receive ladies at his house but had grown shy and given it up. Before the evening ended the resolution was shut and locked.

It is late—I must shut and lock too. . . . My Flushie has just had an escape from the jaws of Mr. Chichester's great dog—he shrieking and screaming and clinging to Arabel's arms! My poor Flushie!

God bless you! Your kindness is too too great!—God bless you—Ever your E B B

Not a word of the *Corn Law* letters. It is very able: what is your mind about the new tax? That Sir Robert Peel! He is 'subtlest of the beasts of the field'.

¹ Samuel Richardson (1689–1761), author of *Pamela* (1740) and *Clarissa Harlowe* (1747–48). Richardson's *Correspondence selected from the Original Manuscripts bequeathed to his Family* was published in 1804 by Anna Letitia Barbauld (1743–1825).

² John Williams (1796–1839), described as the most successful missionary of his time. Author of *A Narrative of Missionary Enterprise in the South Sea Islands* (1837). He revisited England in 1834: E B B heard him speak at Sidmouth and was much impressed by his 'exceeding benevolence'. On November 20, 1839, he was killed and eaten by natives at Dillon's Bay, in New Hebrides.

[50 Wimpole Street]
March 30, 1842

. . . Indeed I never did read or even make believe to listen to all the debates of a session—and if I seemed to listen, be sure that it would be '*make believe*'. I like Lord John Russell for a certain nobleness and simplicity of purpose, which one does not see in that narrow paltry slippery artful (without *art* as you say) statesman Sir Robert Peel. I have the sort of dislike to that man which some people have for cats or spiders—a half-fear and half-contempt. There is more nobleness of instinct in a 'schoolboy's' oratory than you find in his; which gives no breathing-room much less a breathing-out, for a generous sentiment. The man's ideality is in his father's mills . . going towards manufacture—and indeed his whole mind rather revolves like a mill-wheel than advances or aspires. In regard to *powers*, there is not a redundancy of it on either side, I readily grant to you. The country is sinking on one side like a willow tree, for the lack of power—for the want of a supporting soul. We have hands enough, and tongues rather more than enough, but of souls there is a deficit. So it appears to *me* . . .

[*50 Wimpole Street*]
April 1st. 1842
Isn't it *spring*?

. . . Often and often do I look back, leap back in spirit
over the great gulph of darkness between my *now* and my *then*,
and think of the moment when the door was first opened to
me of the permission to love you. Did I ever tell you just how
it was? Mr. Kenyon had been asking me, asking me,—like a
king beseeching a beggar to take a dukedom—pressing me on
all sides with kindness to pass an evening at his house to see
Wordsworth. Now I would have gone on a pilgrimage to see
Wordsworth ever since I was eight years old—and if the
indispensable condition had been pebbles within side of the
pilgrim shoon, I would have gone even so. But at the end of a
pilgrimage, I should have seen Wordsworth alone in his niche—
kissed his feet and come away . . and he peradventure
wouldnt have seen *me*! It was altogether different going into
Mr. Kenyon's den of lions and lionesses—and I was frightened
into absolute shame at the sort of roaring implied by my
imaginativeness. I know Mr. Kenyon was half angry, thro'
all his kindness, at my long drawn perversity—and I was near
crying in the conflict between what I wished and feared, and
what dear Mr. Kenyon tried to press beyond the fear. Who
can judge aright for another who has lived a peculiar life, in
no sort of society except of books, and shy at the best, as to
manners? 'I loathed that I did love'! Well—at last the
temptation took the form of a softer devil. He, not the devil
but our dear friend, asked me to think no more of the great
party but to consent to come to a very small one, where
Wordsworth would be again—*and Miss Mitford* . . and then
he told me of your gentleness and dearness. So then I said
'Yes'—half ashamed and half afraid still!—and then again in
the morning came a note from him to propose my going with
himself and *you* . . and *you*!—to the Zoological gardens. Oh
how I remember the words—I am sure he measured them so
as to encourage me into some estate of common sense—'you
will become acquainted' (thus they ran) 'with an amiable
person whom you will be certain to like, and who is prepared
to like you'. Prepared to like *me*! I resolved at once to go,

114

and set my teeth as for the desperate purpose of it—couldn't do anything during all the interval at books or writing—dawdled about . . walked up and down stairs, looked out at the window—said to myself so as to keep myself firmly buckled up in resolve, 'I shall be glad *after it is over*!—I shall be glad I have seen her, all my life afterwards (O unconscious prophetess!) and in the meanwhile it will only be a few hours pain'. Think of me as you please, but I do assure you that when the carriage was heard to be at the door, my knees trembled so that it was a hard thing for me to get down stairs to it. And then . . the first sound from your lips which reached my ears . . embleming all the rest . . was said in reply to something Mr. Kenyon said and I could scarcely hear in my confusion, something to the effect that I 'should have a protectress now'. '*I hope, a friend.*' Those were the first words I ever heard from your lips—and there was a tone, a significance of kindness in them which went beyond the words and made me love you in [a] moment. I loved you before as all the world does and for much the same reasons—but the heart-to-heart love began just then! You were Caesar to me in a moment! Dearest friend . . bear with me as you have done. It is for *you* to bear with *me*! . . .

Poor Mr. Browning! Was that extreme irritability of nerve supposed to be occasioned by the disappointment, or the exercise of an overwrought faculty?[1] After all I cannot wish with you that he turned to occupations of less excitement. In the first place, *could* he so turn? In the second, dare we ask silence from such a poet? It would be like asking a prophet to forbear his prophecy,—he has a word to speak from Nature and God, and he must speak it!

Certainly Mr. Browning does speak in parables—and more darkly than . . even . . some others of your friends. But he is a true poet. I estimate him very highly—and so do you—and so must all who know what poetry is and turn their faces towards its presence willingly.

The 'Rhymed Plea' is admirable 'after its Kind'—but with all my true and admiring regard for its author and his writings I could not be content to receive it as sole comforter for the absence of higher inspirations.

My prose style like Carlyle! To remind anyone in the world of Carlyle were praise enough and too much. Miss James's praise made me feel glad for a moment—as if it could be true.

And yet you are quite right. He does not write pure English—no, nor quite pure German—nor pure Greek, by any means. But he *writes thoughts*. He reminds me of Leibnitz's plan for an algebraic language,—altho' *his* plan is not algebraic—but he *writes thoughts*. There is something wonderful in this struggling forth into sound of a contemplation bred high above dictionaries and talkers—in some silent Heavenly place for the mystic and true. The sounds do come—strangely indeed and in unwrought masses, but still with a certain confused music and violent eloquence, which prove the power of *thought* over *sound*. Carlyle seems to me a great prose poet. At any rate he is a man for the love and reverence of all poets, seeing that he, almost sole among the present world's critics, recognises the greatness and the hopefulness of their art.

I, presume to offer my admiration to Mr. Carlyle, my dearest friend! No—you have not spoiled me quite up to that point or pinnacle yet.

Thanks upon thanks for the lovely violets. They deserve to lie enfolded in your letters—I wish I deserved to receive them, as well!

May God bless you ever. They always drive me away from you with this post hour. Say how the face-ache is!—and go on to love

Your own grateful

E B B

¹ Robert Browning was at this time deeply absorbed in an unlucky passion for the theatre. He was mortified by Macready's refusal of *King Victor and King Charles* (published on March 12, 1842, but written several years earlier) and *The Return of the Druses*; and angered over his procrastinations with regard to *A Blot in the 'Scutcheon*. 'So runs this idle life away, while you are working!' he wrote bitterly to Alfred Domett on May 22, 1842. (*Robert Browning and Alfred Domett*, ed. Kenyon, p. 36. Smith, Elder, 1906.)

[*50 Wimpole Street*]
April 25, 1842

. . . I saw Mr. Kenyon for a short time the day before yesterday—and Mr. Wordsworth does not come to London quite as soon as was in his first intention. Mr. Kenyon told me a story which I must tell you though he told me to tell nobody—because you who live so close to whole groves of roses must be sacred to Harpocrates all over—I rely on your secrecy. It is what Mr. Wordsworth says of his daughter's marriage— she having married last year Mr. Quillinan, *your* Mr. Quillinan, *my* Mr. Quillinan the author of the 'Conspirators'.[1] He says 'I am satisfied with the marriage, but I really dont see why I should. For my son in law is a Roman Catholic—and an Irishman—and a widower—and the father of a family—and a beggar'!! . . .

[1] Edward Quillinan (1791–1851), described by Matthew Arnold as a 'man unspoil'd, sweet, generous, and humane', after years of opposition on her father's part, married Dora Wordsworth on May 11, 1841. Three years later Wordsworth wrote: 'I will not bind myself, circumstanced as Dora is, to make her any fixed allowance . . . That she may be somewhat straightened, acting as she has chosen to do with my strongest disapprobation I deem fit and right.' (Selincourt, p. 1217.)

[50 Wimpole Street]
May 21, 1842

. . . Mr. Kenyon and I were longing so for you, two days ago when he was sitting in this room. 'Oh!'—he said 'how I do wish she were here—*living* in London! We might all pet her and do all the honor we could to her, and enjoy her delightfulness! Instead of that, she must, in some degree at least, be thrown away upon the society round about Three Mile Cross—in a degree she must!' Of course I said yes and yes and yes to it—and so that's the way in which we modest people wish you to belong to *us* as the only relative position in the world not altogether unworthy of you. . .

Dont let me forget to tell you that Tennyson's new volumes rapt me in Elysium.[1] *New*, they are not altogether—the first of them containing every poem of those formerly published which the poet intends to live. Of the new poems we may say, there is less of the quaint peculiarity, more individuality, more *power* in the sense of nervous utterance, more thought under the obvious ordinary forms, and *less* of that high ideality which distinguished the old Tennyson lyrics, and includes always,— however occultly a higher degree of philosophic thought than the critical world wotteth of. That is my doxy about the poems—the poet being divine as I always felt him to be . . by

his steps—as the Greeks detected the godship of their gods.
Well!—but what I wanted to tell you was that one of his
idylls . . perhaps the most beautiful of all—nay, certainly the
most beautiful of all, was by the author's confession in a note,
'suggested . . by a pastoral of Miss Mitford's'—or 'by one
of Miss Mitford's pastorals'.[2] It made my heart leap up to see
your name—as 'at a rainbow in the sky'! I think it will please
you a little. I think within myself that fancying myself *you*, it
would please *me* a good deal—I think such a godship of
Tennyson!

The story is your beautiful one of the son marrying against
his father's consent—and of the manner in which his child
after his death, is adopted and embraced, after a Ruth-scene in
the cornfields.

Mr. Wordsworth goes out of town on friday: but it is only
for a week or two to Harrow, and his intention is to return.
He has been holding his court royally in London—breakfasting
five or six times every morning, and taking evening refresh-
ments as polyglotically. His wife bent over his chair, as Mr.
Kenyon stood by some evenings ago, and said, stroking his
'sublime grey hairs' gently . . 'Ah William—you are tiring
yourself'! Do you not like to hear it?

To pass to a lower personnage altho' still a royal one, I
was glad to be told two days since by one of my brothers who
had it as a true tradition from somebody called 'a silver stick
in waiting' a Colonel Read, that the only gentleman with whom
the queen shook hands at her last drawing room was Lord
Melbourne. And her eagerness of joy was obvious both in the
act and the manner. Poor queen!—there may be good in her
yet: and it is a merit (*as from a queen*) to be cordial to a friend
in adversity. To do another thing attributed to her by silver
stick . . i.e. hating Sir Robert – – is a merit in anybody. . .[3]

Dearest dearest friend, how I do trample on your forbear-
ance with wooden shoes and on every possible occasion. Bear
with me still—love me so as to make it possible. Do write to
me. The longer I think of the silence the blacker it looks.
Surely you received my last long letter?

God bless you ever and ever:

I am sure I am yours *so*

E B B

¹ *Poems, in Two Volumes*, by Alfred Tennyson, published on May 14, 1842.
² The poem is *Dora*, based on Miss Mitford's *Dora Creswell*. (*Our Village*, Vol. II. 1826.)
³ In September 1841 Sir Robert Peel succeeded Lord Melbourne as Prime Minister.

[*50 Wimpole Street*]
June 30, 1842

. . . I could thank you down ten pages for your letter with the storm in it, and Mr. Mainzer's ¹ choral visitations, for the calm. I walked step for step with you in that tempestuous wandering, and enjoyed the excitement without the wetting—which was perhaps as well for me. For *me* to stand in the rain just now out of pleasure and adventurousness would be a sort of invocation of the Devil—a reading of the Lord's prayer backward—a daring of evil influences beyond what is at all tolerable as good. But a few years since, how I used to do it—how I rejoiced in doing it ! A hundred times, in the country, when the rain was raining waterspouts, continuous Niagaras, have I jumped out of the ground floor window, to enjoy till my breath stopped, that natural shower bath. Can anything be more exhilarating than the sense of being rained upon from Heaven ! A pouring rain with the sunshine threading it as in April, 'close and silent' as I said myself in the verses which were happy enough to please you. Do you remember how Bacon,—not least great in that feeling,—bared his head reverently in the rain,—so to do homage to 'the descending Spirit of the universe' ? ²

All of which is very pretty sympathy as coming from one friend to another who has been caught in a thunderstorm and soaked to the skin ! But you did not catch cold,—you were not the worse you said at all,—and so I let myself take as much pleasure from the story of your adventure, as the enchantment of the story teller 'did in such case make and provide' . . .

Dear Mr. Kenyon has gone away. He came on sunday to say goodbye—but I had just gone back to bed with a heavy depressing headache, and so I missed the goodbye. He told Arabel that he should be back again in a fortnight certainly—which I can scarcely be very glad of as it will be only to prepare for the longer absence on the continent. Still I am not like you—I applaud 'the design' of the continental wandering.

And I think that under certain circumstances I would extremely enjoy doing the exactly same sinful thing. Think of the German pine woods!—and again, those of the Appenines! Think of the Alpine glories—thrusting into the sun's face their everlasting snows! Who wouldnt be the better for bathing in beauty his senses and his soul? I wish I were with you at this moment, in the heart of the Brockens!—while *you* perhaps simply wish *me* there! . . .

George is on the circuit—dear fellow! Oh this hot weather—the concatenation of wigs and hot courts and legal opinions and *no* business! How oppressive it all must be to him!

I doubled back the leaf just now and caught a glimpse of my graphic and 'by no means common' expression about the Alps—and it made me smile as it wont do *you*, at the remembrance of a story which Mr. Kenyon told me of the late American minister. Lord Aberdeen had just come into office, and the point was doubtful how far he would make himself agreeable to Mr. Stephenson.[3] Said the latter sublimely—'Let him put on airs with *me*! I should like to see it! I would just take two steps backward—draw myself perpendicular up!—and look at him as cold as the snows upon the everlasting hills'!

There is the story of which my 'everlasting snows' reminded me. It is transplanted from Mr. Kenyon's and my confidence into yours and mine. Pray do not let it go further.

Of the same Mr. Stephenson it is narrated that since his residence in England, he looks at *everybody* as cold as the snows on the everlasting hills—and as high too. Did you know him?

Give my love to Dr. Mitford—and 'in the interstices between the intersections' of visitors and letters, oh remember how tenderly and truly I am your

E B B

[1] Joseph Mainzer (1801–51), singing master at the College of Treves. He settled in England in 1839, where he started a paper called *Mainzer's Musical Times*. His book, *Singing for the Million*, Part II, was reviewed in the *Athenaeum* on July 30, 1842. The title was adopted by Hood as the subject of a humorous poem.

[2] John Aubrey engagingly describes this springtime practice on the part of his lordship.

[3] George, the fourth Marquess of Aberdeen (1784–1860), Secretary of State September 2, 1841, to June 5, 1846. Andrew Stevenson (1784–1857), Congressman from Virginia, Speaker of the House of Representatives, was minister to Great Britain from 1836 to 1841.

[*50 Wimpole Street*]
July 4, 1842

. . . Another attempt—or assumed attempt on the queen's life! [1] A boy—having the appearance of an errand boy,—and the pistol loaded with tobacco pipes—and a stander by snatching it out of his hands while he was preparing the gunpowder in the park! What is this strange popular mania of queen-shooting? What is the motive?—and what the end? In the meanwhile the despots of the earth sit safe—the Austrian emperors remain according to Mrs. Trollope, 'our angels'—and nobody thinks of even smoking a tobacco pipe at them, much less of shooting it. It is only citizen Kings, and liberal queens that their people address themselves to shooting! I am very angry—angry and sorry and ashamed. Who shot George the fourth? Not even I—says the sparrow. Poor Victoria! Let the coolness be what it may, there is an under current—she is a human being and a woman!—and is moreover conscious that of those who reproach her most, nobody has said that she has not wished to benefit her people according to her light. And the end of it all is,—she is set up for a mark to such little boys in her dominions as are pleased to play with pistols! It is worse than bad.

I hear that people go now to see the poor queen leave the palace for her drive with a disposition to be excited, with an idea of seeing her *shot at*: there is a crowd at the gates every day! Mr. Hood [2] proposes in an epigram in the last New Monthly, to change the name of Constitution Hill for Shooter's Hill [3]—but the subject is too grave for jesting on.

By the way, were you not amused by Hood's letter on the copyright, in the Athenaeum? [4] *I* was, and far more so, than by those elaborate merriments which however adroit and clever,—and he is the master of his Art,—do sometimes rather weary me than make me gay. Do you not confess to the same feeling? Laughter as by literature professed, seems to me like religion as by law established, rather legal than cordial. And however this may be in general, the effect of Hood's gaieties are very particularly in my experience gravities, from one end of the Comic annual series, to another . . .

[1] In July of this year, and two months after a previous attempt at assassination by one John Francis, a 'hunch-backed wretch' named Bean shot at the

carriage in which Queen Victoria, Prince Albert, and King Leopold were driving.

² Thomas Hood (1799–1845), the humorous poet who, suffering all his life from ill-health and insolvency, once said 'there's not a string attuned to mirth but has its chord in melancholy'. *The Song of the Shirt*, published in *Punch* in 1843, is probably the poem by which he is best remembered to-day.

³
On a Certain Locality
Of public changes, good or ill,
I seldom lead the mooters,
But really Constitution Hill
Should change its name with Shooter's !

T. H.
(*New Monthly Magazine*, July 1842.)

⁴ *Copyright and Copywrong*, Letter IV. (June 11, 1842.) Letter V appeared on June 18, 1842.

[*50 Wimpole Street*]
July 18, 1842

Before your letter came my dearest dearest friend, I was on the edge of one just ten times—and now, since its coming, I have suffered some three days or four to pass without a word. The truth is, I have felt rather depressed and *disagreeable*—in the sort of spirits which inclines one to lean *back* from one's friends for their own dear sakes—and I thought to myself that you would be quite as well, . . in fact, quite *better*, without having anything to do with me. Papa went away suddenly last week for a few days (he has returned now) to look at an estate near the Black Mountains—and their shadow fell upon *me*. I have been anxious, *pre*-sentimental . . disgusted without a reason—or to speak it more briefly, altogether disagreeable.

And now to speak, lest I forget, of your kind castle-building, or rather cottage and bower-building for me my beloved friend ! If I could see you I should be content to forswear the roses—nay, *that* is not a compliment, for I am content as it is. If I had my 'choice' like Hercules and Pomfret,¹ I would stay here, instead of going bower-hunting. The impressions gathered during my absence were of an ineffaceable character—and so are those of the comparative peace and calm, and positive blessedness of my return. I have a large room with air enough and silence enough—I am as tranquil as if I lived 'down in a leafy dell' : and presently I shall get down into the drawing-room—for *show rather than use*—, because you see, I cant possibly receive my sister's visitors, and shall [?] put everybody out of their way directly I go down. But as to leaving London, suppose I went a few miles away and Papa went with me—first there is the risk of moving, then of fixing in a lodging—and whether the fuss of the whole would be profitable, I question much. As it is, I make clear progress every week—get up at twelve in the morning—and attach to my daily walk with Crow, an appendix of 'standing alone', which I accomplish almost as well as when I was nine months old. Let me touch a finger, and I do it—otherwise I stagger, waver, have a tendency backwards or forwards—and altogether, this new pedestal of mine is as I say, far more glorious than safe. But it is a proof of new strength. Two months ago, my knees bent like paper if all my body's weight were not lent away from them,—and to sustain it even for a moment is decided progress. And now do try to imagine yourself into my place and prejudices and memories and *Being* generally. Think what calm is around one now—and how natural it is for me not willingly to stir from the scene of it.

Yes!—you would find contentment in London my beloved friend—there is everything here except the waving trees—everything in London except the country! We lived at Sidmouth for two years, and I who always from my first childhood loved the coast with [word illegible] unconscious enthusiasm, liked Sidmouth and very much *dis*liked the thought of being fixed finally in London. It would be difficult to find fit words for the feelings of depression with which the first week of our living in London abounded to me. There was a sense of impossibility that I could ever live on so. The narrowness of the streets, . . the *want of horizon* . . pressed through my senses to my soul, till I struggled to pain [?] with the new obstruction. But in a fortnight I was better—in a month, satisfied; in two months, quite happy; free in spite of the streets . . wishing myself no otherwhere; enjoying the grass and trees of the parks as truly and rustically as I ever did country in my life—with a disciplined imagination and fresh inward senses, and desirous of no more. Just so, would it be with you, my dearest friend. This London is a wonderful place—the living heart and centre of an immense circle of humanity—the fountain of intellect—of Art in all its forms—of the highest memories consecrated by genius : it is your Fletcher's London, our Shakespeare's London, my Chaucer's London . . 'this citie of London,' said he, 'which is to mee so dere and swete'! And then what a miracle it is to the imagination, and one under which mine cannot cease to thrill, to sit still and silent and serene in a room as tranquil as this, considering what a great roar of life and greatness is without! You would like my London, my beloved friend, if you knew it well and quietly : not in a whirl of company and sight-seeing, but well and quietly as I do from my sofa. You may be sure Flushie likes it. One might take Flushie for a citizen, to see the pleasure he has in looking about him at the shops, or going to the parks or to Hampstead—and in a carriage if you please : he would far rather go in a carriage.

While Papa was away, Flushie and I went into his room to sleep, so as to give place to the cleaners. Flush did not hesitate about going—he would not stay behind for the world—but he was very glad indeed when all the cleaning was done, and he and I could come home. . .

You speak mournful words my dearest dearest friend – – I scarcely dare to look back to them : only such words must be remembered. Well!—if you 'die in a poorhouse', I shall either have died somewhere before, or be dying or living under the same roof. Be sure of *that*—and surely you *were* sure of it even when you wrote those words : or else (which I am loth to believe) you do not love me well enough to understand *how* well I love *you* . . .

As to Mr. Kenyon, – – I scarcely know how to answer—I know so few of his admired ones that I am not qualified to sound the depth of the admiration. Shall Mrs. Niven [2] be a 'hot ploughshare' to prove him? Shall we commit him to that proof, dearest friend? But he has not come back yet.

Your ever attached E B B

[1] John Pomfret (1667–1702), Bedfordshire clergyman and author of *The Choice* (1700), which describes the pleasures of a literary and rural life.

[2] Mrs. Niven, *née* Vardill, was a friend of Miss Mitford's. She was the client in a very remarkable case, the issue of which—'whether a Scotch marriage could pass an English estate'—was decided that year in the House of Lords, after twenty-one years of litigation.

[50 Wimpole Street]
July 22 [1842]

I hope you have received the newspaper my dearest friend, containing Col. Dundas's high treasons.[1] The want of chivalry all around us is rather more singular than becoming—and whatever the poor queen's faults may be, I am at a loss to understand how she can have deserved it all. Oh yes—the whipping, as Dr. Mitford suggested it, is the only fit remedy for the assassinations—and you will see that Sir Robert Peel has decided it so. The paper spoke of her being 'much affected' by the last attempt,—I wonder if it is true. In any case, she must *feel*—whether the outward sign be given or not. . .

As to the cross-stitches—or stitches alas! of any sort, . . I am ashamed to say how useless and unaccomplished my fingers are in respect to them—and the more ashamed because I feel conscious that people may suspect the fault, of the *vanity* of a merit—by way of pedantry and the like. So when talk begins of work—German wools English threads and the rest, I make haste to change the subject or to look on one side and escape the imminent exposure. Oh!—you cant think—you can scarcely imagine, my awkwardness when I pretend to work! Such pricking of fingers, and knotting of thread, and sowing backwards in certain evolutions, instead of forwards! I ought to have been well whipped at six years old, and then—that is, now—I should whip better. As it is, I once knitted an odd garter, and embroidered an odd ruffle, and committed fragments of several collars, and did something mysterious, the name of which operation has past from my head, toward producing the quarter of a purse—yes, and made several doll's frocks, and one or two frocks for a poor child of mine adoption— and that is 'the head and front of my *att*ending' to the duties belonging to my femineity. *You* who are excellent in all things, will make an effort and forgive me—but the *effort* will be necessary. The best excuse for me is—that the Occupation was never put to me in the form of a duty. I had nothing to mind or do, needle-ways for myself or others. And then, my beloved friend, I was always insane about books or poems— poems of my own, I mean—, and books of everybody's else— and I read Mary Wolstonecraft [2] when I was thirteen—no, twelve! . . and, through the whole course of my childhood, I had a steady indignation against Nature who made me a woman, and a determinate resolution to dress up in men's clothes as soon as ever I was free of the nursery, and go into the world 'to seek my fortune'. '*How*', was not decided : but I rather leant towards being poor Lord Byron's *page*.

So, altogether, you see,—you will allow, my dearest indulgent friend . ., that I am one degree less 'good for-nothing' than might have been, à priori, expected.

Ever your
(as proven) unworthy and attached E B B

¹ 'Lord Worsley is to-morrow night to ask a question of Sir Robert Peel in the House of Commons, as to his knowledge of certain expressions said to have been used by one of her Majesty's aides-de-camp respecting his royal mistress at a dinner party consisting (we believe) of members of the Caledonian Hunt. The expression imputed to this aide-de-camp, the Hon. H. Dundas, is so gross and indecent that it cannot possibly be laid before her Majesty ; but the fact of an outrageous insult having been offered is notorious, and of that the Queen is doubtless cognisant.' (*Morning Chronicle*, July 4, 1842. From the *Observer*.)

² Mary Wollstonecraft (1759–97), author of *A Vindication of the Rights of Women* (1792). She married William Godwin, and their daughter, Mary, became the second wife of Shelley.

[50 Wimpole Street]
July 26, 1842

Angry with you for *importunity* my beloved friend—angry with you for *love*! Why what stuff can you suppose me made of, to suppose *that*? On the contrary—I thank you from the bottom of my heart for caring to think and write and be persuaded about good for me in any possible respect—nay, I would rather *act* upon your opinion than upon any medical opinion,—which might send me, for aught I know, to Madeira quite as soon as to Hampstead. Oh how perverse I am! Mr. Kenyon told me so on sunday—and on this tuesday I am sure of it—how perverse, how perverse I am! But 'I hear a voice you cannot hear' and 'I see a hand you cannot see', and all my omens bid me stay where I am—and then, I am under a vow, that I *never will* leave my family for health's sake any more. It is my vow. I have wept tears of blood for going: I will never do it again . . .

And now, you are to reward me for my docility and obedience (I deserve most of your praises full as well as this of my own) by sitting down directly if you please, and telling me the whole story about Miss Pickering.¹ Oh!—you *are* a knitter of a mystery! I am curious to the very extent of my capacity. 'Bridecake—bridecake.' Why do you mean, can you possibly mean, that Miss P. the second, *signified* to you that Mr. Kenyon proposed to her or meant to propose to her, or considered her directly or indirectly 'par amour'!? Is that your meaning? Now I do beseech you, . . if any compassion for or sympathy with an unfortunate victim of curiosity remain with you, tell me your story. I wont tell it over again to Mr. Kenyon—be sure of *that*: but if I see him before he goes abroad, I *will* assuredly ask him if he is acquainted with Miss P the second, and how she stands in what Howell calls 'the horizon of his love'. I may say *that*—all except the last word, for which of course I should give small change. I may look in his face and talk of Miss P the second and think . . metaphysics. I wont betray you dearest Miss Mitford—not for a wilderness of bridecake—so do, do, open your chronicles in my sight!—and consider the weakness of our common womanhood by eschewing further delays!

It seems to me that (talking of womanhood) your pen and ink odiosities do beguile you (for *you*) into wonderful injustices sometimes. For instance, isn't it hard for women in the majority,—hard for them not as 'great writers' but as petticoated creatures, to go down hill in that dreadful metaphorical sense of growing old? Dont they slip down, creep down backwards, and send all spectators over the stiles? Do the devotees to German stichery get down any better in general than the Miss *Ps*? I trow not. And even if you are right in straightening your remark within such limits . . why you should be tenderhearted my dearest friend and consider. Miss P. the first, wishes to propose,—Miss P. the second, to be proposed to. Now how effective can the most active exertions towards those meritorious ends, hope to be, without a little youth for a groundwork? One might faint nine times at forty, and dead away, and in vain, when the mere asking for hartshorn at eighteen would *do* it. The inference is clear—it is better to be eighteen than forty, for marriageable women—that is, for women resolved on being married—and it is clear to me besides that your Miss P the second, is far from being such a 'fool' as your Master Ben took her for. . .

Well!—and dear Mr. Kenyon came to see me on sunday. It was cold and rainy by the lakes, and he and his companions (oh! who were they?) were forced to have a fire every day as it came. He saw Mr. Wordsworth by two half hours, and thought him out of spirits—'depressed' was the word—suffering much from his eyes, and wearing a green shade. He did not go near poor Mr. Southey whose case is worse and worse—not recognising even his wife.[2] He didn't see Mr. Hartley Coleridge! I asked him if he had enjoyed it all,—and he laughed and told me not to ask questions. And yet, and yet . . if Mr. Crabbe Robinson was one of his companions, . . Miss Baillie was another! Yes—it is true. And the circumstance was not so much told to me as betrayed to me,—which makes it significantly true. . . Oh bridecake, bridecake!—was this the Miss Baillie who travelled into Devonshire?—to Ross?—the very same. Whether the Miss *B* shall clash finally with the Miss *P.* you know better than I do—but verily I am beginning to think that this dear Mr. Kenyon of ours will come to belong particularly to somebody distinct from us, in *bridecaka bridecakorum* . . .

Will you give my love to Dr. Mitford? Will you try to go on to love me?

Your E B B

Ah—thank you for the honor you dreamt of for one of my brother's! May your lovely young friend be as happy as love can make her,—and something richer, presently! Will you assure her by some opportunity, of my earnest good wishes? What a dreadful story this is (running the clubs I hear) about Lady Winchelsea's robbery (supposed) of Lady Augusta somebody's jewels. Mr. Kenyon told me that they were traced to Lady W—and that Lord Winchelsea, noble and chivalrous in all things, and confident and indignant in this, placed his wife's jewel case in the hands of the lady robbed—the lost jewels being found in the case! *Can* it be true?[3]

---

[1] Ellen Pickering (?–1843). Compelled to take up writing, through financial losses in the West Indies, she earned, it is said, £100 a year by her pen. Author of *The Fright* (1839), *The Quiet Husband* (1840), *The Expectant* (1842), *The Grumbler* (1843).

² After the death of his first wife, Edith Fricker, Robert Southey married
Caroline Bowles in 1839. At that time he was already suffering from softening
of the brain, and lived for the rest of his life in a semi-coma, scarcely able to
recognize the members of his family.

³ 'I have heard from several London people the details of Lady — and
the robbery of the jewels; it is amongst the most remarkable Events of my
time—and very frightful.' Sydney Smith to Lady Grey, Sept. 19, 1842.
(*The Letters of Sydney Smith*, ed. Nowell C. Smith, Vol. II, p. 892. Oxford,
1953.)

[50 Wimpole Street]
August 18, 1842

. . . First of all, let me tell you that I am not 'naughty'
anymore, but good—that I have been downstairs into the drawing room three times, and that I am going—that is, . .
meaning to try to go . . out in a wheeled chair along the
pavement before our door. *Isn't* it good of me? And isn't it
a close imitation of your plan for me about the wheeled chair
in a garden?—*as* close and good an imitation, I mean, as *I* can
perform, of *you*?

Flushie was in agonies to see me carried into the drawing
room. He hates the drawing room. It is Blue Beards' lock up
room to him. He wont go into it for anybody; and if carried
in, as I was, he trembles all over and makes a dash at the door
by his very first opportunity. But dear faithful loyal Flushie!—
he wouldn't see *me* taken there without going too! Down he
darted after me!—and after an affectionate *devouring* scene
upon the sofa in which I underwent a whole series of condoling
kisses, he laid his head upon my shoulder and never left me
until I went home again . . up stairs! But I think that
Flushie will approve of the wheeled chair. Even Flushie
will! . . .

The story is, that the queen has discovered a plot against
the further flourishing and well-being of the Prince of Wales,
by straying one sad day into the nursery. There, sate the nurse
Mrs. Lilly, embracing the royal baby . . while *both* 'cheered
and inebriated' by the contents of a certain brandy-bottle
dearer than royalty. She was sent off instantly—but just in
time (within a few days I was told) to lose two hundred a
year for life and a commission in the army for her son.¹

You have never told me what you think, how you feel

rather (for surely it is a matter of love and admiration and exaltation) about Tennyson's poems. Are they not *great*—divine?

In the meantime poetry does not harmonise the land! There is a continual cry in the streets of 'second editions' 'dreadful conflicts between the military and the populace' 'shocking burnings of property' and all such horrors as may be said or sung. It makes me half nervous to lie upon Papa's floor (my habit during these burning broiling days) and hear the bloodthirsty chant along the pavement. And Spittalfields is expected to be up every day, which is comforting! So much for the subjects of congratulation dwelt upon by the queen's speech. She had better have congratulated Mrs. Lilly!

Goodbye my beloved friend! I wish I had some good news of you and Dr. Mitford—yet do *not* write so as to weary yourself. A packet will go

[The rest of this letter is missing.]

¹ Nevertheless, when, on April 25, 1843, the Queen was safely delivered of a Princess, 'Mrs. Lilly, the monthly nurse' was once more in attendance on Her Majesty.

[50 Wimpole Street]
August 22, 1842

My beloved friend you distress me much by the description of your new sad anxiety.¹ Oh that I could do more than my affectionate and most sympathising prayers and thoughts can do, towards giving you some help and comfort. But my hands are tied while my heart goes out to you in full devotion. Tell me my dearest friend, if there is anything which appears to you possible for me to do,—and do a little justice to an affection which would fain prove itself beyond words,—by *trusting* it beyond them.

There is one thing which occurs to me but which quite trembles to put itself forward so as to solicit your notice. And yet I do not see why I should fear to ask you to receive from me what under similar circumstances I would take from your hands in a moment—and I never could understand why it should be found harder to *act* upon rights of love than to talk and feel upon them. And all this preface to a bagatelle—but it must be *telle*.

So dearest Miss Mitford, I have just to say to you that if twenty pounds would be of the slightest use to you, they are here—lying by me and of no use to *me*—, and shall be sent to you instantly and without the admission of anybody into the *aside*. Thro' the love and loss of precious friends I have shares and fund-deposits which Papa takes such kind care of in reference to my 'ill-odour' of imprudence and a possible futurity, that he does not let me touch more of them than what he trusts me with for pocket-money—and I mention it only to prove to you that you deprive me of nothing, not even of pocket-money, in receiving this poor £20 which I have just received from Mr. Dilke.[2] All the harm you will do is the making me glad and proud, overmuch perhaps, . . that you would make use of me as a friend—and indeed I am quite aware that I myself do use a friend's impertinence in offering such a trifle to your thoughts. But your being just now in peculiar circumstances makes it appear just possible to me that the suggestion . . gives me courage in fact to write this multitude of words upon naught and to hope and trust that you will not be displeased with me for writing them.

May God grant that since the last postscript, your dear patient may have rallied and rewarded your watchfulness. I do not say—'Leave off watching—spare yourself!'—because there are necessities of Love as well as of Life, and I know that *you* of all in the world, cannot deny them. But I know also and grieve to think, that you are wearing yourself out – – injuring your health, trampling under foot your spirits,—and that *I* cannot help it. This is grievous indeed.

May God bless and comfort you and help you availingly, as only He can, O my beloved friend.

My 'aside' aside! And let the word be '*send it*'—and let the word live on *between you and me*. Am I not

Your own E B B

[1] Dr. Mitford, who had recently had a seizure which left him partially paralysed, was now a helpless invalid, requiring 'five women to attend to him, and two men', besides the constant presence of his daughter, who was prevented by his demands from earning the money required to meet the situation.

[2] In payment for a contribution to the *Athenaeum*: possibly *The Book of the Poets* which appeared June 4–August 13, 1842.

[50 Wimpole Street]
Sept. 27th. 1842

Yes, my beloved friend . . now I see quite what the tears meant. You are not satisfied with *the marriage*—rather hopeful than satisfied—rather fearful than hopeful.[1] And since your telling me of some things and being silent of others, I do not wonder at the fearfulness and the tears—and I dont like what you say and what you avoid saying of the bridegroom—and I dont like the fashion of the courtship,—and least of all, do I like the *portion*. Oh, for a woman to have a dowry which can by any possible calculation be *worth a man* . . how great is her misfortune! Grant to me my dearest friend that, after all, the heiress is accursed above the poetess: and I will grant to *you*, and willingly, that the happiest woman of all, hides deepest and most quietly by the hearthside of domestic duty—without an aspiration beyond.

As to this bride and bridegroom, you are not to mind *much*, the contrast between them,—knowing how contrasts in love and marriage have flourished into proverb and borne very fine fruit. Yet I confess I dont like my own idea (however I came by it) of the 'merry bridegroom',—and am of opinion that if a lover of mine should laugh at the church door, I would spare his walking any farther. Why surely a merry man out of Robin Hood's gang, might by one 'touch of nature', be grave on his wedding morning. I do *not* like such merriment out of place! Yet he might love her—he might *love* her, after all—and may God's mercy avert whatever evil is 'just possible' too.

No—I cannot express to you how it touched me that you should have wished to give away your treasure, your 'Lucy Anderdon', to a brother of mine. But then you see, none of them are rich enough yet to think of settling—and George who in virtue of a profession by which he makes five pounds at intervals, is nearest the mark, could only have fallen in love and been miserable at the very best of it. And then George has a magnanimous theory about the impropriety of accepting a fortune from a wife! I believe he thinks it very immoral indeed,—even worse than marrying without any fortune. He is waiting now to have 'three thousand a year' for a minimum, as a preliminary to falling in love. If he had seen your darling, probably his opinions upon various subjects would have suffered a change—and he is so good, so upright, so persevering to work and so high-minded to work *out of the mud*, so strong where strength should be, and so soft where softness is admissable, that I could not wish him to change otherwise, even for a darling of yours. And she might not have liked him, you know, as he is. Who can tell? Love is a mystery. It must be best as it is—and I do hope, happier. Try to think it so. . .

Your own

E B B

There is a little more time—and now I will tell you what helped to make me so silent some time ago. I was *naughty* first, you know—that is agreed—and besides troubled in my imagination. Once upon a day, towards noon, I heard that Papa had gone away early as the dawn. Gone—vanished—and I never dreaming of his going! Gone down into Herefordshire, to look at an estate for an investment. Well—scarcely had I 'triumphed gloriously' over the ruffling of this news, when Septimus diverged from Latin and Greek into fencing with his tutor upon that part of our domains commonly called 'the leads', without 'buttons' and without masks—the consequence of which was that the tutor's weapon flying out struck the pupil's eye. Poor Set nearly fainted—and upon the nearest physician being sent for, Dr. Mayo, he shook his head,—'knew nothing about it',—the 'bone between the eye and brain was slight',—'did not however think the brain injured',—'did not think the eye destroyed'—but 'they had better send for a surgeon'. Liston ² was here directly of course: and I am thankful to say, no real injury had occurred,—altho' one half a quarter of an inch higher, and the stroke would have been, he said, instantaneously mortal.

I knew nothing of all this until the next day, through the consideration of my kind dear people—but even to hear that such things *had been*, made me turn quite sick and throw down my pen. A black eye with the sign of a cut upon the lid, remains to signify the evil—and no more. The Divine mercy is great. He might have died—died on the spot—and Papa away! Papa is not away now. Three days or four brought him back again,—and the estate does not seem to be very much worth going so far to look at—so that my troubles have come to a timely end.

God bless you in the midst of yours, and soften them out of their name.

[1] 'At Swallowfield, Berks, the Rev. W. E. Partridge, Vicar of Ilmer, Bucks, Chaplain to the Earl of Buckinghamshire, only son of C. A. Partridge, esq. of Cotham Lodge, Glouc. to Lucy-Olivia-Hobart, only surviving child of Oliver Anderdon, esq. Q.C.' (*The Gentleman's Magazine*, November 1842.)

[2] Robert Liston (1794–1847), Fellow of the Royal Society, and Professor of Clinical Surgery at University College, London. When he amputated, it is said that 'the gleam of his knife was followed so instantaneously by the sound of sawing so as to make the two actions appear almost simultaneous'.

[50 *Wimpole Street*]
Oct 15th 1842

Yes!—and when you say that Mr. Townsend complains of the obscurity of Mr. Browning, you should add that your Elizabeth Barrett does the like, of both of them. Nevertheless Mr. Townsend and I are not peers of Mr. Browning's. I have a high admiration of Mr. Browning and recognise all the poet in him, if a little of the riddle-maker—often great thoughts, which while they love the cloud, have the glory of the lightening. He is defective in *harmony* it strikes me : but the power of objecting dies away before the palpable presence of poetic genius everywhere, from Paracelsus to these last dramatic scenes.[1] His conceptive faculty is far beyond Milnes's : and Mr. Townsend's is none at all . . at least in exercise. Do you observe of Mr. Townsend that capable as he is of pretty thoughts, beautiful thoughts, most poetic thoughts, he has no idea whatever of attempting a *whole* of poetic creation ? I have doubted whether the defect arose from his habit of giving broken moments instead of whole days to composition—or whether from a deeper source ; and I do suspect that it is from the deeper source . . .

Ah—the chloride of lime ! It *is* very purifying to the air, and its appropriate unpleasantness you may perhaps fumigate away with the pastilles. Here are two more boxes of the latter, waiting to hear if you will have them. I am so very very glad that the grapes were acceptable, and I shall send you more of the same on Monday. Do, I beseech you, keep out in the air as much as possible. Otherwise you destroy yourself and *unavailingly* . . . My hopes are full of much future happiness for you, and perhaps of some happiness to be enjoyed with you,—and if you destroy yourself now, if you ruin your health for ever by a sacrifice without usefulness, what shall I say to you? *Be* persuaded, my beloved friend.[2]

And now I will tell you of a kindness done to me by your friend Mr. Haydon. Henrietta and Arabel both went to see the cartoon some days ago,—nay, many days ago,—and were delighted, full of admiration. He showed them among other pictures, an unfinished portrait of Wordsworth for which he sate this last summer,—and upon the sight of which Arabel exclaimed,—'Oh, how my sister would like to see this!' 'Then she *shall* see it' said the kind Mr. Haydon: and accordingly on the very same evening, the picture was sent to me,—and here it is still, because I was desired to keep it until it was sent for. Is it not kind? And the sort of pleasure the picture has given me I should describe with difficulty. A magnificent head, its white hair glittering like a crown! I mean to send a sonnet back with it as a witness to my feeling.

May God bless you my beloved friend, and your dear sufferer—I think of you all day long.

Ever your E B B

---

[1] *King Victor and King Charles*, 'Bells and Pomegranates', No. II, was published on March 12, 1842.

[2] But neither the entreaty nor the outcry of her friends could persuade Miss Mitford to relinquish her post at the bedside of her ailing father. The root of this devotion was a deep one. While still a schoolgirl at Hans Place, she had written: 'I hope dear Tod [Dr. Mitford] will take care of his dear head! His poor Mam Bonette [M R M] is not able to fly, or she certainly would come to Reading to nurse him, and she is the only one that nurses him well. But dear Mumper [Mrs. Mitford] must not be jealous, as she knows his Mam was always his head nurse.' (L'Estrange, Vol. I, p. 19.) His head nurse she remained; and for the rest of his life no one was permitted to relieve her of the privileges of that long-coveted situation.

[*50 Wimpole Street*]
Friday, Oct 19 1842

. . . Thank you for your kind tolerance of my sonnet on the picture. Do you know Mr. Haydon is so pleased with it

that he talks of sending it to Mr. Wordsworth, and requested
me to publish it in the Athenaeum, on account of some impossible good which he attaches to its publication.[1] Of course, I
could not say 'no'; but whether Mr. Dilke may not, remains
to be proved : for Mr. Haydon says rightly that the Athenaeum
people dislike him, . . are cold to him . . as they are indeed
to the whole world of art, with the exception of musicians.
Before I sent the sonnet away yesterday, I tried to alter that
line with 'releast' to the end of it,—but could not, for the
better. The Sonnet structure is a very fine one, however
imperious, and I never *would* believe that our language is
unqualified for the very strictest Italian form. I have been
exercising myself in it not unfrequently of late.

Ah—you speak more severely of Mr. Browning, than I can
say 'Amen' to. Amen would stick in my throat—even suppose
it to rise so high. There is a unity and nobleness of conception
in 'Pippa passes' which seems to me to outweigh all the riddles
in riddledom—and verily a great many 'lie hid' in that same
'Pippa'. Give me my choice,—only give me my choice,
between Mr. Milnes's genius and Mr. Browning's, and you
will see if I dont take the last and say 'thank you'. I am sure
I ought to say it for what your goodness leads you to say of
me—but indeed, indeed, Pippa, dark as she is, is worth all those
rhymes you speak of—in my eyes, not blinded by friendship.
Do you know that Mr. Browning is a great favorite (I mean as
a man) of Mr. Kenyon's ? Mr. Kenyon spoke to me warmly
of his high cultivation and attainments, and singular humility
of bearing. And he is weak in health too ! I should like to
hear you praise him a little more, indeed.

I have had one or two kind and interesting notes from
Mr. Haydon, who speaks of you as admiringly as I like almost.
'She is a noble creature' he says—'never flinched in all my
misfortunes'. I like *him* too, and am grateful to him. But as
to seeing him yet and here, . . oh no, my dearest friend, I
couldnt ! Why, do you know, that, last summer, Mr. Wordsworth had himself the infinite kindness of proposing twice to
Mr. Kenyon, to come to see me,—and Mr. Kenyon said 'no'.
Not that *I* said 'no'. I could not have articulated it to Wordsworth ! I could rather do so to the queen. But 'no' was said ;
and now, how could I say 'yes' to anybody in the world ?

Next summer, perhaps, it may be different—but who am I, who talk of next summers?

It is very cold—which is probably not likely to be injurious to your dear patient. Of the Kenyons, I hear nothing at all.

I smile in triumph over your feeling about Anna Seward's letters.

Ever your most affectionate

E B B

Some more grapes shall go to you on Monday—supposing that I do not hear before that he cannot take them.

[1] The sonnet—*On Mr. Haydon's Portrait of Mr. Wordsworth*—was published in the *Athenaeum* on October 29, 1842.

[50 Wimpole Street]
Oct. 23rd. 1842

. . . Mr. Kenyon's servant must be a 'character', from what Crow tells me of him; and I have often and often been amused at her report of his way of talking grandeur and literature, as to how '*we* had conversation-parties' and how '*we dined* all the cleverest people in England' and how 'my master talked better than . . any woman in the world'. There, was a comparison! . . . Mind you never divulge my impertinence to dear Mr. Kenyon—or he may be angry with me and his 'gentleman', who is a very learned gentleman, be sure, with an air of sitting 'on Olympus' top' all day long, and of counting poets, if not their syllables, on his fingers, . . 'siding the Gods'. Crow 'couldnt remember', she said, all the poets he talked about, – – but '*we* live very much with the poets'! I hope you smile a little. The lions roar even down the back-stairs, dont they? At any rate I am very very glad that dear Mr. Kenyon is coming back. I do like to see him and to hear him talk! He comes into this room like a flash of lightening, for suddenness and contrast and power,—and like sunshine, for calmness and gentle cheerfulness. He is my epitome of society—and even apart from the regard I have for him, I should miss him exceedingly, and rejoice that he has done for the present with Italy and Germany . . .

[*50 Wimpole Street*]
Oct. 27th 1842

Thank you my beloved friend, for your delightful thrice welcome letter, which at my bed-side 'bade goodmorrow' just as I opened my eyes for the day. Welcome it was, once or twice, as from *you*; and thrice, as bringing such a better account of your dear patient beyond the reach of my hopes. Never lark sang more pleasantly than your letter did! By the look of it, on the outside, I who am a prophet, knew that he was rather better than otherwise; but, to be sure, to be so well as *that*, did reach beyond the best of my hopes. I congratulate you,—I thank God for you my beloved friend! And I wait for the sign of your hand about the grapes, eager to send them both for him and you: and pastilles besides, . . I must not forget . . and the chocolate and salts. . .

What it must have been to you to pray with him again— and to hear his voice speak love again in the old tune! Is your Vicar a gentle simple man?—you have never praised him to me. Papa is my chaplain,—prays with me every night; not out of a book, but simply and warmly at once,—with one of my hands held in his and nobody besides him and me in the room. That is dear in him,—is it not? And he with his elastic spirit and merry laugh! One might as little expect such an act from the youngest of my brothers (at first sight!) as from him. When I was so ill he used to do it constantly I think, and altho' I could not understand what he said, through the wanderings of my mind at that time, yet I had a sort of vague satisfaction in seeing him kneel down there and in feeling that he was praying for all of us. It was strange, my state *then*, and looks to me from hence like a dreamed of dream! I am sure I never prayed myself for a long while. I seemed to lie too near to God to pray—as if the sword were close to my neck, and I, lying without hope or fear, could not *speak* to the striker. It was power and weakness meeting together—my sense of power in *Him*—my sense of weakness in myself. It was no doubting of His mercy, none of his love—but the Hand had struck me and I could not speak. . .

So you think me old enough to have twenty gentlemen in my bedroom if I please, according to the order of the garter! Agreed!—but then, but then—this Papa of mine would, even if I were fifty, most certainly demur to it. He is twice as 'proper', do you know, as I am who have the misfortune to be a 'good for nothing poetess'! He is indeed. . .

Mr. Haydon sent my sonnet to Wordsworth—did I tell you? And to my astonishment, to my great great pleasure this morning, a note very gentle and gracious, from Wordsworth himself was in my hands! I shall throw myself at Mr. Haydon's feet for procuring me such a pleasure!—he was the *means* of it obviously! The great poet speaks of the obscurity of the line you remarked upon, and suggests an alteration which unhappily is just too late for the Athenaeum, but which is available for a republication.[1] A letter from Wordsworth! Dont tell anybody, but *I kissed it*. And he speaks so kindly of his intention of calling upon me when he was last in London!

[The rest of this letter is missing].

[1] Wordsworth objected to the lines 'A vision free And noble, Haydon, hath thine art released', suggesting in their place 'By a vision free And noble, Haydon, is thine art released'. E B B, however, preferred her own emendation, 'A noble vision free Our Haydon's hand has flung out from the mist'.

[*50 Wimpole Street*]
Oct. 31, 1842

. . . My beloved friend, your most touching letter suggests much cause for thankfulness in all its deep sadness,—and I thank God for you that such things should be . . softening and sweetening to you His dispensation. When I was a child I had fits of fearfulness sometimes. I used to be frightened of the dark, and could not go to sleep unless the nurse sate there with a candle; and I well remember how I used to think . . 'I shall not like to be grown up because then I shall have nobody to take care of me,—nobody to *trust to*'. Distinct, very distinct, is my recollection of that feeling. It is pleasant, yes, necessary *to trust*—and to trust what is above us: and the strongest and wisest of us stand before that great eternity and among the secrets of life and death like children in the dark. How delightful, how consoling, that your own beloved sufferer should *trust*, before he sleeps!—and that you who are in a more painful situation, should trust too through the pain! I am glad he likes in particular the apostle John—because I myself do delight in that part of Scripture beyond all the rest. I have a notion too that altho' Paul is more difficult, John is more deep. There is a depth of Love everywhere—serene thro' its profundity. What can there be in language more divine than the seventeenth chapter of John's gospel? We hear in it the last beating while on earth of the heart of the Redeemer,—holy, tender pathetic,—distinct as the murmur of pure rivers, from the complex and contrarious uproar of creeds and controversies,—and *we*, learning so the full loving nature of that Heart, learn also the sufficiency of what we trust. That seventeenth chapter of John's gospel is my system of divinity. Nobody learns from it when to wear a surplice and when a gown, or when to light the church candles and when to put them out,—but the divine love in the Saviour, and the believer's safety through it, are as clearly *there* as the sun and moon in Heaven, and are *enough*! *My* peace I give you. Not as the world giveth, give I unto you. Let not your hearts be troubled, neither let *them be afraid*' . . .

And now let me stand in the sun for a moment before I say 'goodbye'. I shall come to the rescue of poor Mr. Browning,—'out of the spirit of contradiction', you will be of opinion. But consider! He is very fond of his mother and his sisters! [*sic*] And instead of accounting it effeminacy that he should fear their 'taking his horse away from him', I call it affectionateness that he should not bear to do what would occasion them anxiety.[1] If he had been afraid himself, he would himself have abjured the horse—and that *we* might have called effeminacy—but love, love, . . who dares say a word against the influence of love? It is strongest, be sure, with the strongest . . .

[1] In December 1840 the Brownings moved from Camberwell to New Cross. Robert Browning's uncle, Reuben Browning, who lived close to the newcomers, kept his horse in the stables of their cottage, with the result that the poet could ride at will, a privilege which is said to have inspired the galloping lines of *Through the Metidja to Abd-El-Kadr*.

[*50 Wimpole Street*]
Nov. 8, 1842

My beloved friend, I must write a few words to you and then be done—for silence is out of the question for today

again, and our friend, Mr. Hunter has come from Brighton to
see us and will be in this room in ten minutes. I have often
mentioned him to you I think, and his little girl who was my
'Little Friend' [1] in the poems, and is a great girl and friend
just now, of sixteen. You know he is a dissenting minister of
wide acquirements. He has a chapel at Brighton and wishes
to take private pupils besides and has one young man already, —
and *likes teaching*—which is so wonderful to me that I consider
it an idiosyncracy. But a person of high talent he is certainly,
and full, too full for happiness, of sensibility—that is, the power
of suffering is not sufficiently balanced by the energy to act,—
which produces a despondent character very painful to witness
the working of sometimes, in so dear a friend.

I have not seen Mr. Kenyon since the first time. He is
carried away by the social stream of course—and perhaps, . .
perhaps . . has never thought of me again! There's ingratitude of my secret thoughts, for you! But I cant help thinking
such things of him indeed—try as I may—and kind as he is!
He lives in such an unnatural whirlwind or whirlpool or both.
One can as little expect another to remember one in such
circumstances, as to take notes while he tumbles down Niagara.

But I must remember at last to tell you something he said
to me when he was here. It was not said in an àproposity to
your opinions yet it reminded me of them. He said that
Coleridge said, that every great man he ever knew, had something of the woman in him, with one exception: and the
exception was Wordsworth. Now, mind! The observation
was intended as no reproach to great men generally, but
praise—and the subject defined had no relation to *effeminacy*
(strictly speaking) but to softness . . tenderness! So I in my
perversity, put your remark and Coleridge's together, or rather
plunge yours into Coleridge's and leave it there liquidated!

They are coming! I hear them on the stairs! My beloved
dearest friend,

[The rest of this letter is missing.]

[1] *The Little Friend*, inspired by Mary Hunter and the halcyon days at
Sidmouth, was published in 1838 in *The Seraphim, and Other Poems*.

[50 Wimpole Street]
Nov. 14, 1842

. . . And now to tell you why I did not write. I have been overpowered with sadness and headache, and the heart-ache-feeling of . . 'If I do write to her I shall only do her harm'. My poor dear friend, Dr. Scully ! He is gone !—died last saturday, after the fluctuating painfulness of a three months' illness. And there, has broken the last thread which connected me with that fatal place,—there, is embittered the last association—and now from the largest association to the least, all is bitterness in relation to it. Oh, if I believed in local curses, I should know where to find mine. Think of living for two years in a place and of gathering *nothing* from it but grief—and speaking advisedly I say *nothing*. For to be silent of what is indeed with me unspeakable, the only two faces which I was obliged to see professionally and which associated themselves subsequently with kindness and gratitude,—are *both* darkened by death ! A strange coincidence of sadnesses. And I liked the place once—I really did—after the first gloom of my arrival there, which struck to my heart strangely. (I thought at the time) as if I felt grief in the air ! No strangeness is it, that the place should now be dreadful to me. The very name sounds like another word for sorrow. And I smile sometimes at my own weakness of verbal superstition, when I catch myself shunning the articulation of the name, and saying 'when we were *in Devonshire*' for 'when we were at *Torquay*' . . .

[50 Wimpole Street]
Nov. 18, 1842

I am so tired ! Which is scarcely a word to begin a letter with—and yet it is so true that it comes out of its place of peroration ! I wish I had written to you first of all,—and then I might write to you delightedly as usual. But Adam's curse waits even upon the letter-writer, and I was obliged to answer those three letters of Mr. Boyd's in one of mine, for he was very angry . . IS . . will be perhaps in spite of all—and why ? —why because I wont agree with him that Wordsworth is at

best, a *third rate* poet, and cant in fact write poetry in the true
sense, the least in the world. I asked him to read the sonnet
on Westminster bridge, among other passages—but the only
thing that struck him in it, was 'the profanity' of the 'Dear
God'. So he and I must talk and agree in Greek alone, for
the remainder of our lives.

Talking of Greek, Mr. Haydon has sent me lately a translation of the Gorgias of Plato, prepared for the press by his son
in law.[1] It is an excellent and spirited translation; but I
venture to think it inelegant and have said so. Plato uses
music as we do air for articulation,—and it does not do to
translate him into discords. Suppose Mr. Haydon should be
offended at my saying my thought about it! But then what
could I do? I was asked—and I always make it a point of
speaking the truth upon every such occasion. It is the only
means left to me (besides the moral motive) of giving any value
to so poor an opinion.

My ever dearest friend, how I rejoice that *the day* has past.
I quite dreaded it for you. Ah those birthdays! Mr. May [2]
is very very right. They burn our sorrows deeply in—that is
the most obvious use of them. For my own part, not even my
stupidity about remembering dates and numbers which is so
complete that I remember no birthdays except one or two or
three out of all the multitude we commemorate, there are just
one or two which prick me to the heart every year and make
me wish to forget *myself*. As to my birthday, nobody lately has
spoken to me of it, on the day of it, . . it is so impossible for
me who am not given to much weeping, to repress the tears
and deep emotion, which are excited by the remembrances of
past joys and holidaytimes and family unwounded affections.
Oh, Mr. May!—how right he is. Mr. Boyd's faculty of remembering dates . . I believe he has a recollection for the anni-
versary of every day in the year, forty years backwards, . . I
would not possess on any account. I prefer my stupidity. And
to be sure, I am stupid *par excellence* where there is anything to
be done with numbers. I could not tell you the age of one of
my brothers or sisters . . unless it were my youngest brother's,
—and when I told you his once I discovered afterwards that
I had made a mistake by a year less or more. Nay, you may
open your eyes,—but I could not tell you off hand, and without

reference to my books, as they 'calculate' over the Atlantic, how old I myself am. Now nobody would believe that! They would think it was a convenient Ladylike oblivion of a disagreeable thing. But, no!—it is simply a part of the idiosyncracy of my stupidity! I should probably be wrong by a year or two or three, if I attempted to say off hand how old I am—having only the intimate conviction that I am not eighteen nor a *P. . .*[3]

Would that I could see your face for one moment.

May God bless you ever,—and from Heaven and earth—my beloved friend!

Your E. B. B.

[1] The Rev. Orlando Hyman, the son of Mrs. Haydon by her first marriage. Scholar of Reading School, and Fellow of Wadham College, Oxford.

[2] Mr. G. May, the well-known Reading surgeon, was Miss Mitford's medical adviser.

[3] Pardoe—the ever youthful Julia.

[*50 Wimpole Street*]
Nov. 21, 1842

. . . Keep my secret—but I have been reading lately a good deal of the new French literature. Not that I would let it loose in this house for the world, no, nor in any other—but I was curious beyond the patience of my Eve-ship; and besides grew so interested in France and the French through my long apprentice ship to the old Memoirs that I felt pricked to the heart to know all about the posterity of my heroes and heroines. And besides I live out of the world altogether, and am lonely enough and old enough and sad enough and experienced enough in every sort of good and bad reading, not to be hurt personally by a French superfluity of bad. That however is my apology. It shows peradventure a suspiciousness of conscience—and it might have been franker and plainer to have just said 'I was curious and a woman'. The end remaining the same . . that I have been reading these French books. Do you know much of them? You mentioned Victor Hugo to me; and I had held him, long before, for a wonderful genius. So is George Sand—*shameless* as she is sometimes—by which word I mean no activity of indignation against herself

144

R. H. HORNE
From a daguerreotype

and her works generally, which appear to me unduly decried—
but a bare expression of the sort of feeling with which one
regards a woman whenever she leans to the aggrandisement of
the physical aspect of passion. For the rest, she is eloquent as
a fallen angel . . and often free from the taint, and great
consistently. A true woman of genius!—but of a womanhood
tired of itself, and scorned by *her*, while she bears it burning
above her head. Then there is Eugene Sue,[1] and Frederic
Soulie,[2] and De Queilhe[3] . . why the whole literature looks
like a conflagration—and my whole being aches with the sight
of it,—and when I turn away *home*, there seems nothing to be
seen, it is all so neutral tinted and dull and cold by comparison.
Full indeed of power and caprice and extravagance is this new
French literature—a kind of practical palinodia to the Louis
quatorze glories. The want is, of fixed principle. It is as if
the soul of the thinker were given to the four winds and the
multitudinous waters, without hold or compass, and as if in
this great tornado of being she lost sight of the localities and
relations both of Heaven and Earth. Now tell me, what you
think? That it is very naughty of me to read naughty books—
or that you have done the same?

You are a rebellious subject, my beloved friend, of her
Majesty. 'No sensibility!' Yet it was said of her that at the
period of her expected accession she wept day and night,—
which, if it happened to be a story, was a well constructed
and devised one. Well!—I should like to know the rights or
the wrongs of it—for all the Gods know that I have no peculiar
admiration for her *because* of her queenship. It was only
because of something beyond or under it, and taken account
of by my fancy. Mdme D'Arblay's Diary disgusts one, . . and
disgusted *me* to a degree which I will not seem affected by
recording, . . of queen's senses and queen's servants and above
all of queen's condescendances and sweetnesses. Surely there
is more freedom now at Windsor. Surely it is more lawful now
to be tired or hungry even, in the presence of Majesty. Tell
me if you do not think there may be some improvement.
Otherwise I give her up . . that is, her Majesty; and she may
go the way of all crowned flesh, henceforward and for me. . .

[1] Eugène Sue (1804–57), naval surgeon turned novelist. Author of *Jean
Cavalier* (1840), *Lautreamont* (1837), *Les Mystères de Paris* (1842–43), *Le Juif*

errant (1844–45), etc. Described by Jules Janin (*Athenaeum*, May 20, 1837) as 'a romance-writer without mannerism—lively, gay, daring—a jester and a satirist'; and by the *Athenaeum* itself as '*Sue* (not *slow*) poison! the poison of unhealthy excitement and false morality'.

² Frédéric Soulié (1800–47), dramatist and novelist. Author of *Les Mémoires du Diable* (1836–38), *Les Deux Cadavres* (1832), *La Confession générale* (1840–48), etc. 'The natural arrangement of a plot—and the bringing on a dénouement, bold, unexpected, and terrible, constitute his especial talent.' (Jules Janin, *Athenaeum*, June 10, 1837.)

³ Louis de Maynard de Queilhe, of Martinique, was killed in 1837 in a gun duel with his brother-in-law. He was the author of *Outre-mer*, a novel (1835).

[50 Wimpole Street]
*Nov*ʳ*. 27, 1842*

You delighted me, my beloved friend, by your sympathy in my naughtiness; for if you had held up your finger (as seemed to me just possible) and said 'fie', *that* would have been a 'fee fo fum' to me and frightened me tête a tête with my conscience. You are right and wise, I believe, besides being lenient—and what you properly call 'a chapter' in the philosophy and literature of our times, should not be skipped by thoughtful persons for the sake of the apparent want of a moral, when there *is* in fact a moral to all evil as to all good if we send out strong souls to the search. And now I do yearn to make you an accomplice in act as in desire. Oh that I dared to send Saunders and Otley's books to you!—only I dont dare—I cant dare—I mustn't try to dare. I must look to other means—and consider them . . and prepare in the meanwhile, my list, my 'map of the country' to meet your opportunities.

Yes! Victor Hugo stands first of all in genius, I think—and I should say so distinctly if I could make up my mind to call George Sand *second* to any genius living. *He* is wonderful—*she* is wonderful!—he, dramatically, and in action and effect—she, in eloquence and passion. Why Rousseau is cold lifeless loveless, deaf and dumb to her!—and (here is the miserable misfortune!) the *worst* which is offensive in him, is innocent to what is bad in her. It does really strike me to be so—altho' perhaps my impression may have exaggerated itself in my recoil from the occasional position of her *womanhood*. Still there are books of hers, as your Duke of Devonshire said, pure and taintless. 'Les maitres Mosaistes', for instance, may be read aloud by the most proper of governesses to her pupils—, *but* for the damning name, on the titlepage, of George Sand. '*Leila*' again, made me blush in my solitude to the ends of my fingers—blush three blushes in one . . for *Her* who could be so shameless—for her sex, whose purity she so disgraced—and for myself in particular, who could hold such a book for five minutes in one hand while a coal-fire burnt within reach of the other.

To be sure 'Le Roi s'amuse' [1] is very great!—but I who am not *all drama* as you are, . . do consider Nôtre Dame to be the greatness, par excellence, of its . . *poet*. Now answer me as if you were in the confessional. Is not Nôtre Dame a more wonderful work, a more sublime *poem*, than anything which our Scott ever performed or imagined, or saw in a dream when he rested from his Ivanhoe? Can you hesitate—can you *not* say *Yes*?

And have you observed what I have observed (I am sorry to keep you on your knees so long, but you must answer one more question) that Charles Dickens has meditated deeply and not without advantage upon Victor Hugo,—and that some of his very finest things, (all for instance of the Jew's condemnation-hours in Oliver Twist) are taken from Victor Hugo, . . 'Les derniers jours d'un condamnè' and '*passim*'? I admire Boz very absolutely and gratefully . . more than you do I suspect, —but my sense of his power and genius grew grey and weak 'in a single night' with reading Hugo.

Your inference upon the condition of French society, is scarcely too melancholy I must fear, for the obvious fact.

Beranger [2] is admirable—but then he scarcely takes rank (does he?) with 'young France'! He sang, you know, to the destraction of Louis le desirè who did his best to gag him—and the fierce, wild, passionate, and ghastly character of the present literature finds no room for its description on his songs. I have just done reading a romance of Frederic Souliè's which begins with a violation and a murder, and ends consistently with a murder and a violation,—the hero who is the agent of this 'just proportion' being shut up at last and starved in a premature coffin, after having his eyelids neatly sowed up by the fair fingers of his lady-love. The smell of all this sulphur has scarcely passed out of my nostrils! The devils smell so—be sure . . .

Think what I have seen since friday—three more pictures—portraits—and not by Haydon. Writing to Mr. Horne, I said something of this portrait of Wordsworth which stands still in my room—and in reply he said 'Haydon is a man of genius but so opposed in nature to Wordsworth that I cant believe in any portrait of Wordsworth produced by him'. He then asked me if I should care to see another miniature portrait of the same subject by Miss Gillies [3] . . 'the only living artist, I do believe, who can paint a head with a soul'. My answer need not be told—and as a consequence, three most exquisite miniatures, of *Wordsworth, Leigh Hunt and Mr. Horne*, were trusted to me by the kindness of the artist—, sent on saturday and left with me to this morning—and indeed they quite charmed me for the intermediate time. All three heads had souls, there was no doubting—and my dear friend Mr. Horne's had a moustache besides! In relation to Wordsworth's, it did not bewitch me out of my liking for Mr. Haydon's picture,—but it certainly has a sweetness, a serenity, a look of the setting sun, a pathos of genius in old age, which we could not consider seasonable for a poet on Helvellyn. Do you know Miss Gillies's pictures? And do you know that Mr. Browning has published another gathering of poems? [4] 'Dramatic Lyrics' he calls them—but I have not read enough to speak out my mind of them. And did you ever hear of a French authoress yclepped Mad[me] Amable Tastu [5]—or of two little volumes of her's called *Prose*? There is a good deal of beauty and sweetness and not a bit of naughtiness in this miscellany, which contains sundry translations from the English, . . one Irish story professed to be translated from *Miss Hall*,[6] and one from poor Miss Landon and one (with no profession or acknowledgment at all) taken word for word from *you*—the very idyll which Tennyson built a poem on . . the idyll of Dora Creswell and the cornfield − − *adopted* not adapted, and called 'La guirlande' and dropped gently into French as M[dme] Amable Tastu's own production! . . .

---

[1] *Le Roi s'amuse* (1832), a drama by Victor Hugo.
[2] Pierre Jean de Béranger (1780–1857), the great popular *chansonnier* of his

day.   Upon publication of each successive collection of *Chansons*, in 1815, in 1821, in 1825, and 1828, Béranger was heavily fined and sentenced to a term of imprisonment.

3 Margaret Gillies (1803–87), miniature and water-colour painter, who studied under Cruikshank and Ary Scheffer.   While she was 'staying at Rydal to take Wordsworth's portrait', the news came through of the reprieve (on February 1, 1840) of John Frost, the chartist leader, who, for his part in the insurrection at Newport, had been sentenced to be hung, drawn, and quartered.   On hearing of the reprieve, Wordsworth, she said, 'stamped his foot with vexation and rage'.   (*Memories*, by W. J. Linton, p. 167.   Lawrence, 1895.)

4 *Dramatic Lyrics*, 'Bells and Pomegranates', No. III, was published in November 1842.

5 Madame Amable Tastu (1798–1885), author of *Poésies* (1826), *Poésies nouvelles* (1834), etc.   *Proses, recueil des nouvelles, contes*, etc. was published in 1836.   On April 18, 1827, Eckermann wrote, 'Goethe then praised the poems of Madame Tastu, with which he had lately been occupied'.   (*Conversations of Goethe*.   Everyman, p. 195.)

6 Mrs. S. C. Hall (1800–81).   Dublin-born, her stories of Irish life may be compared to the rural sketches of Miss Mitford.   She published more than fifty books, entertained spiritualists and street musicians, and helped to found both the Hospital for Consumptives at Brompton and the Home for Decayed Gentlewomen.

[50 Wimpole Street]
Dec. 4, 1842

. . . I am sorry for Mrs. Dupuy—and really believe and hope better of her mind and heart, than to suppose that she could *die* of the fear of losing her fortune.   You say 'Poor thing'.   Well, and so do *I* !   Still I confess my slowness and obtuseness of sympathy in pecuniary misfortunes generally, and more especially where only one person suffers . . not *for* others, but in himself or herself.   Reduce me to bread and water and a mattrass and a patched garment . . and I should be ashamed before my own soul to shed a tear—I cannot understand these griefs for money's sake—mere personal griefs for money's sake.   They are griefs to be sure, but of the lowest and lightest burden.   Who would not embrace them, kiss them fervently as a great good, in change for other griefs which strike our hearts darken our eyes and bereave our affections?   Who would not?   Not *I* !   Oh that I had my beloveds back, to work for, starve for, beg for in the street-crossings,—work and watch for by day and night !   But it is best for *them* otherwise—though saddest for *me* . . .

[*50 Wimpole Street*]
Dec. 6th 1842

. . . My dearest dearest friend, may God preserve you from any future form of poverty. 'Part from Flush.' No indeed you shall not! What a thought! And to have sprung too from a word of mine! Forgive me for saying it. Dear dear Flush! Oh yes! To be sure, poverty is an evil. I never felt the actual pressure—never did. And then I am not alive all over to the hypothetical pricking of it, as some people are. For instance, I should feel nothing stronger than a little vexation, and even that not long, . . if I were forced to go away from this house to . . I wont say to a cottage in the country where I might plant ivy, and be poetical and selfsufficient, . . but to a little lodging-room over a grocer's shop. It wouldnt grieve me, to be forced to live on spare diet . . 'a raddish and an egg',—or to dress in dimity and a patch. None of these things would 'trouble me'. Nor would it *humble* me to have to say 'I am poor' . . .

Ah—my poor dearest Papa! How I remember the coming of that letter to apprize him of the loss of his fortune—not down to the point of 'elegant competence' but very far below it! He was surrounded by his family—and they, so young— and not educated,—and with not one prospect amongst them. And the letter came—and just one shadow past on his face while he read it (I marked it at the moment) and then he broke away from the melancholy, and threw himself into the jests and laughter of his innocent boys. That was the only shadow seen by any of us, with a direct relation to those evil news! And in all the bitter bitter preparation for our removal, . . there never was a word said by any one of us to Papa, or by him to us, in that relation. He *suffered more*, of *course*, and he suffered in proportion to the silence: but he bore up against the mortification and the anxiety, gallantly admirably— as you would do, my dearest Miss Mitford: and the reserve in matters of suffering is a part of his nature and not to be disturbed by the most tender of those who love him. Even now, I never say 'Hope End', before him. He loved the place *so*. The circumstances of our leaving it (it was seized under a mortgage) were full of mortification to him, and to us for his sake. It is a beautiful place—and people crowded to see it under the pretence of purchasing,—and our old serene green stilness was trodden under foot, day after day. And we had to hide, even away from our own private rooms, where we used to be safe from all the world,—and to hear in our hiding-place the trampling and the voices of strangers through the passages everywhere, and in the chambers which had been shut up for years from our own steps, sacred to death and love. It was a miserable time, I thought then—miserable for the sake of love and not for that of a mere lost possession. Miserable I *called* it. But in proportion to what has happened since, I do call it a happy time—thrice happy and blessed. . .

When I opened Mr. Horne's portrait, I started back as if I caught sight of your bludgeon. Imagine a high-browed and broad-browed head, absolutely bald, appearing to the fancy as if all the glistening auburn ringlets belonging to it, had fallen down to the base of the head and expended themselves in whiskers and moustachios! The features are very handsome—the nose delicate and aquiline, the eyes a clear blue, serene and elevated,—the mouth strikingly expressive of resolution—the complexion quite colorless, almost to ghastliness—with a Rembrandt light full on it. I assure you, I started. What Papa meant by 'no peculiarity' I cant conceive. He says it is very like indeed—and very peculiar it assuredly is— very peculiar and very expressive. Somebody cried out 'Its like an assassin',—and somebody else 'Its like a saint'. A very fine head certainly!—with a fifth Act in the very look of it! But I deprecate the moustache, and half believe and hope that it has been cut away since the picture was painted. He has a noble generous nature in spite of all the moustachios in the world, and to match his poetic genius.

May God bless you ever and ever

Your [signature obliterated by seal]

[*50 Wimpole Street*]
Dec. 13, 1842

I feel grateful to all the dear people, my beloved friend, who have been as you say, kind to you—and very grateful for their dissuading you from the attendance at the funeral,[1] which would have been quite too much for you even with your idea of privacy . . quite too much—likely to be altogether overcoming to you . . . My beloved friend, when Papa came to me last night and prayed with me his usual prayer, it was not prayed in forgetfulness of you. I did not say to him, 'Let us pray for her' : he did it out of his own mind and quite from his heart as you would have known if you had heard—and I kissed him twice instead of once afterwards, because it touched me. During your trial he has asked of you every day. I do not show your letters—except occasionally—even to him—but he knew that I had them, and always asked, and was very grave indeed after the bad news. Indeed I must not dwell most on him : for all of them, my sisters and brothers too, put twenty questions to me after every post, and think of you with the strongest interest and solicitude.

Here too is Mr. Haydon who has just written to me of you . . 'Her kindness and devoted attention to her father, will be a blessing to her remembrance to the end of her life' . . .

How wrong, critically wrong of Leigh Hunt to call Tennyson *sensual*. It seems to me quite wrong. Take his Sleeping Beauty for an instance, and see. He has not flesh and blood enough to be sensual—his forms are too obviously on the surface to wear pulses. His representation of beauty in that poem and otherwise, is rather the fantasma of beauty, than the thing. You can no more touch or clasp it, than beauty in a dream. It is not less beautiful, for *that*; but less sensual it *is* . . . *I* could have written Lockesly Hall and the Two Voices!! Ah my dearest friend, I fear you think a whole mountain too high of me. I know, I wish *I had* written them. I would rather have written them than any poem of the day—which is an answer to your question about Browning . . .

May God bless you my dear dearest friend! You shall hear again from me tomorrow.

Your own

E B B

[1] Dr. Mitford, who died on December 10, 1842, was buried in Shinfield Church on December 15.

[*50 Wimpole Street*]
Dec. 14, 1842

I thank God for you my beloved friend, most earnestly. This is merciful goodness in Him! This is worthy of you—worthy of you and of your beloved one who is gone. This calm, and readiness to be satisfied with the heaviest pressure of the Divine will, . . this outward working of your inward assurance of his happiness . . this is all reasonable as well as religious, and to my mind, the most worthy tribute to the dear and venerable memory, which is in your power to pay. . .

You are probably quite right about the superfluity of the latter stanzas of Lockesly Hall, altho' I did not observe it at the moment. I always *mean* to buy those poems—and had it been done, I might have, as commentators say, 'examined the text'. Now I simply trust to you and am the further, probably, from error on that account. That Lockesly Hall *burns* with life and passion—what is your reason for refusing to the poet, the *constructive faculty*? I have been thinking and do not come to a result. It appears to me that there is more evidence in these volumes *for* the probable possession than against; and that such a strong tragic soul works in the last poem we have spoken of, as would soon, if it willed, supply itself with a body. The 'Two Voices'! What an astonishing power of subtle thought in a silver-vibrating language! He takes a high place, by that composition, among those metaphysical poets, who have (not Cowley as Johnson dreamed) [1] but that high prince of riddledom, the thoughtful Lord Brooke [2] at their head.

I have heard that Mr. Tennyson prefers to all his other works the 'Vision of Sin', at the end I think of the second volume or near the end. Do look at it. The opening is full of power,—the versification wonderful, giving proof of a master's hand . . and *wrist too*. Still, and notwithstanding Hazlitt's dogma about authors always being right in the appreciation of their works—in which by the way I am tolerably sure that Mr. Hazlitt was wrong, . . I cannot rank this poem even *with* the poet's highest—much less *above* his highest. Can *you*?

Mr. Browning's last 'Bells and Pomegranates' I sigh over. There are fine things—yes, and *clearly* fine things. But there is much in the little (for the publication consists of only a few pages) which I, who admire him, wish away—impotent attempts at humour,—a vain jangling with rhymes. . I mean of *mere* rhymes . . and a fragmentary rough-edgedness about the *mounting* of some high thoughts. It is astonishing to me that it occurs to nobody else . . but when he rises into the Drama . . his manner of being graphic and passionate reminds me so of Mr. Landor that I am absolutely startled. There are no particular imitations, but the manner strikes me as identical. It *did*, in that magnificent, passionate scene in Pippa Passes, which Mr. Horne so justly praises. Is my imagination in fault? I should not be sorry if it were. I admire Mr. Browning; and recognise him always as a true original poet whenever I consider, and that is not seldom,—how great a thing it is to be one . . .

¹ Of the 'metaphysick style', Dr. Johnson wrote that 'Cowley adopted it, & excelled his predecessors, having as much sentiment, & more musick'.

² Sir Fulke Greville, Lord Brooke (1554–1628). *Certain Learned and Elegant Workes of the Right Honorable Fulke, Lord Brooke, written in his Youth and familiar exercise with Sir Philip Sidney*, was published in London in 1633. In it are included *The Tragedie of Alaham*, *The Tragedie of Mustapha*, and *Coelica*, containing *CIX Sonnetts*.

[50 Wimpole Street]
Dec. 17, 1842

. . . I do trust that this lovely, unduly warm weather, this Christmas June, may last, so as to admit of your taking long delightful drives and walks and whatever may be good for you. There is a little sitting-room next to your bedroom—isn't there?—and this is the room you occupy? I sometimes dream to myself of that 'vision of delights' of which I cant yet be exorcised, at Hampstead or Kensington . . of taking an unfurnished cottage at either place with a strip of garden where you might live as still as a 'country mouse' and yet have access to the city cheese. What an idol would in such a case be set up for the citizens, to the sound of harp sackbut and dulcimer and all manner of instruments! How you would hold in your hand, the golden Key, to the best society—artists, poets, and the canaille of Dukes! And yet how free you would be from the pressure of the ungovernable mob, who have afflicted your leisures so, at Three Mile Cross, and delayed you with curious eyes. No place so quiet as London, if one pleases to be quiet! Both the matter and the manner of society becomes here a matter of choice. . .

I sent Père Goriot, with the three novels of M^dme Dudevant [1]—because it is my belief that I never mentioned to you the name of Balzac, and that he *is*, nevertheless, the most powerful writer of the French day next to Victor Hugo and George Sand!—that he completes the *triumvirate*. Père Goriot is a very painful book—but full of a moody reckless power, dashed with blood and mud. It appears to me the most powerful work of its writer, I have read—and also the most open to tenderness. I like it the best—and also admire it the most. He is less a poet than either Hugo or George Sand—less ideal—less eloquent—nearer to the ground, . . deeper in the mire and sinning less by permitted passions, than by the influence of social corruptions. To me he is very revolting— cold and bitter with the sight and slough of evil . . to be shrunk from, as at the touch of a worm. Yet many of the *Scenes de la vie priveè* besides Pere Goriot and others of his books, are fine and ineffaceable—and I hope that you will think those words of *Père Goriot*.

[The rest of this letter is missing.]

[1] The married name of George Sand.

[*50 Wimpole Street*]
Dec. 21, 1842

My beloved friend, you were magnanimous in not adding to the opium—far more so than I should be. I say nothing against opium. It would be mere hypocrisy if I did. Under the denomination of morphine, I take life and heart and sleep and calm from opium, and praise it gratefully whenever there is room for my voice—and am persuaded that it not only assuages the spirits but in my particular case does positive *good* to the lungs by equalising the general circulation. Vivat opium! And may you and I live by its means!—moderation

155

which is good in all things, say the copy books—being very particularly good, we must admit, in this.

Still, with your peculiarity of bodily habit, I can understand how even a 'moderation in opium' may affect you injuriously—and why you should be more than others, guarded against an excess. The sleep after the nine miles' walk, was better than an opiate sleep. Do go on walking, that you may sleep sound, as by a cornfield of poppies—and have their colors in your dreams. And tell me if you sleep. And tell me if you dont sleep. Because as you have discerned, it is right of you to tell me the real bare truth, so that I may be glad and sorry accordingly and unmistrustingly.

Your righteous indignation on the subject of Ma^{dme} Dudevant, is responded to from the foundations of my temper and moral economy. It is precisely what I expected from *you*—and I beseech you to understand clearly that I did not send *Jaques* to you with any idea of his being admired. I wanted you to see to the horizon of the moral turpitude as well as of the intellectual power—and because I would not, *could not*, send you *Leila* a serpent book both for language-color and soul-slime and one which I could not read through for its vileness myself, . . I sent this Jaques, which seemed to me to stink less in the *phrase*, altho' the bearing and countenance and general moral tone are identically bad. Your observations seem to me the very lightenings to suit the offence. The triumph of sensual tendencies over, we will not say personal purity, but the common virtues of gratitude, friendship, and maternal duties,—and the representation (which the thing called a *struggle* is simply intended to make) of the *impugnable* nature of those same sensual tendencies, . . would be vile and debasing to the very eyes which read of them, if they were not read as a lie, and a gross lie, against the humanity of womanhood. . . *Indiana* less revolting as a whole leans alike and with the bent of the author's peculiar womanhood, to the sensual and physical—and yet that work does appear to me very brilliant and powerful, and eloquent beyond praising. Nay, I do consider *Jaques* to partake of all high qualities of rhetoric and language, on each side of the serpent's hiss. I am very sensitive,—I believe far more than I ought to be, . . to *style* and language. I could read a book upon a walking stick, if it were written eloquently, and delight in the eloquence. Style is music to me : I cannot help my pleasure in the beauty of it. Now, to my mind and ear too, the bare *french* of that wonderful genius Victor Hugo and of this brilliant monstrous woman Ma^{dme} Dudevant, is french *transfigured*. . . It is not french—it is french no more. We recognise nothing like it in Voltaire—and the previous (so called) classical writers. It is too sweet for french,—and too strong—and above all, too numerous. It is something like the 'voice of the charmer' . . to me.

In regard to Victor Hugo, I do certainly (ah my dearest friend, it is best to speak the truth !) differ a little with you. It is easy you say 'to be monstrous. So it is—very !—far be it from me to deny the facility : but the extravagances of genius are very different I must observe to you, from the exaggerations of mediocrity. The extravagances of genius are easy only to genius : and genius is not common. I honor Walter Scott for much—but never for *his knowledge of human nature*. It seems to me that he *paints* human nature—that he looks at it pictorially and conveys it to his canvass in its attitude and garment of picturesqueness—thinking at least as much of the setting of the folds, as of the beating of the heart. He is more a painter than a poet or philosopher. It is an outside view of humanity—not the view our Shakespeare took ! Am I very very wrong. I speak as it appears to me. . .

Post going—I break away from I cannot wait to examine what critical nonsenses. But ever yours—that is sure – –

ever your E B B

[*50 Wimpole Street*]
Dec. 28, 1842

. . . Ah my dearest, dearest friend, how could you, how could Mrs. Niven let you, go along that road again in the dark to meet another bludgeon ! ¹ It was very, very wrong. And then for you to be ill afterwards ! Those hysterics !—and your strong, energetic, magnanimous nature to be rent and shattered like that of the least of us women, by those terrible attacks ! I know what they are too well. Yet I dont cry and laugh in them—or shriek—but am convulsed and lose the power of swallowing. I *used* to suffer so. It is not the case now. Do do, my beloved friend, give yourself rest—repose. You have thrown yourself into society before your spirits are fit for it— and if I dared to say so, Mrs. Niven is a companion less suitable to the circumstances than a duller and more ordinary talker. My suspicion is that you did not suffer that night merely from fear acting upon a morbid state of nerves. You are excitable, and were naturally excited and kindled by that peculiar strain of conversation you have described to me, – – and then the reaction of the silence, and darkness caused you to sink and be overwhelmed. And my suspicion goes very near to a persuasion. . .

You are of course right about Andrè [2]—but you will smile to hear that I have not read that work yet. You will think that it isn't naughty enough for me. The truth is, that it has been absent from Mr. Saunder's library whenever I have sent for it—but I have sent again today and hope to be successful. You say not a word of Pere Goriot. Did you throw it into the fire in a paroxysm, and are you afraid of abashing me by telling me? It is a very powerful work—altho' the road through it is muddy, and noxious to the nostrils. And after all—we talk loudly and aright . . with a righteous indignation,—against this and similar works – – but to look back on the imaginative works of a previous century, of Marivaux [3] and Crebillon,[4] and compare – – why the books of La jeune France are clean and holy to them. Do you remember what Gray said about his idea of paradise being to lie all day long on a sofa and read eternal new romances of Marivaux and Crebillon? And did you ever look at—I dont say *read*—the 'Sofa' of Crebillon fils. I sent for it once in the innocense of my ignorance, and after a quarter of an hour's turning of the leaves dropped it like a burning iron. It is the most disgusting sensual book I ever *tried* to read—but *didn't* read, I do assure you. This post, this post. Time gallops when I write to you.

Ever your own

E B B

---

[1] About a month previously, while returning at night from Reading, the gig in which Miss Mitford was travelling was attacked by two highwaymen armed with bludgeons. Miss Mitford escaped with a severe shaking.

² A novel by George Sand, published in 1835.

³ Pierre Carlet de Chamblain de Marivaux (1688–1763), novelist and dramatist. Author of *Le Jeu de l'amour et du hasard* (1734), *Vie de Marianne* (1731–41), etc.

⁴ Claude-Prosper Jolyot de Crébillon (fils) (1707–77), novelist and dramatist. Author of *Les Amours de Zéohinizul* (1740) and of *Le Sopha, conte moral* (1745).

[50 Wimpole Street]
Dec. 30, 1842

There are occasional florid passages, to be sure, in Ma^{dme} de Stael ¹—but 'the rosy-fingered Aurora in prose' whom Pope used to hate so much, is not predominant in her—and I never never could think, my dearest friend, of comparing her to Hervey. The French critics cried aloud I know, and spared not, against her want of *classicism* and departure from the models. Let them cry! Who can be insensible to the warmth of colouring, the masterdom of outline . . the eloquent weeping and laughter of her *style*. It is eloquence. . . So I do venture to disagree with you, very humbly, in regard to what I cant help considering your underrating of one of the Duality of great women produced by or affiliated in France— Ma^{dme} Dudevant being the second. Ma^{dme} de Sevignè ² is an intellectual Grace—Ma^{dme} Dacier ³ a learned writer : a woman of genius, neither of those can pretend to be. France must turn, with the crowning due to *genius*, to her Corinna and George Sand. . .

Now I am going to tell you of a present I have received. My dear brother Charles John—he is the eldest of those left to us—very kind, warmly affectionate, sensitive beyond what is happy for him, and so unfortunately nervous as to shrink from general society and observation . . to refuse even to dine down stairs when *women* dine here . . most unfortunately shy and nervous which infirmities an impediment in his speech has done much to increase and *to be increased by*—well, he, my dear brother Charles John, brought me, the evening before last, a very precious present. Can you guess what it is? It is the engraving from Mr. Lucas's portrait of *you*, my beloved friend, framed very prettily in satin-wood ; and he gave it to me, dear kind fellow, as 'the present he thought I would like best'. If you had seen his dear face—how it shone and glowed at once with love and shyness! He had wished, he said, to give me a present—and he had great difficulty for fear of my not liking what he selected,—but he thought he *couldn't* make a mistake in choosing a portrait of Miss Mitford, particularly as it seemed to him very like indeed'! Wasn't it dear and kind? And dont you guess that both for his sake and your sake I have banished Spenser's castle from under Papa's picture and replaced it by yours?. . .

No—Moxon [4] wont have my poems. George went to him before he left us for the circuit, and he was infinitely civil and 'did protest' like a bookseller, his 'respect for Miss Barrett's genius',—the only drawback being that he preferred having nothing to do with her. He said that he happened to be personally connected with several poets, and from mere personal motives had been drawn in to publish their poems—that they did not sell . . that Mr. Milnes's did not sell—that Mr. Tennyson's sold the best—indeed he might almost say that his last volume had succeeded—that Wordsworth's were only beginning to sell—and that poetry being at a discount, his (Mr. Moxon's) object *now*, was to form quite a new connection. There! Nothing could be more unhesitating and decided, George told me, that [*sic*] his answer. . .

This morning I had a very cordial letter from Mr. Lowell,[5] the poet of Boston—and he asks me to send him a few poems for a Magazine he is originating (which I certainly will do, because the Americans have been so good natured to me) and to solicit Mr. *Tennyson* for something, if he should be of my acquaintance. But—alas, alas,—not for Mr. Lowell but for *me*: Mr. Tennyson isn't of my acquaintance—I do not, so, 'side the gods'.

Mr. Kenyon is at home again. In his goodness he called here the day before yesterday, not to see me but to leave Macauley's ballads for me to look thro'.[6] How kind!—how *too kind for a scandal monger*!

Mr. Haydon too has given me, *given me* two pages, nearly, of Keats' poetry written in the poet's hand.[7] The world is prodigal to me just now I think! . . .

Your own affectionate

E B B.

JOHN KENYON
From a drawing

¹ Madame de Staël (1766–1817), author of *Delphine* (1802) and *Corinne* (1807). De Quincey described her as 'a hideous-looking creature, with a huge structure of bones about the shoulders . . . Her chest, especially when viewed *en profile*, was, as a London wit remarked, like a chest of drawers.' (*Recollections of Hannah More. Tait's Magazine*, December 1833.)

² Madame de Sévigné (1626–96), in whose delightful letters, published successively in 1726, 1734, and 1754, is to be found a vivid reflection of the daily life and preoccupations of the aristocracy of the seventeenth century in France.

³ Madame Dacier (1654–1720), French scholar and translator of the classics. In 1699 her prose translation of the *Iliad* was published, followed in 1708 by a similar translation of the *Odyssey*.

⁴ Edward Moxon (1801–58), publisher and verse-writer, author of *The Prospect, and Other Poems* (1826). In 1833 he married Lamb's adopted daughter, Emma Isola, and established his publishing house in Dover Street.

⁵ James Russell Lowell (1819–91), American lawyer and author. His literary journal, *The Pioneer*, ran for three issues only, coming to an end in 1843. His works include *A Year's Life* (1841), *Conversations on Some of the Old Poets* (1843), and *The Biglow Papers* (1848).

⁶ *Lays of Ancient Rome* by Thomas Babington Macaulay, was reviewed in the *Athenaeum* on November 5, 1842.

⁷ The manuscript contains the last portion of *I stood Tip-Toe upon a Little Hill*. At the foot of the second page Haydon has written 'A Fragment of Dear Keats poetry and writing, given to me by him and by me to Miss Barrett; December 30th 1842. B. R. Haydon.' (*The Papers of Lt.-Col. Moulton Barrett: Sotheby Catalogue*, June 1937.)

[50 Wimpole Street]
Jany. 4, 1843

. . . Oh my dearest friend, you little guess at the *sort* of *shyness of shyness* which my poor dearest Stormie (as we call him) suffers under, if you suppose that I could, *dare* to read to him all your kindness said. It is a sort of shyness which prevents anyone from saying before him 'he is shy'. He shrinks from the shadow of his own personality—from being talked of or looked at or reasoned about. Not one of us would *dare* to make an observation upon his stammering, for instance, altho' it is rather a nervous affection than a physical defect, and not at all bad in its degree. Knowing that he held you in high estimation I read to him what you said in your goodness, about 'feeling sure that he and you would be friends' and that you had been 'interested' by his appearance of 'sensibility'. My dearest friend, he flushed up to the temples, walked about the room in agitation, reproached me gently (he is much attached to me, dear fellow, and when he doesn't think of *you*,

M   161

makes me a grand exception to the female race, to the great amusement of all the house who delight in stirring him up to the climax of his anti-womanism!) reproached me gently for saying a word to you about the giver of the picture . . about naming *him* to Miss Mitford!! My dearest friend, I was confounded! I might have guessed it—but I overlooked the possibility—and stood aghast at the consequence of my imprudence. I missed all about the shyness—it was just the idea of being distinguished by you, of being selected for observation, which startled him. Ah—it is so unfortunate! And *he* so affectionate, so generous, so right-minded in all things! It is a worse shyness than yours was, my dearest Miss Mitford—because it is the sense of what he considers to be a natural defect, this stammering, on which it is founded—and because he does not struggle. Papa sent him with George to the Glasgow university, a few years ago—and he began by being brave, by attending all the lectures and reading his own Essays in the presence of the Collegiate body. He did it for some time perfectly well and without hesitation—but one morning, his nerves were weaker than usual and he became excited, and the impediment was distinguished in the reading. In the cruel brutal animal spirits of early youth, some of the students *laughed out*. He stopped in a moment—was silent ; and fell back into his seat covering his face with both his hands!— and never from that moment could remonstrance or persuasion move him from his resolution of reading in public no more ; and he left the university, much to Papa's vexation, without even taking his degree there as George did, because the few words which it was necessary to speak in public in order to it, he *would not speak*. And the shadow has fallen upon his life from that time to this. . .

[*50 Wimpole Street*]
Jany. 7, 1843

. . . Flush is quite well again—thanks to you and Ben— and screams no more. As to London I persist in thinking, tell Master Ben, that London agrees with him perfectly. He has quite as much exercise here as he had in Devonshire—frequently in the parks, and occasionally as far as Hampstead : and he might have more if it were not for his excessive *fineness* as to society, which prevents his choosing to go out with anybody except Arabel or Crow—or Sette on the sunday afternoon when the two great dogs are taken out *en grande compagnie*. Not Mrs. Trollope on the right hand of Prince Metternich, could rejoice more in la crême de la crême, than does my Flushie.[1] Call it fineness, or call it cowardice . . he is unpersuadable by and inaccessible to the majority.

Certainly, as people represent to me, he leads an unnatural life in this room of mine—but how can I help it ? He wont leave me for anybody in the world except Crow. He likes my brothers and sisters and Papa or Trippy [2] to come into the room—overwhelms them with salutations—plays with them joyously—of Arabel he is particularly fond and deserts my side to lie in her lap and kiss and play with her,—all the time they and she and remain in my room. But the instant, anyone of them says 'Flush will you go down stairs with me', . . he darts off as if they had struck him with an instrument of violence—darts off and rushes to me throwing himself into my arms, kissing me for protection pushing earnestly *into* me with glittering dilated eyes as if he would seek there some innermost security. Is it not both strange and pretty ? Papa asks him 'to go down stairs with him' everyday, and the effect is invariable—upon which Papa always says 'What a fool that dog is',— and *laughs*. Nobody can help smiling, really, to observe the effect of the solicitation. Flushie *runs* as if a cat were running after him—and *that* is the climax of his possible terrors and fastest flights.

He likes to go out to walk, though,—he likes *that* to ecstasy, whenever he is sure of his company. And if my brothers *ask him* to go out . . his agitation between his taste for the thing and his dislike of the escort generally ends by his beginning to cry. He puts his head on my shoulder and begins to cry—just like a child who complains of *being teased*, and cries ! They always tell me that Flush is a spoilt child, and really he does sometimes remind even myself of one.

I have no doubt that Ben was right as to the cause of the screaming ; but Flush is quite well now—and when you see him you will agree with me that he is improved in beauty and roundness and grace. Was he *four months* or *eight months* old when he came to me? Tell me—for I forget, and want to be reminded. With all his love for this dark silent room, he never was more gleesome and vivacious than he is now—more given to leaping and running, and stealing gloves and doing all sorts and conditions of mischief. He might be a puppy still, as far as his 'wild oats' are concerned. And then, when the play-fellows are gone, to lie so gently and silently and closely to me—'What should I do without my Flushie! . . .

¹ Mrs. Trollope, who arrived in Vienna on September 1, 1836, received an invitation to the British Embassy, where she was taken in to dinner by an attentive Prince Metternich.

² Mary Trepsack, E B B told Miss Mitford, was 'a very dear old family friend of ours, who lived *simply as a friend* in Papa's family, has held him an infant in her arms besides each of his infants, and now having lodgings in a street near to us runs in and out (she can still run I assure you) of this house and calls us "her children!"'. [March 3, 1842.] She died 'at a great age' in 1856.

[*50 Wimpole Street*]
Jan. 10, 1843

No—I should not dare to propose such a thing. None of us dare to make any allusion to the defect—and when Papa has laid in his way books professing to let one in to remedial systems, it has been in vain—he will not be persuaded. The excessive sensitiveness to the defect is far worse, infinitely worse than the defect itself—which if it were *mine*, I should think very little about. I dare say Mr. Darley's is of a more distressing character. Stormie, dear fellow, will talk with no sign of it, when he is unexcited and unabashed. At moments of excitement on the other hand he can scarcely articulate at all—and he is very excitable indeed. Say a word against O'Connell – – and the whole evil becomes developped! My dear dear Stormie! Yet it does not affect his spirits. He is joyous enough with *us*—and eager about politics. The shrink-ing from society is unattended by any moodiness or melancholy —altho' enough remains, of course, to vex Papa a good deal and to fill us all with deep regret.

I shall feel more for Mr. Darley since I have heard this of him—and the meaning of his word '*mask*' I already understand the bearings of.¹ Yes!—it struck me that in one or two notes of his which you allowed me to see, there was an undue proportion of *classicism*. Now *vive* Romanticism, in our letters at least! it is dreadful to be wise all day long—and I like to have what Cousin ² calls 'l'homme et le grand homme' both together – – sometimes peradventure liking the first better than the last. But Mr. Darley! I dare say I should like *him*, for all the classicism! I do like the poet—and the poet (depend upon it) altho' you and Mr. Kenyon dont think so, is the innermost man, the most real man of all. I dare say I should like Mr. Darley, whether in letters or conversation. What I *dont* like in him, is his crossness—his acerbity—his acrimony—his want of sympathy for his brothers in literature. *That* I dont like—and I confess that my knowledge of it has given me a sort of distaste to the individual, and made me feel cold at moments when I recognise his genius most confidently. . .

Mr. Haydon and I are great friends, I assure you; and he has ended (now I tell you this in confidence) he has ended—considering me as a sort of Abstraction called Elizabeth Barrett, before which it would be impossible to blush or tremble,—by confiding to me a MS autobiography unseen before by any human eye even in his own family.³ Only the first part, reaching to the beginning of his Academical career, I have yet seen; but I am much delighted and interested, and look forward with staring eyes towards the remainder. It is full of blood and pulses—and of the detail of life—and of the *life-agony* of genius. You may imagine whether I am pleased or not! But you had better perhaps, my dearest friend, *not* say to Mr. Haydon that I had mentioned to you even the existence of this MS—for if the Abstraction, the daughter of Ens, and cousin of the quiddities, once gets a reputation for prating, . . there, will be an end to the confidences! He has twenty five volumes of Journal, he says, which he once thought of sending to me but afterwards found out that 'they *cant* be sent'. How vexed I was when he found it out! But the Autobiography consoled me in some sort: and Northcote Opie and Fuseli ⁴ have appeared on the scene already. Now you see! I was bent on making you as jealous of me (almost) as I am of Mr. Kenyon for certain reasons you are 'ware of'. Your introduction of me went a good way with Mr. Haydon—and then my state of adversity—and then my genius for making unknown friends with whom I am intimately acquainted all except their faces !—these three things overcame him.

May God bless you my dearest, dearest friend !

Your ever attached

E B B

¹ 'My impediment is, as it were, a hideous mask upon my mind which not only disfigures, but nearly suffocates it.' George Darley to Miss Mitford, August 22, 1836. (*Friendships of M R M*, ed. L'Estrange, Vol. II, p. 6. Hurst & Blackett, 1882.)

² Victor Cousin (1792–1867), author of *Cours d'histoire de la philosophie moderne* (1841), *Rapport sur la nécessité d'une nouvelle édition des Pensées de Pascal* (1842), etc.

³ *The Life of Benjamin Robert Haydon*, drawn from his Autobiography and journals, and edited by Tom Taylor, was published in June 1853.

⁴ Like John Opie, the Cornish Wonder (1761–1807), James Northcote (1746–1831), author of a memoir of Sir Joshua Reynolds, was a historical and portrait painter. His emaciated appearance inspired the remark that he looked 'like a rat who has seen a cat'. The paintings of Fuseli (1741–1825), translator of Winckelmann, reveal a strong interest in the supernatural. His influence is to be seen in the work of William Blake.

[*50 Wimpole Street*]

Jany. 14, 1843

My dearest friend I seem as if I had been holding my breath since I wrote last to you,—and certainly I should not have failed to write yesterday if I had not been crying instead. Dont be afraid—there was no reason for the crying !—at least, no new reason. I am not fretful in general,—but when I once begin to cry, for something or nothing, I cant stop myself—and it was just so with me yesterday, until Flush, dear little thing, grew quite uneasy and set himself to administring a series of medicinal kisses on my lips and eyes which made me laugh again in spite of the world and Mr. Varley's stars.¹ I couldnt get up spirits, nevertheless, to write to you. And even today you wont think me worth much as a correspondent. The philosophy of crying is, to be sure, an even *more* foolish thing than Philosophy generally, very often is. We never have got anything by it since the moon was first cried for by a fine baby. . .

In the matter of my most excellent modesty and humility

in which (O santa Maria!) I exceed so infinitely certain of my contemporaries, I am almost afraid, if I say what is in my mind, that I may fall from the third 'story' of this high reputation in your esteem of me—and yet I *must speak* . . like others of womankind, . . at whatever risk. Well then!—my dearest dearest Miss Mitford—you will try to be patient with me and I will try to take courage and altogether disagree with *you* on the subject of *originality*. What! I am never original—Tennyson is not original—nobody is original *now*! And you dont tell me to destroy every word I ever wrote—and you hold Tennyson to be a poet—and you consider the world *not at an end*? My dearest friend, I do disagree with [?] you with all the powers of my understanding. Voltaire said—(did he not somewhere?) that there are only eight distinctive comic characters in the universe of humanity, and that they had been written out. But *you* are not Voltaire. But in this matter you write Voltaire . . *a little*!

'So she sets up to be original—does she?—this modest E B B'!

Ah, be merciful! She would not 'set up'—she admits your right to set her down, if she did. And yet she acknowledges freely that any single poem of hers which was to her conviction, *not* original—that is, which did not express a direct impression from nature to the mind of the writer unintermediately received and which did not convey to the reader's mind a fresh breath or new aspect of nature, intermediately received,—such a poem I would destroy willingly, gladly, righteously, and never look back upon its ashes. Perhaps this proves a want of modesty in me: for certainly it proves my convictions of what Poetry ought to be to assume the name, and of what poets ought to be to assume the name. And now, dont let us talk any more about *me*. I only *aspire*.

But Tennyson . . not original! Ah my beloved friend!— what is genius—but the power of expressing a new individuality? Would all the finishing in the world move the soul into another attitude, as certain of those poems do? Surely, surely not! No more originality now? Have we seen to the bottom of that infinite of Nature, which reflects God's! Surely, surely not! If I thought so, I would throw away all these poems, and 'walk softly all day long' as in a universe worn out and annulled.

Art and literature should be names of memories to me, for evermore—mocking an impossible substance.

But my hope and belief are, that to be 'original' is as possible and not harder now, than in the first days of the creation—and that every writer who is at once true enough and strong enough to express his own individuality, is original as Shakespeare was. I hold Tennyson to be, strictly speaking, original—and Browning!—and Milnes, in a less degree. Passing to prose, your own Village and Belford Regis are original—and if others write in your manner, they *Mitfordize*. . .

Three days ago, Mr. Kenyon brought a picture for me to see—a painting in oils—an *ecce homo*—by a young artist yet unknown. The crown of thorns is there, and the blood-drop falling from the temple, as in Guido—but the face has a distinct character. The broad brow is knit between the eyes, losing nothing of its majesty in the anguish—and *they*, with the serene will burning in them, look divinely onward, until your own eyes seem to fall before their *look*. It is a divine picture to my feeling. We had a candle to throw the right light upon the face—and really that light appeared to startle it into projection and actual life. And this was painted in a garret! Genius has not withered from the world, let us be very certain. . .

Forgive my various impertinences—do!—forgive me for the sake of my crying-fit yesterday. I may have cried away the greater part of my modesty and my sense, without knowing it.

Your own

E B B

[1] John Varley (1778–1842), painter, art teacher, and astrologer. A very strong man, he enjoyed boxing; when tired of boxing, he and his pupils would toss Mrs. Varley from one to the other across the room. At the post mortem on Varley the surgeon said of his organs that they were in such perfect order that they looked 'as though they had never been used'.

[50 *Wimpole Street*]
Jan. 15, 1843

My dearest friend, do believe (to go on where I left off) that Fame, reputation, the recognition of a master-power available for goodness or for truth, I undervalue as little as anyone in the world, and never did undervalue. Perhaps, if the secret hearts of us were beheld, I value it even more than you do. I *think I do*. I think, for instance, that you, as your Miss Austen did and as Mrs. Radcliffe [1] did, care more for the respect paid to you on mere social grounds, than you care for any acknowledgement of your power as a writer and on literary grounds. I think that you have a sort of satisfaction in saying 'People do not talk literature to me'—or 'people like me for myself better than they do for my books'. I think moreover, that you have a tendency to laugh to scorn, as far as your goodness and dearness of nature will let you, the pain of that wrestling for merited distinction under which so many great hearts have groaned aloud – – I think your tendency is to doubt the reality of this sort of pain, just as you say that mine is to under-rate poverty-pains. . .

But—oh my dearest friend, is not real fame, Milton's fame, different from the pseudo shadow called by men popularity? And is it not an historical fact and worthy of all consideration, that poets who have leapt into popularity have *generally* perished from fame? And have not true poets who have also become popular poets at once, been so for reasons independent of their poetry . . and even of their powers? Was not Byron's popularity (and he was a true genius though Mr. Serjt Talfourd refuse ten times to turn the patronage of his eyelids upon Manfred's castle) owing in great measure to his worst faults—and then again, to his stories and eloquence . . things apart from his poetical genius? I think so—it appears to me so. My beloved friend, if I had the power you would dream for me, and double *that*, I should not even then be indifferent to *praise*,—because I never pretend to that virtue, (or vice?) of such indifference,—but I never would write a line nor unwrite a line with the intent of being popular among a contemporaneous public. Here is a fact! The Rev^d. Robert Montgomery [2] is at this moment, as far as the sale of books can prove anything, . . and it certainly proves success with the multitude, . . the most popular poet in England. Even Wordsworth after more than half a century of conflict, cannot talk of eighteenth editions. Robert Montgomery is the most popular poet. Poet!—'poet-ape' Sir Phillip Sidney would call him. Do you know his 'poetry'?—the sound and fury of it, and nothingness of signification? *He* is the most popular poet in our England! And this is the meaning and worth of 'popularity!'

I mean to make you value more Mr. Browning; so I am going to send you with Ma^{dme} de Genlis' Alphonsine, Heinrich Stilling's [3] Autobiography which you must keep for my sake, and Browning's last Belles [*sic*] and Pomegranates. Certain of the poems should not, I think, have been published,—but several of them are very fine and individual—'original', my dearest friend, according to my impression and conviction. They are at least *new to me*. We must speak after our experience. And in relation to this subject, as I read this very morning Schindler's [4] interesting memoirs of Beethoven, . . that true genius Beethoven—that Goëthe of music—(you do justice to Beethoven's genius I am certain) I came upon these words—'Beethoven always bore in mind that a Mozart had preceeded him and that another might follow him. He *ever cherished high expectations of the future, for he fervently believed in the omnipotence of the Creator and the inexhaustibility of nature*'

Now that is just my creed—and I do believe that when you wrote what you did about the exhaustion of originality generally, some naughty body or mind (mine perhaps!) had been teazing you with commonplaces into an utter despair of the possibility of anything better. Confess, my beloved friend! Now wasn't it so?

As for all you say about me in particular—about the want of clearness, and the propriety of blotting and burning pretty freely, *I* confess it all. You are always right my dearest friend, —you always must be *when you blame me*—and I am always frightened when you do—because the faults *which you see* must be large indeed. You would have thrown me into despair by the 'originality' remark, if you had not applied it also to Tennyson—else, I should have died on the point of the knife. . .

Your attached

E B B

---

[1] Ann Radcliffe (1764–1822), author of *The Mysteries of Udolpho* (1794), and the originator of the Gothic-romantic novel.

[2] The Reverend Robert Montgomery (1807–55) became, in 1843, minister of a proprietary chapel in St. Pancras, where the ladies of his congregation 'made and presented to him, in the course of a single season, one hundred pairs of slippers'. Author, among much else, of *Satan, a Poem* (1830), *Woman, the Angel of Life* (1833), and *Luther, a Poem* (1842).

³ Johann Heinrich Jung ('Jung Stilling') (1740–1817), surgeon and Professor of Political Economy. Author of semi-mystical romances, and of an autobiography which was translated into English in 1835.

⁴ Anton Schindler (1795–1864). A close friend of Beethoven, and his first biographer.

[50 Wimpole Street]
Valentine's day. [February 14] 1843

. . . Are you aware that Mrs. Sigourney ¹ in her new publication of 'Pleasant memorials of pleasant lands' has given to the public a detached passage of a letter of yours, at once graphic and touching in its filial tenderness? Had she done only *that*, it had been well. But even *I* shrink back from the publication of the fragment of a letter from Mrs. Southey, showing how her husband had not written his own name for two years,—could scarcely be supposed to recognize her,—and had been shaken in health and partially in intellect ever since the insanity and death of his first love and wife, Edith! Now to cut out of a letter that tender mystery and coldly print it among 'Pleasant memorials' seems to me,—yes, even to *me*, . . who when you and all the world were a little cruel to poor Miss Sedgewick, shook my relenting head, . . the most inexcusable sin in its degree that has been sinned by man or woman. Yet the book which sins so, appears to me an amiable book, a pleasant book, a book with heart and head in it. It is a mixture of prose and verse . . and smiles in the spirit everywhere. Not much power, to be sure, in either prose or verse – – nothing beyond pretty description and gentle sentiment!—still it is an amiable book—and it is 'wondrous pitiful' to see it so deformed. Mr. Southey wont mind perhaps —but his children *will*—and we all start back before this lifting of the grave-cloth on a face more sacredly removed than by Death, from the public gazing.

Have you heard yet of the new tragedy by Mr. Browning? —and of its *success*—for it *did* succeed? ² Mr. Kenyon saw it acted at Drury Lane and witnessed the sensation in the house, the tears upon stedfast faces, the silence and applause not offered but compelled. It is a fine production, I think, – – this

171

'Blot on the 'Scutcheon' – – and though only in three acts, you must not lift your dramatic brows in derision of these three. As a composition, I seem to be aware of a little weakness towards the close—but I always believed that Mr. Browning was a master in clenched passion, . . concentrated passion . . burning through the metallic fissures of language—and this last trial of his, and the last but one 'The return of the Druses' [3] do not cause me to waver. You shall see them both before long. And yet you half-frighten me from sending you Mr. Browning's poetry. Promise not to say again that it was a pity he missed being . . an attorney . . an engineer . . a merchant's clerk . . what trade was it? . . .

Moreover, my dearest friend, I do rather, nay, to be honest I do *quite*, entirely . . disagree with you as to 'obscurity being the fashion' in these latter days upon the earth. Take away Mr. Browning—and Mr. Townsend, who is scarcely before the public—and your friend – – and who in the world else can you account obscure and misty among the poets? Mr. Tennyson has some hard parts—but you do not complain of him as a son of the mist. Therefore I defend the times against your imputation!

But I cant do that or anything beside a moment longer today. I write in the dark without a metaphor and the time of posts is at hand.

Do you try a fumigation of tobacco for that pain in the face which I grieve to hear of? It is imperious over the nerves— and if you call it an unpleasant remedy, why pain is a still worse evil. *Do not write to me. I ask that of your love!*

Ever your attached Valentine

E B B

[1] Lydia Sigourney (1791–1865), known as 'the American Hemans'. Author of *How to be Happy* (1833), *Pocahontas, and Other Poems* (1841), etc. Sentimentality combined with a preoccupation with death was a notable characteristic of her work. Her publication of Mrs. Southey's letter gave to the world the first intimation of the nature of the Poet Laureate's illness.

[2] *A Blot on the 'Scutcheon*, a tragedy in three acts, 'Bells and Pomegranates', No. V, was published on February 11, 1843, the day of its first presentation at Drury Lane. Extracts from a letter written by Joseph Arnould (*Robert Browning and Alfred Domett*, p. 62) gives a vivid account of the atmosphere of 'bad feeling, intrigue and petty resentment' in which the play was produced.

[3] *The Return of the Druses*, a tragedy, 'Bells and Pomegranates', No. IV, was published in January 1843.

[50 Wimpole Street]
Feb. 16th. 1843

If any one of my brothers, my beloved friend, should have had it in his power to express in some slight way the respect and interest which they *all* feel towards you, it must be *George*, the only one who can stand yet by himself. I write to explain this, lest the other name which is sacredly dear and sorrowful to me, should be applied wrongly. But Papa's own name is the same—*Edward*—and as Mr. Kenyon, dear Mr. Kenyon, often calls him by it, the mistake probably arose *so*.

You say nothing of your health and power of sleeping—and as you *did* write in spite of me, I wish you had told me how you were. Do *not* write again—*not soon*—and hereafter when you do, let me have some sign of your being better.

Yes! Mr. Macready, from all that I can understand, behaved execrably to Mr. Browning: would and would not act his play—and at last acted it *for damnation*. This is friendship—but notwithstanding every possible disadvantage, the poetry triumphed—and *that* was victory! Mr. Kenyon who was present, bears witness to the emotion of the full house, . . to the living tears and compelled attention.

'And those who came to mock, remained to *weep*'.

I agree with you, however, in regretting that the poet should,—having a choice,—expose himself to such malignities and vulgarities. Doing so, . . as Paul Courier [1] said of Napoleon when he wanted to be an emperor, . . , 'il aspire à descendre'.

Yesterday I had a heap of newspapers and magazines from America,—so full of kindnesses to me personally, that I forget the boundary line catastrophe altogether.[2] Among the literary newsmongering from England, your laying the foundation-stone at Reading is mentioned of course.[3]

Is your dramatic Montague the Eleonora Louisa Montague [4] who writes occasionally, or used to write, in the Athenaeum? But dont answer this question or any other. Dont write to me, now while you are oppressed with much writing, my dearest friend. Only keep in your mind how truly I love you and how my thoughts wish all good to you constantly.

Your E B B.

¹ Paul Louis Courier de Méré (1772–1825), brilliant pamphleteer and classicist. Author of *Pétition pour des villageois qu'on empêche de danser* (1822), *Pamphlets des pamphlets* (1824), etc.

² A dispute between Britain and the United States, relating to the boundary line between English and American territory west of the Rocky Mountains.

³ At Reading, on September 1, 1842, Miss Mitford had laid the foundation stone of a new reading-room.

⁴ Eleanora Louisa Montague was the author of *Edith of Graystock, a Poem* (1833), *The Landgrave, a Play in Five Acts in Verse, with Dramatic Illustrations of a Female Character*, etc. (1839).

[50 Wimpole Street]
March 25, 1843

I should have written yesterday my dearest friend, but Mr. Kenyon came with the Scissors of a Fate and cut off the remnant of the day before post time. And now, first of all, lest I forget afterwards, . . about the chocolate. I will make . . that is, more reverentially . . I will ask Papa to enquire in the City whether any West India ships have brought a supply, and send it to you according to my success. His own ships return in the summer—but he may have means of supplying you earlier. It is almost unlucky—because the prepared chocolate I could always have it in my power to send you. Nevertheless I hope in Papa !

No—I have seen Bewick ¹ only in extracts—therefore you are justified in reproaching my ignorance—and I dare say I was perfectly wrong in supposing him to be a mere scientific writer without a soul—as wrong as if I had fancied the same thing of Buffon.² Bewick did not however write all his own books . . as of course you are aware : and an old eccentric Northumbrian clergyman who was one of his writers, was one of my unknown correspondents years and years ago, and amused me much with his quaintnesses of thought and word. *Mr. Cotes*, the name was ! Ah ! I am glad I recollect it at last ! For the name of a friend, vanishing out of one's head for a moment, makes one think of sack cloth and ashes and all sorts of propitiations !

Well ! Mr. Kenyon came to see me yesterday (dear Mr. Kenyon !) and he brought and read to me a letter from Mr. Wordsworth to Mr. Crabbe Robinson speaking with great feeling of the release of the poor Laureate. Although it *was* a release, the letter said, – – yet he, Wordsworth, could not consider the removal of a friend of his youth, without depression of heart—and then he went on to say that, invited or not to the funeral, he would attend the body to the grave. Mr. Southey died at last of typhus fever – – having had an apoplectic fit a few weeks ago—so that he passed through many forms of death before he entered into its rest. It is equally impossible to lament that *he* is gone who stood in the world with a wall of darkness between him and us so long— and *not* to feel sadness in some degree when we think of Southey among the dead !

Mr. Wordsworth had the goodness to send for me, in the same letter, a printed but unpublished poem of his own, and of some four pages, 'with his very kind regards'.

This of course has delighted me ! The subject is Grace Darling ³ . . .

Ever your attached

E B B

¹ Thomas Bewick (1753–1828), wood engraver. His *Select Fables* appeared in 1784, *The Quadrupeds* in 1790, and *British Birds* between 1797 and 1804. The text of *Water Birds* (second volume, 1804) was by the Rev. Henry Cotes, of Morpeth, to whom, in 1828, E B B sent her poems for criticism. (Barrett Sale. Sotheby's, June 1937.)

² George-Louis Leclerc, Comte de Buffon (1707–88), the celebrated natural historian. His collected works were published in forty-four volumes in 1835.

³ *Grace Darling*, composed early in March 1843, and privately printed. 'I was slow to send copies of *Grace Darling* about except to female friends, lest I should seem to attach too much importance to the production, though it was on a subject which interested the whole nation', wrote Wordsworth on April 1, 1843. (Selincourt, p. 1158.) The subject of the poem, dealing as it did with a scene of shipwreck and drowning, caused E B B 'such extreme pain as to incapacitate me from judging it'.

[50 Wimpole Street]
May 1, 1843

Ever dearest Miss Mitford, you are better I see—you are stronger—you are growing to be wicked. Think of your travelling round the world to investigate gentleman's ages from red books and other sorts of books ! ¹ I am astonished at you ! Why the next thing will be (it is dreadful to think of !) that you

will be penetrating into *ladies' ages*! Can your Bath friends
have any sort of notion what a serpent they are nourishing in
their bosoms?

Even if I had no remorse, I couldn't help you to Mr.
Landor's chronology,—seeing that the only edition of his
poems which I have, is not the first one . . no, nor an early
one at all. But prove him sixty five which he may be, or
seventy five which he cant be,—and if he chooses to be Lothario,
and if ladies fair choose him to be Lothario, what cause do
you show why he shouldn't be Lothario? If Cupid sits in his
eye, a grey eyebrow overhead wont prove an alibi—he may be
'a dangerous man' after all his three warnings . . and if you
address a fourth warning to his victims, apprizing them of his
longevity, . . they will be none the less victimized, be sure!
. . . So you cry out about the rain already! Be politically
economical of your interjections, I advise you—for verily,
when you get into Devonshire, the surprise will be, not when it
rains, but when it ceases to rain. Even the sun is used to the
rain in Devonshire, and shines through it.

In comes Mr. Kenyon while I write, and interrupts my
rain and sunshine. . . Such a characteristic note he has read
to me from Mr. Landor!—it has quite amused me!—so much,
that if you will make oath never to tell anybody . . not
Celia . . not Rosalind . . not *nobody*, . . I *must* remember to
repeat to you the last sentences.

—'One Quillinan, I hear, has been writing against me in
Blackwood. This is funny. The things may be called *Quillinan-
ities*'.[2] 'I hear'—just as if he had not seen or felt! He tells
Mr. Kenyon that Mrs. Southey complains of having lost half
her income by her marriage (which Mr. Kenyon however
doubts) and thinks that Sir Robert Peel should give her a
pension.

You surprise me by your account of the low state of literature in Bath, for I had always fancied that Pen-and-ink had a
certain predominance there. Which reminds me . . Mr.
Kenyon speaks kindly of the P[3] . . and very compassionately.
Poor thing! She is of the West Indians and fell down their
cataract . . from splendor in the New Forest to labor and
sorrow among the booksellers. One of her sisters is a governess,—her brother an invalid . . and herself a laborious

worker. We must be sorry for her and interested in her, I think.

But I dare not write any more,—I am afraid so, of being too late for the post. Yes, *number two* is decidedly scandalous, and wont do for the compositor of this 1843.

Your own

E B B.

Poor Ben! I certainly *am* sorry that you did not take Flush with you. He would have enjoyed the travelling and have learnt to be a dog of the world; and then his conversation would have done you good. . .

[1] Miss Mitford, who was on a visit to Bath, had written to E B B to ask her to discover the exact age of Walter Savage Landor, whom she found 'enchanting the wives, making jealous the husbands, and "enjoying" altogether the worst of reputations'. (Landor, in 1843, was sixty-eight.)

[2] In order to defend 'the venerated author of the *Excursion*', on whom Landor had thrown 'obloquy', Edward Quillinan published in April 1843 an *Imaginary Conversation, Between Mr. Walter Savage Landor and the Editor of Blackwood's Magazine.* 'Please to tell Mr. Kenyon with my kind regards', wrote Quillinan to Crabb Robinson, 'that I shall be well content to be let off so easily by Mr Landor as by a pun on my *Quill-inanities*, if Mr L. is content to take no rougher notice of my comments on his *Quill-insanities*.' (Morley, Vol. I, p. 500.)

[3] Miss Pickering. She died of scarlet fever later in the same year. She left an unfinished novel, *The Grandfather*, which was completed by Elizabeth Youatt in 1844.

[*50 Wimpole Street*]
May 4 [*1843*]

. . . Altogether, that you should remain another week at Bath, appears to me a wise step . . leading to enjoyment! I approve of it in spite of what you tell me about your presentiment of danger from arch-enchanting bishops at Prior Park, – – for after all, I am not very much afraid that you will ever put your conscience in the keeping of the most fascinating of men. The good sense and clear judgement predominate in you too much—you are not a woman to go over in a rapture and a puff of incense into the belief of an infallible Pope—and therefore I am not afraid. For the rest I would not willingly speak with disrespect of Roman catholic christians.

I have come into Papa's room, the adjoining room to mine,—for the first time today—to have the windows opened and a little dusting done . . which will make me cleaner and more exemplary tomorrow. The consequence of living through the winter in one room, with a fire, day and night, and every crevice sealed close, . . you may imagine perhaps by the help of your ideal of all Dustlessness, latent and developped. At last we come to walk upon a substance like white sand, and if we dont lift our feet gently up and put them gently down, we act Simoom, and stir up the sand into a cloud. As to a duster or a broom, seen in profile even, . . calculate the effect upon us! The spiders have grown tame—and their webs are a part of our own domestic œconomy,—Flush eschews walking under the bed. The result of which is that I am glad May is come, that I yield to that necessity at once. May God bless you— and give you health,—and gladness by its means! Write to me—do! Your writing reeled from your pen in this letter! I never remember observing that it trembled so before. May God keep you, my dearest dearest Miss Mitford.

Yes, I have been in Bath twice—once when I was quite a child and we travelled *through* it and I did not stir from the hotel door—and once on our way from Herefordshire to Sidmouth, a few years since,[1] when I was too weak and out of health to stir from the hotel window. We spent one night there on the latter occasion, and I gathered my impressions from my place at the window (– – of the York House) and in passing through the streets. . . As you found by my letter, and as I always said, Bath is the very ideal of a town to me,—worth a hundred Cheltenhams, notwithstanding those noble avenues which almost save Cheltenham! But as a *town* . . I choose Bath: it is a fine birth of its own hills – – marble of their marble, heart of their heart—almost grand with their spirit. The Bath town-scenery is the noblest I ever saw . . apart from associations—and if I had to live in a town which was not London, I would rather live at Bath than anywhere, I think. . .

But I must tell you first that Mr. Browning is said to have finished two plays, one for Charles Kean and the public, the other for himself and Bells and Pomegranates.[2] I am sorry. He appears to me capable of most dramatic effluences and passionate insights—and it would be wise in him I think to spend this faculty upon poems which the sympathizing could read, rather than on plays cast to the mercy of the Great unwashed who cant read right. And besides . . you will say, (altho' *I* have the grace to feel that I oughtn't to say it . .) acting a play of Mr. Browning's, is like reading a riddle-book right through without stopping to guess the answers! Something like . . perhaps. Yet after all, he is a true soul-piercing poet—and it is easier to find a more faultless writer than such a one.

Mr. Kenyon met four and twenty . . not fiddler's . . but harmonious spirits in different degrees, at your friend Mr. Chorley's the other evening. The new German wonder Mr. D . . . . . (I really am afraid to write him down, so little sure of him am I) raised thunderclouds and lightenings out of the pianoforte . . and Moscelles,[3] who is only a demigod followed the miraculous with his heroic—and Adelaide Sartoris [4] sang like a spirit—and Mrs. Butler read Shakespeare. And your Mr. Chorley lives in an enchanted house in Victoria Square . . (a new square with tiny houses)—in a sort of golden . . not 'vinegar-bottle' . . but *vinaigrette* . . with ceilings and chairs of gold, and hangings of silken crimson. 'It is like a jewel-case', says Mr. Kenyon—and Mr. Chorley lives like a ruby in the glory of it. . .

May God bless you, dearest friend. I never heard Mr. Jay,[5] and very likely should not admire him—but he is a good man with wide influence.

Ever your
E B B

[1] In August 1832.

[2] *Colombe's Birthday*, a play in five acts ('Bells and Pomegranates', VI), was published at the end of April 1844. 'I made it for the use of Charles Kean, to whom I read it', Browning told a friend in 1877. 'They would have acted the play—but in perhaps two or three years to come, and in the meantime I was to keep it unprinted—whereupon I withdrew it, and included it in my *Bells and Pomegranates.*' (*Letters of Robert Browning*, ed. T. L. Hood, p. 179. Murray, 1933.) E B B's letter seems to confirm W. C. De Vane's surmise (*Browning Handbook*, p. 172. Murray, 1935) that the drama *A Soul's Tragedy*, although published in April 1846, 'was probably written in 1843'.

[3] Ignaz Moscheles (1794–1870), a brilliant pianist, who was Mendelssohn's head of the piano department in the Conservatory at Leipzig.

[4] Adelaide Sartoris (1814–79), the singer, was the younger daughter of Charles Kemble, and sister of Fanny Kemble (Mrs. Butler).

⁵ William Jay (1769–1853), dissenting minister, described by Sheridan as 'the most natural orator he had ever heard'. His writings were very popular; his *Morning Exercises in the Closet* (1829), going into ten editions.

[50 Wimpole Street]
May 13th 1843

. . . Dearest Miss Mitford, how are you? Mind you tell me in all detail in the *great* letter which I am looking for every morning. The want of sleep evidently proceeds from over-excitement if not over-fatigue: and I exhort you to make to yourself quieter afternoons,—to cease to walk at three o'clock, and to cease to talk at nine, . . and watch the effect of that preparation of tranquillity upon the night's rest. If I did not prepare myself in some like manner . . shut myself up from all degrees of talking by eight oclock in the evening . . all the opium I put my trust in, would fail in procuring me any night-sleep. I smooth my soul and senses as people do their pillows,—and then, after a while, I may sleep perhaps.

I am mournful at heart today—and this is the cause. Today we received a sad account of our poor young cousin, little Cissy Butler, to whom with her sister, my aunt Miss Graham Clarke has been as a mother since they lost their own; and who has been pronounced consumptive by the medical men at Cheltenham. She is about fifteen years old, . . a gentle, delicate-looking and moving and speaking little thing, with a sweet smile and a self-forgetting nature, and an affectionateness of spirit which has its part both in earth and Heaven. She was with her sister and my aunt in Devonshire, part of the time I was there—and then, three years ago, I saw her for the last time—and a dear gentle child she was then! This last winter they have spent in Cheltenham, and ever since Christmas, she has had a cough, the account of which I did not like, and which prepared me in part for the melancholy news of this morning. Still, we can hope . . and if we *can* hope, perhaps we ought to hope. I think of myself—and how the stethescope reported equally ill of my lungs, and how I am alive still and better!—and then I think again, that it may please God to spare her, and my poor aunt who is breaking her heart about her! Mr. Shaw, the medical man, famous, they say, in such cases,—has commanded mutton chops and porter for her, and will not give an opinion upon probable results, until his system has been tried. Dear little Cissy! May God bless her—dear child!

Moreover . . by way of a *little* evil . . Lady Margaret Cocks [1] has come to London and asked to see me; and I who said 'no' to the same question from the same questioner last year, was ashamed to say so this year, and yet was vexed in saying 'yes', past your comprehension and sympathy. Every day *after two* I am in an agitation—watching for double-knocks . . palpitating at footsteps . . leaping from my sofa at hypothetical voices – – growing cold and pale in each cheek at the excess of my own fantasy, when a mouse's stirring gives it opportunity! Ah!—you have no sympathy for such childishness: and yet the suffering is none the less actual for the lightness of the occasion. I wish she were come—and gone—that so I might be serene again—I dread her like a thunderstorm! She is kind enough—too kind, you will suggest, for my ingratitude,—and sensible enough, . . and something of an old friend. But to see her is an inexpressible effort to me. Oh! there, again is that eternal knocker! But no—it isn't Lady Margaret!

Flush went to Hampstead yesterday and spent a delightful day, said his companions, running racing, leaping through the green fields. For Arabel and Octavius had tickets, in common with their friends the Miss Mackintoshes, to see Cardinal Wolsey's bed, . . a splendid fabric of tortoiseshell and ivory, presented to the little prince of Wales by its proprietor Mr. Thompson,[2] and waiting in his cottage at Hampstead the queen's pleasure for its removal to Windsor. An ivory chair too, in which a Pope had sate, formed a part of the present— and 'it should have been larger' said the donor 'only Her Majesty was too proud to come herself to inspect it'. Prince Albert went—and stood there, according to tradition, two hours, three months ago—since which, Mr. Thompson has given up the ghost at ninety six, leaving everything over and above his presents to Victoria, to Gregory [3] editor of the Satirist, a relation of his own. . .

May God bless you, my dearest friend! Ben is excellent.

I am your own affectionate

E B B

¹ Lady Margaret Cocks, EBB said, is 'an old friend of mine, who was kind to me when I was a child, in the country, and has not forgotten me since, when, two months in the year, she has been in the habit of going to London. A good, worthy person, with a certain cultivation as to languages and literature, but quite manquée on the side of the imagination . . . calling "Pippa Passes" "*pretty and odd*" . . .' (*Love Letters*, Vol. II, p. 127.)

² John Thompson, known as 'Memory-corner Thompson', made a large fortune as a brewer's surveyor, and furnished his house, The Priory, Hampstead, with a collection of antique furniture. He died on March 6, aged eighty-six. (*Gentleman's Magazine*, July 1843.)

³ Barnard Gregory (1796–1852) married a niece of John Thompson, and inherited the latter's money. Gregory's paper, *The Satirist, or the Censor of the Times*, throve on scandal and the systematic blackmail of its victims. In private life, Gregory is said to have been 'gentlemanly and retiring in his manners and possessed of a good fund of anecdote'.

[*50 Wimpole Street*]
May 29, 1843

. . . Mr. Kenyon was at Mr. Chorley's the other evening, and from thence went to Mr. Babbages' ¹ where he met among divers notabilities, Mr. Borrow the Gypsey.² You know, or you ought as soon as possible to know, Borrow's 'Bible in Spain' and 'Gypsies in Spain'. He is full of genius – – you may *almost* call it genius, . . and earnestness of purpose, – – a strange wild energy living in his eye, ear, and voice, and giving out life all around,—as picturesque on paper as a gypesy on a moor, and a sincere man and upright! Mr. Kenyon says that he looked 'every inch a' . . *man*, as he stood in Mr. Babbages drawing-room, . . with six feet three of height, bone and muscle, . . grey large earnest eyes, aquiline nose, determined mouth,—fit to be the lion he was! The story goes that he dined with Mr. Milman ³ and others at Murray's some days ago, and that the conversation turning on Spain he said quietly . . 'My good fellows, none of you know anything of Spain except what you learn from romances', – – upon which (incredible to be told,—too ludicrous to be credible!) the good company, being far too good in an aristocratical sense, to be addressed as 'good fellows', showed their sense of the insult by rising from table in a body and walking out of the room! The story runs so!—and I only *tell it*! . . .

Your

EBB

¹ Charles Babbage (1792–1871), mathematician and inventor of various calculating machines. Peculiarly sensitive to sound, he was, it is said, 'the implacable enemy of organ-grinders'.
² George Borrow (1803–81). Born at East Dering in Norfolk, where his father was a recruiting officer. Between 1833–40, as an agent of the Bible Society, travelled in Russia, Portugal, and Spain. *The Gipsies in Spain* appeared in 1841, *The Bible in Spain* in 1843, and *Lavengro* in 1851.
³ Henry Hart Milman (1791–1868), Dean of St. Paul's in 1849. Author of *A History of the Jews* (1830), *History of Latin Christianity* (1854–55), etc.

[50 Wimpole Street]
June 23, 1843

Oh your Miss Brabazon! Surely she must have been steeped in a cauldron of Ink to have rendered herself so disagreeable to you! What 'bad books' did she write? ¹ I do not remember her name in my 'letters'. Certainly, if she knows how to write, she doesn't know how to behave;—or your whole experience (of her coming for a month, and grumbling over her dinners, and inviting herself into your friends carriages,) would have been a good deal modified. I could not help laughing! It was so bad as to be good. The brass was so very Corinthian! Do you know there is something sublime in the self-reliance which could determine one to spend a month with a stranger of European reputation, and order fish for dinner? That is not an every-day deed of a commonplace woman—it would be unattainable to four fifths of us! Tell me what books she wrote. . .

I sent Mr. Horne's twenty five copies of the third edition of Orion ² to you this morning,—and I sent your message to *him*, half an hour afterwards: and, whether he goes to you immediately or not, I am sure he must be touched and gratified by your true kindness and hospitality, for which I infinitely admire you, and which will stand in prodigious contrast to *our* conduct here in Wimpole Street. Think of my dear naughty Papa's never asking him to dinner! He called on Mr. Horne by his own impulse . . and through a kind wish, quite unprompted by me, of acknowledging kindnesses done to me—but you see the never asking him to dinner makes the calling worse than nugatory. I am very vexed at it! The obstacle seems to be a kind of shyness of your Pen and Ink—

and a feeling of . . 'he will lack entertainment here' – – and just the same thing prevents his asking Mr. Kenyon, his own college friend and cousin, and my friend . . the only friend (almost) I see in my prison. And unfortunately we never any of us can 'reason high' with him, as Adam did with the angel Gabriel, in relation to anything done or undone—he is master as he ought to be! It would be impossible for anyone to persuade him that Mr. Kenyon could dine anywhere out of a draught of epigrams, with a lion's hide for a table cloth, except by constraint and as a matter of sacrifice. So I remain vexed . . moralising on what dear Mr. Kenyon's inferences may be. How *you* were permitted to run the risk of being dull and degraded here, I do not know—except that your affectionateness to me overcame your *prestige*,—'Dearest Dread!' . . .

Alfred (commonly called Daisy) and Sette and my two little cousins took Flush with Catiline and Resolute the other day to Hyde Park, to see the Review! Flush in an ecstasy of terror at the sight of the crowd and military assemblage, prancing of steeds and flashing of swords, howled up to the sky, as if he saw the moon there; and the moment after, threw himself upon Alfred, aspiring to be taken up in his arms. But when the artillery thundered along, it was past sustaining any more. One might as well be in a battle you know, and he doesn't pretend to be a hero—and so, down he fell upon his back without a sound—in unutterable and immoveable dread!—and Alfred thought he had fainted. When however, he turned round to look at him again . . to feel his pulse, I suppose, and administer hartshorn . . the patient had disappeared! They looked everywhere—no Flush! Had he vanished into a drum?—or been blown away by a trumpet? Nobody could tell! He had left the field of battle 'either with his shield or *on* it'; and not a Spartan of them all, could enter into farther particulars!

In the meantime my hero, on recovering his breath, turned his back on the 'pride, pomp and circumstance of glorious war' and ran away home as fast as his little bantam legs (Flushie's legs are exactly like a bantam's!) could carry him. When he arrived, everybody observed that he looked 'as if he had been frightened'. Very likely indeed! He refused to go out of doors for that day and the next, and has embraced very strong views, I apprehend, of the iniquity and insanity of military glory,—being henceforward and in that relation, of the strictest sect of – – *the quakers*! My poor Flushie!

He never barks for joy either—except when he goes out with the great dogs who always bark, and so inspire him. Think of Flushie's taking pepper (cayenne) with his chicken, . . and having a particular liking for ginger cake . . so strong with ginger as to light up a little flame on your tongue. There's social corruption for you! . . .

You are not well, my dearest friend? Is it right of you to give up your exercise in the poney carriage?

Ever your affectionate
E B B

¹ An Elizabeth Jane Brabazon published *Stories from the Rectory* in 1840.
² *Orion*, an Epic Poem, in ten Books, was published at a farthing: Horne stipulated that no person should be supplied with more than one copy; and that no copy should be sold to any person who called it 'Orïon'.

[50 Wimpole Street]
June 30th 1843

Dear dear little Flush! How frightened you must have been—and how glad we *both* are that he is better! No!—*my* Flush never has been 'seriously ill'. He was unwell, sick, and without appetite, for several days once—but he was never very bad indeed . . not so bad as not rather to enjoy than otherwise the nursing and the patting and the pittying pertaining to his state of indisposition. My Flush is very fond of pity—and we suspect him of making the worst of his grievancies upon most occasions. Who says that vanity, coquetry and affectations are peculiar to our humanity? *I* dont, since I know Flush. I cannot pretend to such an opinion, as long as I see him preferring the coffee cup to the saucer (to the obvious inconvenience of his nose) for the sake of drinking his coffee after my fashion—and sneezing as hard as he can contrive, . . when I hold up a bottle of eau de cologne with the cork in it— and sneezing by the same unnatural effort, when he sees Crow about to light a candle,—because the matches are kept in a bottle too; and the noise and the sudden flame frighten him ; and he considers that the most emphatic way of expressing his disapprobation is to sneeze at the offence ! And then, his pleasure at being praised . . called pretty—told that he has pretty teeth ! He will hold his head still, and his mouth half open, for minutes, until you have exhausted your admiration on his teeth—and triumphs in a succession of collars—and even, the other day, took a fancy to a bracelet on Arabel's arm, and would not be satisfied until she took it off and lay it over the back of his neck. If all *that* is not personal vanity, I really do not know what is ! But he never, although breathing this stagnant simoom commonly called London air, has been 'seriously ill'—and a dog-dealer being in the house the other day and examining his mouth, told Crow that he never in all his experience, saw a house-dog in such a faultless state of health.

Did I tell you that it is Flush who always calls me in the morning ? He always does. Crow comes into the room and pours out the water before she brings it to my bedside—and as soon as she enters the door, there is Flush, leaps up and gives me one kiss as a signal that she is coming. He is gone to Chelsea to-day with Crow for an excursion—set off in high spirits, with the full sense of a pleasant day before him, leaping and dancing ! . . .

[*50 Wimpole Street*]
July 6, 1843

I cannot help the oozing forth of my Io triumphe . . although it is by no means my dearest friend, *my* turn for writing. Mr. Kenyon came yesterday—and he had just been reading, he said, 'Pride and Prejudice', . . driven into making an acquaintance with Miss Austen in despite of his anti-novelism, by the buzz of admiration which beset him from Mr. Harness,[1] and others. Mind, he was quite unaware of your and my ever quarrelling on the subject : he spoke to me of his impressions therefore innocently and freely, not knowing but that I myself might be wearing out the knees of my soul before her statue. And these were the words he said . . 'I am astonished ! absolutely astonished ! There is excellent, nay, admirable good sense—distinction of character, sufficient

if not subtle—(I do not think it is very subtle!)—an under-
current of humour,—a natural and flowing style—that is all!
I am astonished beyond expression that she should be praised
as some persons praise her. I like the book very much—I
could read a hundred such books - - I like these correct
pictures of middle life. But the class, whatever her excellence
in it, is *low*—and I am much struck with the narrowness—the
want of all aspiration towards, or instinct of the possibility of,
enlargement of any kind . . the want of elevation . . the
poverty in what is called *intellect*'. I do not pretend that this
is a verbatim report; but as far as the sense goes it is a very
fair piece of Boswellism, and I cannot refrain from sending it
to you. And do, my dearest Miss Mitford, consider that if I
who lie under the disgrace with you, or at least under the
disadvantage, of an imputed and acknowledged tendency to
mystical and out-of-the-world distractions, may be suspected
of a prejudice involved in my own faults, against such writers
as Jane Austen, . . Mr. Kenyon is not subject to any such
suspicion, . . Mr. Kenyon is a man of the world, and no
dreamer, . . acute, studious of life and character . . dis-
inclined to vague speculations . . averse from theological
ecstasies! And yet he uses words as nearly as possible as I
should select them to express my own opinions. I was struck
as he uttered them. I could almost have clapped my hands,
with a 'By heaven, he *echoes* me'! Only that where he missed
the 'intellectual' I missed the 'spiritual' besides . . the latter
being the worst want, . . because 'intellectualism' as the word
is used, is not common to all men, whereas 'spirituality' more
or less *is* common to all men. 'Man is a religious animal', and
has instincts beyond this conventional life, let him own or
disown them. And now you will be for disowning *me*! . . . .

You must not, you shall not give up 'pen and ink'—use
and abuse them! And the pleasure, the pleasure! What
pleasure is like the pleasure of pen and ink work—when you
are in the heart of it? Is it not the intense consciousness of
Being—twenty senses instead of the natural complement—a
doubling and tripling of the powers of life? And then, the
great priveledge of throwing *work* between Life and its shadow:
and between yourself and all natural trouble and sense of
frailty, Art and its ideal! Who could forgo such a grace,

having once received and exulted in it ? Surely not *you*. Nay, certainly, and positively not you—and there's an end of it !

Mr. Rogers talks of travelling with Eastlake to Munich—which for eighty years and more, is very well indeed.[2]

And Mrs. Coleridge (Coleridge's daughter) has written a controvertial appendix to a new edition of her father's 'Aids to Reflection' which is longer almost than the work itself, and consists of a treatise on Baptism and subjects appertaining to it, directed against the Puseyite views.[3] Although controvertial it is singularly impartial and gentle ; and with some dullness and lengthiness, is very honorable to our sex through its learning integrity and dexterity in reasoning. I think you are acquainted with her ?

How is your Flush ? I do not hear from you . . and groan within myself as the post comes and goes, making no sign from you to me !

May God bless you ever !

Your
E B B

Have you heard from Mr. Horne about the geranium ? He declared to me that he would write directly to you, to beg you to individualize the honor by modifying the name to the *Horned Orion*, instead of leaving it among the stars vaguely. Did he write ?

[1] The Rev. William James Harness (1790–1869), a life-long friend of Miss Mitford's, and the man to whom Byron had wished to dedicate *Childe Harold*, refraining only 'lest it should injure him in the church'.

[2] Samuel Rogers, the banker poet, was at this time eighty years of age. Sir Charles Eastlake (1793–1865), Keeper of the National Gallery, became President of the Royal Academy in 1850.

[3] Sara Coleridge (1802–52), the youngest of the poet's children, in 1829 married her cousin, Henry Nelson Coleridge. She published in 1837 a fairy-tale, *Phantasmion*. The 'controvertial Appendix' was an *Essay on Rationalism, with a Special Application to the Doctrine of Baptismal Regeneration*.

[50 Wimpole Street]
Saturday. July [22] 1843

How might I be inspired by the genius of quarrelling into writing a controversy for a letter ! But I resist the demon, and he flies from me. Only to be sure my beloved friend, people might wonder (as surely as I might quarrel) how . . not how I came to love *you* – – because *that* could never by any combination of oppositions become wonderful to anybody—but how *you* came to love *me*. For you see how we differ ! There is scarcely a sentence in your letter to which I could not find a nay ! And I am afraid the differences go *farther down* than you appear aware of yourself. It is not that we differ only by one of us caring for the ideal and the other for the actual,—but that what *you* appear to call the ideal, is the very actual with *me* . . as perhaps it will be with you, upon reconsideration. What ! Is it not true that the soul *is* as actually, as your best seedling geranium? . . that our hold upon the spiritual world, and the prophesy of a spiritual futurity within us, *are* as actually, as any impression coming to us by the senses ? Is not God an actual existence ?

I do not like controvertial divinity thrown into a novel as a vehicle, any better than you do,—and if you mean only *that*, by deprecating tract-novels, I will go with you. But that you should determinately exclude from representations of humanity one side of its aspect and the largest and highest proportions of its bearings—that you should praise Scott for being defective in the chief poetry of human nature . . comes with a great clash against my gravest opinions. I will not however argue the point, which is rather for reflection ! . . .

Mr. Kenyon said once to Mrs. Jameson—(he told me this story himself—) 'Life is a jest.' 'Oh', she answered, 'do not say so !—life is a serious thing.' 'And what',—he retorted excellently well,—'what can be more serious, more melancholy, than the idea of life being a jest.'

Now my dislike to Mr. Lever [1] is founded on the fact that he believes life to be a jest, *and its being so, another jest* ! His talent, his power, I do not for a moment deny. Are you not carried away by your sympathy with energy and power ? At any rate, not even for your sake, my dearest friend, can I cease detesting and loathing this uproarious Irishman. I have tried to like him—and could not succeed even so far as tolerating him. . .

Mr. Borrow *is* a very original and characteristic writer. I was delighted with his book—only he who appeared to you to want 'spunk', seemed to me to be a Dare-all. Want physical courage! Mr. Borrow! Well—but the Bible society committee was not satisfied with him. They call him wild I believe and wanting in gravity : and they suspect him of being inventive. I honor the Bible Society,—but I admire Mr. Borrow, and like him all the better for putting off the conventional demureness of a pattern missionary, and daring to be a *man* 'in spirit and in truth'.

All these words have I driven before me like a flock of sheep in a hurry and a dust. Forgive me a hundred rashnesses of thought and illegibilities of pen.

You are not well! Dearest dearest friend—you walk enough, and drive enough I hope?—and lie down on the sofa instead of sitting on a chair, when you pause from exercise? Tell me how you are. The Statira is expected in the docks on the tenth of August, – – having been detained by the bad crops in Jamaica, four months after her time—and I shall hope soon to beg you to try some more of my cocoa.

May God bless you always.

Most affectionately yours

E B B

¹ Charles James Lever (1806–72), an Irishman, who once practised as a physician. Author of *Harry Lorrequer* (1837), *Charles O'Malley* (1840), etc. In 1849 E B B and her husband met Lever at the Bagni di Lucca. 'A most cordial vivacious manner, a glowing countenance, with the animal spirits somewhat predominant over the intellect . . . you cant help being surprised into being pleased with him, whatever your previous inclination may be', E B B wrote to Miss Mitford. (*Kenyon*, Vol. I, p. 411.)

[*50 Wimpole Street*]
August 1843

Thank you my dearest friend for your letter! I waited for it eagerly and opened it without reverence to the seal. After all I am of course a little disappointed by your *impression* : a want of refinement really not being the thing I expected to hear of.¹ How is it that such varied mental acquirement, and such poetical sensibility and imagination should fail in forcing upwards and outwards a polished surface? It is a mystery. Is it that the learning by rote of conventional forms by the process of association, proves to be more essential to the manners and what is called 'breeding' than a training from within? I am a little disappointed. And yet you like him you say. Well—I am disappointed nevertheless. In what you describe as the straining after wit, I miss my phantasma even more than in the want of general conversational power—it seems to involve a want of the good taste I had taken for granted. Because there really *is* in his letters and prose papers, a tact a delicacy . . a 'gentilesse' as Chaucer says, . . from which I argued much. I am disappointed—cant help it—should be, if he sang like a nightingale. Oh!—the guitar does not console me a bit. I love music and can admire a musician—but we do not look to Orions for cachuchas . . but for a high sphere-music. . .

Mr. Taylor has bewitched you I think—and not without a charm of power. Ah—but it is not a sufficient argument for me against Mesmerism, that he did not experience it himself. That some organizations have an inaptitude, is a first principle in the system . . . Mary Minto describes her after sensations very differently from your female friend, as delightful, luxurious—she thinks of nothing but Mesmer. Who was the famous physician who suffered so acutely from Tic douloureux that he is said to have stamped, in his agony, the bottom of his carriage out? I forget the name at this moment. That physician, Mr. Tulk [2] operated upon day after day, throwing him into magnetic sleeps oblivious of any pain in the course of five minutes, though he could not sleep otherwise by night or day from his state of suffering. *Mr. Tulk says so*—I believe him to be a man of honor—yet to judges in general, the evidence is of course insufficient . . .

Now I must tell you! I have had a letter . . a note, . . which has charmed me, touched me, made me feel inclined both to laugh and cry—a touching and most gratifying note from Miss Martineau. [3] She has sent me a little book of hers called 'Scenes of Palestine', in its second edition this year : and had she taken witch's counsel as to the choice of words which best and deepest should please me, she would not have sent the book to me with other words than are actually employed by her . . . She is a very noble woman—and her least word would give honor to me—still more such kind words as

these—and I cannot (you see I cannot) help telling you of
them, knowing that you love me enough to be pleased in my
pleasure. Do you know her? personally—or by letter? She
says that she has 'almost forgotten to desire health and vigour
in the keen sense of enjoyments which bear no relation to the
body or its welfare'.

There is that kind dear Mr. Kenyon! He proposed to me
yesterday that I should go in my chair to his house in Regent's
Park and stay there for two or three hours lying on the sofa
and looking on the trees, safe and silent from all the world,
whenever I pleased—I and Flush and one of my sisters! Such
a kind thought—so like him . . suggested so considerately
and affectionately! If I can get used enough to the motion
of the chair to manage the distance and the cross-stones, I will
really do it before the summer closes—at any rate I will dream
of it—I told him that I would set it by as my dream, and should
like it the better for its association with his kind thoughts. He
is a sort of male Grace of all kindnesses . . is he not? If you
can find him a female Grace to suit him (and the lady you
speak of promises excellently well) pray try to bring them
together—for he deserves every species of felicity inclusive of
the hymeneal. My impression however is, that if his marrying
again was probable, it has ceased to be so. His brother's
marriage seems to be enough for him—enough to supply him
with the sort of home-warmth which a single man advanced
in life must sometimes feel the lack of . . . She is not *too*
young—thirty seven or eight, Mr. Kenyon says; and he is not
too infirm . . crippled as he is in hand and foot,—to delight
in hearing her singing voice as it passes all over the house and
round it. Only once since they came, has he been out of the
house—and only twice has she: they live in the light of one
another's faces, and all beyond is in shadow. Well!—that is
love—is it not?—and with more romance in it too, than often
goes to the making of many a youthful marriage where white
and red meet carriage and four. . .

Oh—I like the Germans. I honor and love the Germans!
I love smoke for their sakes . . be it imagination-smoke or
tobacco-smoke; and if 'Grease and beer' are harder to bear—,
I love the Germans nevertheless. If I were strong and free as
you, you would hear of me keeping witch-sabbath on the

Brocken, with a tame will o' the wisp running beside me. I should be running myself all over the world—I should be at Paris—(there is a chivalry in the French which I like) - - I should be in Italy—I should be longest in Germany—I should be in the Alps and Pyrenees - - I might be peradventure in the eternal mist of Niagara. Seriously and certainly I should very much like to spend the next three years in the midst of new lands and strange souls—I should very much like it—but far, far is the dream of it.

I agree with you in every thought and word you spend [?] upon public weddings,—and am happy to tell you that I never was at such a thing in my life as any one of them. Once indeed I was at a wedding . . poor Annie Boyd's—but we met at the church and separated there; and *that* was enough of it—and too much for *her*, poor thing, who has had reason to sit in ashes ever since. . .

May God bless you my dearest friend! Not until October? —I sigh to think of *that*. George says that Orion is much admired upon the circuit—*and* . . I sent you a salmon yesterday.

Most affectionately yours

E B B.

[1] Richard Hengist Horne had been invited to Three Mile Cross to stay with Miss Mitford. E B B's interest in the visit was intense. It is evident that she was not only disappointed, but exceedingly vexed, at Miss Mitford's unfavourable reaction to the manners and personality of the author of *Orion*.

[2] Charles Augustus Tulk (1786–1849), Swedenborgian and philanthropist. He was the father of twelve children, and when staying with his daughter, Sophia Cottrell, in Italy, he frequently visited the Brownings at Casa Guidi.

[3] Harriet Martineau (1802–76), novelist, journalist, traveller, philanthropist. Author of *Illustrations of Political Economy* (1832–34), *Deerbrook* (1839), *Feats on the Fiords* (1841), etc.

[50 Wimpole Street]
August 17th. 1843

MY DEAREST FRIEND,

I have two letters of yours to thank you for and to reply to—and my first word must be that I am heartily and deeply sorry the visit in question should ever have been paid to you— and that I should be so, even if the sad catastrophe of your being unwell, had not crowned all which was otherwise disagreeable. I am disappointed and sorry to no common degree—and shall never cease to be so while the subject can recur to me. Certainly it was unwise and inconsiderate in Mr. H. to stay so long and to give so much trouble . . in the way too of such supernumerary things as a bath three times a day. There was a want of consideration which was unbecoming to a stranger in a lady's house, and which was unlike everything I ever observed in him from the first day of our intercourse down to this morning. At the same time I am inclined to believe that 'want of consideration' in the literal sense . . in the sense of 'want of thought' and not want of feeling for others, . . was at the root of the evil : and that nothing was really farther from his intention than inconveniencing you or yours by either the ablutions or the determined staying. Recollect my dearest friend, that not once, no, nor twice, not coldly, no, nor indifferently, did you press his coming to you, insist on the honor and pleasure which his presence would do you,— represent in those cordial words, which none use more gracefully than yourself, how your house and carriage were at his service and how likely he was to flourish anew in your air of Arcadia. Recollect that at first he meant to spend only one day with you, and that it was by the force of your own enchantments you determined him to change his plan and go to you in August instead of June, that he might have more time to rejoice in your hospitalities. It seems scarcely gracious to recall these things to you—and yet there is an obvious justice in doing so—which you will not disallow,—now that the evil and visitor are vanished. . . When Papa asked me how you liked Mr. Horne, I answered cursorily (for I would not tell the whole) that you thought him unpolished, . . and that he had stayed too long for your convenience. Instantly Papa exclaimed . . 'There must be some mistake then !—for although he is not particularly polished in manner, he is by no means a *pushing* man—that is certain !' And that *is* certain, *as far as our experience goes*. He has rather shrunk before Papa's advances than even *met* them. There has been a diffidence, which if he keeps it for *us*, is an oddity of virtue. For the rest,—accepting your general impressions as sincere and true, . . I cannot but think that in certain respects the feeling of being oppressed beyond patience has weighed you

194

down into depreciation of his kindness, his degree of unselfishness, and more especially of his *inclination* to honor the genius of his contemporaries. On that last point especially I make a gallant stand . . and throw down my silk glove before the three baths. My dearest friend, if he is selfish, self engrossed, and indifferent to all talent but his own, how is it that some of the most generous critical justice which has been done to the poets of his age has been done by his hand? *There* is a fact against an impression! Ask Mr. Browning, Mr. French—ask his fellow-dramatists Mr. Hunt, Mr. Landor, Mr. Darley and others if he has not praised them generously! That word 'generous' I have seen in Mr. Browning's handwriting and applied to *Mr. Horne* and that he deserves it well from him and others I cannot doubt, judging him 'by his works'.

With regard to learning, he may not be critically learned—probably not—and I agree with you in giving honor (of a sufficiently contracted kind however) to the Porsons and their like . . or rather their unlike,—for Porson [1] had more mind that he could use in his sphere. Perhaps you may be scarcely aware of the limited degree in which even Greek literature is admitted into the universities. There is a story of a professor at Oxford asking with a thunderous brow what a student was reading, . . 'Parmenides Sir' said the student—meaning Plato's mystical treatise. It was a *retort*—and silenced the questioner, who knew very little more of Plato's Parmenides than a [?] self educated man generally knows of the Greek metres.[2] . .

I think it probable that Mr. Horne has read more (perhaps among the classics) than many of these accurately learned men. He sent me a critical essay of his, once, upon Albertus Magnus,[3] which gave evidence of very curious reading in lightly trodden tracks. Moreover I am not like you—for I honor self educated men. Almost all men of genius and some men of learning have been self-educated—and if it were not so, the energy which could struggle with and overcome the opposition of circumstances, is highly honorable, I must consider, in itself. Cobbett [4] was not merely self-educated but imperfectly educated—he knew nothing of liberal literature—perhaps he had not imagination enough to take a polish. We must not compare him with the author of Orion—although in certain positions—he could strike a blow deeper.

Ah my dearest friend, you say (I think) 'You are worse than your client. Go away and leave me at peace'. So I go away. I enclose you however in going a very brief brief from my poor client, which I received together with your letter, – – to prove the contrariousness of certain impressions to and fro.

I have been very dull for some days,—and am glad to hear so much, at least, good news this morning, as that you should be rather better again. My poor little cousin, Sissy Butler was released last Saturday at Cheltenham from all sorrows of the body . . dying softly and in a moment in the arms of the maid who was carrying her into the drawing-room. There had been an end of hope for long—and on the preceding week it had been thought desirable that the medical man should inform her of her situation. She bore the tidings beautifully—a slight quivering of the lip being the only expression of emotion, —thanked him for telling her, and said she was very happy. Dear child—she is happier now! Scarcely sixteen—and the cup of life at her lips! But she is gone 'to drink it new in her Father's kingdom', and selfish is the tear which falls for her. She said to George when she saw him a fortnight ago, with her scant and struggling breath, . . 'Give my love to Ba'. It touched me much. Her poor sister and my aunt go abroad directly.

May God bless you my dearest friend!

Forgive and bear with me—do not talk of me in hyperboles, but love me!

Your most affectionate

E B B.

¹ Richard Porson (1759–1808), Fellow of Trinity College and Regius Professor of Greek at Cambridge.

² De Quincey has described such a scene as taking place, at Oxford, between his tutor and himself. (*Tait's Magazine*, February 1835.)

³ Albertus Magnus (1193?–1280), German philosopher, alchemist, and astrologer.

⁴ William Cobbett (1762–1835), agricultural labourer, pamphleteer, and journalist. Author of the celebrated *Rural Rides* (1830), etc.

[50 Wimpole Street]
August 30, 1843

. . . I have had another note from poor Mr. Horne. I have not yet fallen into the proper key for writing to him. He tells me that you read my House of Clouds to him—'and with

what a melodious feeling she reads poetry'! Ah—but there
was a melody of kindness underneath which is audible also to
me! He praises your Flush as the most benevolent-faced of all
unsouled beings! Certainly you delighted him. He could not
write, he says, and do anything except enjoy!

I shook my head over it all and answered silently – – 'You
never, never, never shall go there again! You have had your
last joy and your last bath there'! . . .

[*50 Wimpole Street*]
Sept. 7, 1843

Poor Flush indeed! My dearest friend, his Catiline is
worse than Cicero's!—never was such a savage, on two feet
or four!

The night before last as it was verging to ten oclock and
Flush had gone down stairs to have some supper, I heard a
great dog-storm in the lower part of the house, furious barking
upon furious barking, cry upon cry of dog and man,—I rang
my bell in fear! There was presently silence however, and I
began to blame myself, as I do twice or thrice a week, for
bearing about terror in my imagination and unconsciously
magnifying noises, when up came Crow carrying Flush. My
poor, poor Flush! Catiline and Resolute are usually confined
in what may be called the back area; and the door of their
prison being left open by some negligence, Flush had come
face to face upon his Cuba enemy in the passage. The noise
I heard was Catiline in savage fury, and Flush in shrieking
agony. Two men were there and several women, but they all
thought that the victim would be utterly worried, so deter-
minedly did the great tusks close upon the little throat, notwithstanding the kicks and blows they could reiterate on the
worrier. At last, Crewes, the waterman, compressed by main
force Catiline's windpipe; and the butler dragged at him
from behind . . and Flush was rescued. He did not attempt
to fight, they say—(how could he, poor little thing?) he only
shrieked and shrieked—and after he had quite escaped he
shrieked again, and then cried softly for a long long time, as if
he were bewailing the cruelty of his fate. Brought up to me,
he could walk only on three legs, being deeply bitten in three

places, besides the old casualty of which I told you before!
There, he was laid down on my bed, and coaxed and pitied,
and washed gently in lukewarm water, and soon began to
receive consolation. By the next morning he was in very
low spirits at not being able to leap up on my sofa. They laid
him on a chair—and he wouldn't be laid on a chair!—he
tumbled himself off and crept close to the sofa and stretched
himself there on the floor. When Crow lifted him up to me,
his eyes beamed and he wagged his tail emphatically. Towards
the evening he was much better, recovering his spirits and able
to touch the floor with the fourth leg—and today, the con-
valescence is obvious and satisfactory. We give him no meat
—except a little partridge from my dinner—milk and biscuits,
or cakes, instead: and he seems to be well in himself, dear
little dog! If you were but to see his eyes when we talk to
him of 'that naughty Catiline'! Catiline!—is he not a savage?
He has such a tiger look!—and immense strength—enough to
kill a man, in ten minutes!

Flush is convicted of having looked out of the Housekeeper's
room window and growled at Catiline, on the morning of the
murder—but if he did, *that*, I maintain, was only a natural
expression of feeling after Catiline's previous conduct to him.
I am in great indignation against the Cuban! 'Generous'!—
you see the length and breadth of his generosity! . . .

No—I do not think with you about Boz or Dickens—nor
did I ever hear of anything unbecoming or undignified in his
manner of receiving last year the American vows of allegiance
and admiration. A true genius I consider him—if of somewhat
less depth and height than the American devotees—and a most
ungrateful man he is, as surely as a true genius! As to his
conduct in America, how would you blame it? How could
he help being worshipped, if people chose to worship him? If
a host of young ladies supplicated him each for a lock of his
hair, how could he help 'their most sweet voices'? He refused
to wear a wig to serve them—and Diogenes could scarcely
under the circumstances, have done more . . or less. But it
is his conduct *since*, which has used all this honor to dishonor
himself—he is an ungrateful, an ungrateful man! . . . [1]

Byron, Coleridge . . how many more? . . were contemporaries of mine without my having approached them near

enough to look reverently in their faces, or to kiss the hem of their garment—and young as I was, I cannot get rid of a feeling of deep regret that, so it should have been.

I think sometimes . . how many were probably nay certainly, English contemporaries of *Shakespeare*, who never stood face to face with Him—and the idea startles me as something unnatural and unworthy.

Have you such thoughts and such regrets ever? Or is my organ of veneration as overtopping as a pyramid?

Abruptly I fall rather than come to an end!

May God bless you!

Ever your affectionate

E B B

[1] In 1842 Dickens visited America, where he was received with rapture. His subsequent account of transatlantic life, in *American Notes*, published in October 1842, and in *Martin Chuzzlewit*, the first number of which appeared in January 1843, deeply offended the Americans, and inspired a charge of ingratitude to his former hosts.

[50 Wimpole Street]
Sept. 20, 1843

My beloved friend I am glad that you are better, and do trust that you will take care for the future and not act upon impulse in confiding yourself, to the elements modified draught-wise. This hot weather is the means sometimes of our being tempted to our perdition—we cannot resist a breath and a shadow,—not if we have to pay double in pain afterwards for a transient relief. When I was free, I used to stand bare headed in the rain, plunge myself headlong into a bath of a long wet grass, . . nay, I have taken off my stockings and bathed my feet with dew—'therefore' you will moralize, 'I am *not* free now!'

My dearest friend, my brothers laughed heartily at Ben's specific for taming Catiline. Verily, they say, Master Ben must come and apply it himself, if it is to do any good here. Think of taming a tiger by biting gently at his front paw! Perhaps Van Amburgh [1] might attempt it. Other people would consider the possibility of said tiger's snapping off their head, in an impromptu retort.

I am blamed however on all sides for my misrepresentations to you of the great Cuban. The fact is said to be that Resolute

is Catiline's heroic spouse (altho' of sons and daughters they
have none), and that Flush being of an aspiring nature, lifted
up his eyes with extraordinary audacity where he ought to
have cast them down, and offered attentions to the lady. It
was flirting with the 'wife of Caesar' in the presence of Caesar,—
and Caesar could do no less for the sake of his honor (goes
the tale) than worry the offender. . . Well! I hope the next
dog stolen away out of this house under the patronage of the
'Fancy', may be the Cuban rather than my Flushie—that's all!

My dearest Miss Mitford, the police could do nothing for
us, – – they seemed quite perplexed and agaze,—having no
notion on which side to look. It would have been satisfactory
to have paid the police : whereas to render, by your own act,
the wicked speculation of those villainous men effectual, and
encourage them, by your own hand, into a repetition of the
evil you had suffered from, is vexatious and repugnant to you ;
when you have breath enough from fright, to think the whole
business over, from one end to another. 'But the dog is not
worth the money', objected Henry [2] to the King of the Fancy—
'you could not sell him anywhere for five pounds. He is
completely untrained—a mere lapdog—and too large for a
lap dog.'—'Nothing to do with it, Sir! Mrs. Chichester's
little black dog (next door to you) is not worth ten shillings—
but she paid me five pounds down before she recovered it.'
It is not *dogs* upon which they trade, but *feelings*. Wretched
men! . . . Taylor holds the reins in his hands of the whole
government. A gentleman, a Mr. Fin . . Mr. . . . oh! I
forget his name – – who lives in Devonshire Place, . . lost the
same dog three successive times, it being each time brought
back to him by Taylor. At last he lost his patience too – – 'Is
it not too bad', he cried, 'that I should be obliged by your
villainy (for I am perfectly aware that you are at the root of
the evil) to pay in this manner for my own dog? And now, I
suppose, I am to lose it for the fourth time?' With unmoved
serenity Mr. Taylor suggested that *that* was by no means
necessary,—and that, upon a certain additional sum being
placed in his hands, he could even answer for the dogs *not*
being stolen for the fourth time. Upon which, the gentleman's
indignation falling into his feet, he sprang up to kick his courte-
ous guest either down the stairs or out of the window—a

design which Mr. Taylor anticipated, by vanishing of himself
. . 'by effacing himself' as the French say. . .

¹ Van Amburgh was an American showman and lion tamer, who brought
a group of lions, tigers, and leopards to Astley's Royal Amphitheatre in the
Westminster Bridge Road. According to Queen Victoria, the 'miraculous'
Van Amburgh had 'a mild expression, a receding forehead, and very peculiar
eyes, which dont exactly squint, but have a cast in them'.
² Henry was the eighth child and fifth son of Edward Moulton Barrett.

[*50 Wimpole Street*]
Sept. 25, 1843

. . . Your Ben is a very fine fellow – – and I am sure I
ought to thank him for his generous sympathies in Flush's
sorrows and mine. . . By the way, Mr. Kenyon was here
yesterday, and told me that Mr. Curtis's coachman told *him*,
in a proposity to Flushie, a story in the high romantic style of
an adventure which happened to a tradesman, a friend of the
said coachman, in this neighbourhood, and not long ago. The
tradesman is a breeder of dogs, a member of 'the Spaniel
Club', and has in his own possession several very beautiful
dogs with the due length of ears and shortness of noses, and
valued by him exceedingly. One day he was at a public
house ; when the conversation turning upon dogstealers, he
inveighed vehemently against them, observing that he never
had lost a dog, but that if he ever did such a thing he would
spare no labour and no expense necessary to reach and punish
the rascals to the utmost rigour of the law. 'He spake' as the
epic poets say—and at the end of two days, one of his prettiest
dogs had vanished. Everything was tried, and every means
failed except – – a bribery of the offenders—and to this,
notwithstanding his resolute intentions, the poor man was
reduced. He was directed (upon yielding to terms) to a house
near the Edgeware Road, and to a room appearing uninhabited
at the top of the house, with a command, that if he identified
his dog, he was to take it up with one hand and lay down a
five pound note with the other. A trapdoor opened in the
floor, and the dog was put up through it, – – and while he
immediately identified it and throwing down the money,
prepared to depart, a voice of one invisible spoke out from the

wall – – 'Go!—go!—and take care of your dog! And re-member the next time you are in a public house, that you keep your tongue between your teeth, and speak no evil of the Fancy.'

This is the sublime of Dogstealing, and as such I recommend it to Ben's and your attention. . . The fault is in the law—and perhaps in the application of the law—for I am as little inclined to aquit the Police, as either Ben or yourself. The Police seemed as powerless as I was. Unless I could tell them where the dog was, what could *they* do, they said! And afterwards, when the theft was proved – – what could *they* do, they said. Oh! they knew of these nests of dog-stealers—and they knew Taylor personally for a 'rascal'—but what could *they* do, they still said. It was the very languor of powerlessness! . . .

[*50 Wimpole Street*]
Oct. 7, 1843

. . . My uncle James Clarke has come to see us, . . you will think us prodigal, in this house, of uncles. Did I tell you that my cousin Leonard Clarke (of the Kinnersley Castle Clarkes . . younger brother of Mr. Eagles's son in law) was going to be married last May to my cousin Isabel Butler a daughter of Sir Thomas Butler's? The bridal-array was chosen, and the orange-blossoms fixed in their wreath, when the pretty little bride put up her lip and sware by yea and nay that she didn't like the bridegroom and wouldn't marry him for the world. He fell into a distraction, and cried like a child,—and she locked herself in her bedroom, and would never see him again. The consequence was a great scandal, and the precipitate flight of the Rejected from the neighbour-hood of his lady's bower. All this chanced last May—and loud and wild was the outcry on all sides of course, in and out of the family, at a conduct of such cold caprice—and if I didnt tell you, it was because I was in a foam of indignation about it, and could not talk of my fair lady cousin without calling her names. A curious consequence of it, was a similar event in Mr. Wordsworth's family, whose son was engaged to be married to his cousin a Miss Monkhouse an heiress. Miss Monkhouse was paying a visit in Herefordshire to her friends the Dews [?], at the time when poor Leonard's misfortune was a general subject of conversation. Upon learning the details, she suddenly appeared much affected and declared to Miss Dew that Miss Butler's case was precisely hers, . . that she was engaged to marry her cousin whom she did not love and could not make happy, and that she would, in consequence, follow the late example and break off her engagement. The engagement was broken accordingly—and the Wordsworths I believe, have been consoled for the vexation, by the symptoms of a strangeness approaching insanity, 'in the order of the going'.[1] Not so however, is the case of my cousins.

A week ago Leonard arrived in town, radiant. He had been recalled. In a letter which he had some accidental occasion to write to my aunt Lady Butler, he wrote cursorily in lover's phrase . . 'I feel for Isabel as I always did, and shall'! The mother showed the letter to her daughter,—and the daughter said that if *he* was unchanged she was so also . . that she had 'thought him *cool*', and that that was the reason of her coolness to him; but that she was ready to marry him *now* if he liked it. And thus it is all arranged back again. Leonard is generous and a lover—and Isabel is, to my mind, either capricious and silly, or weak and a victim—for I cannot help fancying that she has been persuaded or scolded into the palinodia. The marriage takes place instantly—in the course of the present month—and . . poor Leonard, I say still! . . .

[1] In February 1843, Wordsworth's son William became engaged to Mary Monkhouse, an heiress with £20,000. The engagement was broken off in April.

[*50 Wimpole Street*]
Begun two days ago. *Oct. 1843* [Postmark: *October 7, 1843*]

. . . I want you to tell me my ever dearest friend, whether, if you are bent upon Chapel Street, we can do anything for you in the way of arranging the lodging plan . . choosing and taking the rooms etc.—or whether they are predestinated to your use at this moment. . . From eleven oclock every morning you shall have a room here, – – either the dining room or back drawing room – – to receive whatever visitors you please, and to breakfast and dine in *alone*,—I and my room upstairs being your green room . . or 'scrabbled-in background' of the picture. . . As to Papa, he goes away at twelve or a little after, everyday to the city; and we dont see him again until seven. So does George. So does Sette—not to the city indeed, but to Chambers. Stormie, I fear, 'will know you and flee you' as the elements did Kehama—and from my other three brothers and two sisters, I promise you free ground and no molestation. Ah—you are frightened of us I see—we produced an 'impression' on you when you came here last,—and our infantry is worthy, you think, of being ridden away fast from! Try to forgive us this once, and, on condition of 'free ground', accept at least this proposition of the sitting room and the eating and drinking. You shall have your tray—and your room—and your forty thieves by turns— and a full broad liberty in lodgings besides. Now tell me that you want only a bedroom in Chapel Street, and that we may take it for you soon. Will you, dearest friend ? . . .

You are astonished that people go abroad. . I am astonished that they stay at home. Who, with strength and opportunity, should pass into the world of spirits, without a glance at the Jungfrau ?—without looking upward to the mountains and downward to the rivers, . . or standing in the shadow of the pines ? Who should pass away from this form of Nature, without reading its Shakespeare ? Not I, willingly ! Would you be such a one ! Would you ? Oh, for health and liberty, and three years of wandering !—they should not be all wander- ing; for I would settle in some German town for the summer, and in Rome for the winter, and diverge—and share the intermediate time between various shrines of pilgrimage. What !—you would not like it ? *Can* you say so ?

Ever your E B B

[*50 Wimpole Street*]
Nov—1843

My dearest friend I thank you for permitting me to see Mrs. Niven's admirable letter. Her descriptions strike fire out of my desires, and leave me longing 'Oh for a horse with wings'. Am I never never to see Italy with my eyes? Never, in all probability: and it makes me sigh like furnace to think out such a melancholy to an end. If I could go,—if I had strength and liberty,—I would go tomorrow, and divide two or three years between France, Germany, and Italy—and stay longest perhaps in Germany. France, I say,—but it should rather be Paris—because I should care for the insight into men, nearly as well as for the prospects from mountains. What help it would give to the mind,—what help in versatility and aptitude, and variety of association . . to any thinking active mind, alive to clasp, with both hands, the advantages on every side! Is it not true that change in the sensations, and in those ideas more closely connected with the external world, . . must react strongly, deeply, and freshly on the inner Being,—conducing to the fuller development of the Imaginative and Reflective powers? I think so. Not that travelling will make a man wise or imaginative—but that its tendencies are to increase the wisdom of the Thoughtful, and multiply the images of the Poetic. Now I hope you are much the better for this treatise . . . . not pure Bridgewater. . .

Mr. Horne is very kind to 'intend to do' me 'himself'— and although the intention seems to imply what you suggest, perhaps he meant some reference to 'autobiographies' which he may have received from such persons as keep memoirs of themselves in their table drawers for the convenience of editors.[1] I had a note from him this morning—and he tells me not only that the work is to be in two volumes,—but that the *two* (with 360 pages each) are, by contract, to be finished by the middle of next month. Now unless he does it by machinery, or by a flash of lightening, the possibility of this rapidity I can scarcely, understand. For the rest, it seems to me that he must write more quickly than you think,—Orion having sprung upon his feet within this summer,—and Napoleon within a year, together with a tragedy. When he was with *you* . . how could he be expected to abstract himself away from you?—to say nothing of the two angels (hight Katy and Bessie) keeping the background, one on each side!

Did I tell you that Henrietta had been thrown into Mesmeric trances by her friend Mary Minto, four, . . five times lately? The insensibility is not complete, she says,—but the happy impossibility of moving hand foot or eyelid, she has arrived at,—and describes the sensation as a delicious mystery of *something*! Moreover Mary Minto begged Arabel to get a lock of my hair which none but myself had touched, by diplomacy, and wrap it in oilskin,—that she, Mary, might send it to a chief Rabbi of the Magnetisers in Paris, who was to declare straightway the nature of and remedy for my complaint. Instead of being diplomatic, Arabel brought me the note,—and I refused to part with my locks for any such purpose of witchery. My dearest friend, it would have made me as nervous, as nervous and as fanciful as I could well be! I should be lying here by myself, and fancying the mystical presence of a Clair-voyant French soul of a professor! Even Flush wouldnt have been a guard to me! The candles would have burnt blue,—and not a symptom should I have lost, of being haunted! Mr. Kenyon told me I was quite right in refusing the hair. And oh, if you were to hear some of Mr. Kenyon's stories in their grand details—how one body's soul was sent to Bath, and saw such and such a house with such and such pictures, and such and such persons with such and such peculiarities of dress—and how another body's soul went to another house in the country, and described everything in it, except a bronze ornament on the chimneypiece, which, upon enquiry . . had been sent to be mended!! . . and how another uneducated body's unrefined Soul, did, in a trance, utter, in eloquent language, thoughts as deep as Emerson's! And then think of *me* . . full of all those traditions, and with my own natural leaning towards mysticism to give them effect,—left in my solitude to the mercy of my imagination, while a clairvoyant Parisian professor had as tight hold of me by a lock of hair, as the angel of Death could be supposed to have, of a devout Mussulman! Was it not wise of me to deny the hair? 'Very wise', thought Mr. Kenyon!

Thank you,—thank you and Ben, . . for your kindness in the violets. What a sweet memory of the summer,—and promise of the spring!—and I should be puzzled as which, [*sic*] to accept them,—if they were not more fragrant still as a thought of *you*!

May God bless you, my dearest Miss Mitford!

Ever and ever your

E B B

. . . By the way my Flush learnt to count to *three*, in ten minutes yesterday.

¹ R. H. Horne was engaged in his *New Spirit of the Age*, a critical assessment of contemporary writers, which succeeded, to a large extent, in offending both those who were included and those who were excluded. E B B co-operated, secretly, with Horne in the preparation of this work : contributing to the essays on Wordsworth, Landor, and Leigh Hunt.

[50 Wimpole Street]
Dec. 7, 1843

My dearest friend I am so grieved that you should be still suffering from this rheumatism ! And this plan of sitting up all night, which I appeal against with all the forces of my astonishment, and which strikes me as an evil as great as the rheumatism itself—comprehending greater evils !! . . . To think of your sitting up all night long ! I hope K. reviled you with the strongest language she could find—I hope she did.

Oh you must remember the tragedy of Lieutenant Monro— in the course of which, last summer, he fought a duel with his wife's sister's husband and shot him mortally.¹ After that, he fled to the continent, and has only just returned with the intention of delivering himself up for trial. Another atrocious example of the effects of the Duel-system ! Here are two men, husbands of two sisters, quarrelling as any two brothers might do at any hour of the day, about matters of money which becomes a subject of mutual interest with them *in consequence* of their close connection ; quarrelling about sixpences over their tea,—as two testy brothers might quarrel and forget it the next day—and then going out like two savages, with pistols and *friends* (o friendship !) and one shooting the other through the lungs ! There is an end to all ! A little moralizing on one hand—a little sentiment on another—some persons going as far as to regret the unhappy necessity of this commission of murder by grace of society—and a very few, bold enough to protest against its wickedness. In the meantime the murdered man lies still in his red shroud—and his widow raves in a phrenzy. And there, an end. If Mr. Monro recovers from his fever and is tried by his peers, we all know what the result will be—'Manslaughter—and a slight imprisonment'. Poor wretched man! His crime has been the crime of Society—and little right indeed have they to punish him for it. Is it not outrageous that men should act so, calling the crime 'honour'?— 'honorable men'! . . .

If the queen cares for pleasure she has enough of it,—and your magnificent Duke seems to be making a fairy queen of her at Chatsworth, with gorgeous enchantments meeting every turn of her foot.[2] Yes—you are right, I fear I fear! And then again there are reports abroad that she is so low of spirits, so alarmingly despondent at times, that the physicians command every sort of amusement and form of variety to which Majesty can have access. It may be of the physician's misdoing! Pleasure upon pleasure is sure at last, if piled high enough, to reach a melancholy. The senses fall asleep in superfluous enjoyments. And nothing can be more wretched than a man, woman, or even *child*, amused from morning to night. It is better (I sometimes comfort myself with that philosophy) not to be amused at all. When I have tired myself with writing, I am ready to be relaxed sufficiently by a little play with Flushie's pretty ears, or a little dreaming off into a romance,—forgetting the walls of my prison. And I think I could forget, so, even a crown!

Not a word of Mr. Kenyon! I told him he would stay longer. 'No' he said—'I shall *not* stay longer than eight or nine days.' I am sure it is full a fortnight ago since he said so! Dear Mr. Kenyon. I miss him when he is away.

How does your matrimonial scheme get on? Any more evidence *for* or against? Or is the lover's heart in his two volumes pending? I heard from him a day since, with a command for my letters to follow yours to Kentish Town.

My dearest Miss Mitford, do you know anything about that wonderful invention of the day, called the Daguerrotype? —that is, have you seen any portraits produced by means of it? Think of a man sitting down in the sun and leaving his facsimile in all its full completion of outline and shadow, stedfast on a plate, at the end of a minute and a half! The Mesmeric disembodiment of spirits strikes one as a degree less marvellous. And several of these wonderful portraits . . like engravings—only exquisite and delicate beyond the work of graver—have I seen lately—longing to have such a memorial of every Being dear to me in the world. It is not merely the likeness which is precious in such cases—but the association, and the sense of nearness involved in the thing . . the fact of the *very shadow of the person* lying there fixed for ever! It is the very sanctification of portraits I think—and it is not at all monstrous in me to say what my brothers cry out against so vehemently, . . that I would rather have such a memorial of one I dearly loved, than the noblest Artist's work ever produced. I do not say so in respect (or disrespect) to *Art*, but for *Love's* sake. Will you understand?—even if you will not agree?

May God bless you, my beloved friend! Tomorrow you will receive a little fish, which I hope may make itself welcome.

Ever your affectionate

B B

¹ On July 1, at Camden Town, a Colonel Fawcett was shot in a duel by his brother-in-law, Lieutenant Munro.

² 'We arrived at Chatsworth on Friday, and left it at nine this morning, quite charmed and delighted with everything there . . . The first evening there was a ball, and the next the cascades and fountains were illuminated, which had a beautiful effect.' Queen Victoria to the King of the Belgians, 4th December 1843. (*Letters of Queen Victoria*, ed. A. C. Benson and Viscount Esher, Vol. I, p. 637. Murray, 1907.)

[*50 Wimpole Street*]
Dec. 31, 1843

My dearest friend I am ashamed of myself and my carelessness. The seal is gone for ever,—vanished by the crevice through which came my cold!—but the letter is here—I make dishonorable amends for my carelessness by sending it at last. Forgive me my dearest friend.

And while you are forgiving, forgive me for what may appear to you my obstinacy—but if I were to have a consultation of physicians, and they felt the pulse of my windows, and looked into the throat of my chimney, and enquired tenderly after the draught of the door, – – nothing could be done beyond what is done already. I am living in the midst of the precautions which medical men have recommended to me,— have a thermometer to arrange my atmosphere by,—and for my dress, never change it—have two gowns a year,—a black silk one for the summer,—a black velvet one for the winter, the latter fully lined,—and wear them out with the season. I 'tread on silk' in respect to prudence of every sort and kind as regards my health—and I know my symptoms by heart,— understand my pulse when it approaches fever, as certainly as your Mr. May could do,—and am far generally from being the stiffpated selfwilled body you take me to be! For instance, if the spitting of blood were to come on badly, or if a new symptom occurred, I would send for Dr. Chambers without hesitation— I would not risk my life or the peace of those who love me (which is the right way to put it) indeed and indeed. But as it is,—oh my dearest friend—if you were in my situation, if you had passed through my experience and were precisely as I am now,—I am confident that you would act as I do. It is self-complacent to say so, I am aware—but I believe that you would act as I do. Has not Dr. Scully said to me again and again—'It is a case in which we can do nothing'? Again and again he has plainly said or intimated it with a sigh. If certain symptoms had occurred the other day, there are of course active means by which they might be met,—and I should have placed myself in the hands (in that case) best competent to use active means with safety and success. But to prove to you the incompetency of the medical profession to treat successfully these affections of the chest, I will mention to you confidentially that even Dr. Chambers (of whose science and acuteness there can be only one opinion) on failing to stop the bleeding in my case with the common specific of lead, recommended me to a *quack medecine* which had been successful, he said! 'Do not mention my name, or it will all be in the newspapers,—but get the styptic at such a place!' Their science conjectures dimly, and is at fault quickly—and poor Dr. Scully, even when he came to me everyday, did not conceal from me how little he had in his power. 'We want lights' he used to say honestly. . .

For poor Miss Martineau and in other cases besides her's, it may be absolutely necessary to see a physician—or a surgeon perhaps. We cannot judge. I have understood from somebody, that her's was a case of internal cancer—or an affection approaching to it. She spoke you know, of 'displacements'. Probably she suffers, poor thing, far more than I ever have done,—but she does not appear to be so weak as I am even now—and I am strong now to what I once was, you know. Poor Miss Martineau! I do not feel with her throughout her book,—but I look to the mind capable of that production at such a moment, with the most respectful and unqualified admiration.[1] . . . Learn however by the present post, that the book is *not* dedicated to me. Everybody has exclaimed with your exclamation, from its publisher Mr. Moxon, to the most intimate friends of the author—and Mr. Kenyon justly observed that the very supposition is honor enough for me. But he has ascertained that the fact is not so ; that it is *not* dedicated to me—and indeed, without any distinct information on the subject, there are certain passages and allusions which could not possibly be twisted into referring to me. Oh no, my dearest friend ! Neither would the supposition have occurred to you or anybody, except by the bare coincidence of a parallel misfortune. I fit the affliction, and not the honor !—and Miss Martineau required for her dedicateè, a fitness for both. . .

Your always affectionate

E B B

[1] Harriet Martineau, lying ill at Tynemouth, had written in about six weeks a volume of essays, *Life in the Sick-Room, by An Invalid*, a book that Wordsworth, according to his son-in-law, praised 'with more unreserve, I may say, with more *earnestness*, than is usual with him'. (Morley, Vol. I, p. 533.)

[50 Wimpole Street]
Jan. 11, 1844

. . . Mr. Kenyon came to see me yesterday, after his Devonshire journey, and seemed to be glad to be at home. I asked how his brother was, and then he began to tell me that his dream of last year was at an end, and that Mr. Edward Kenyon, being a German at heart and seeing his wife grow paler and paler under the pressure of the social restraints of England, would probably return to Germany without fail, and no later than next summer. . . Altogether there is no hope, I can see, from dear Mr. Kenyon's face, that he can be permitted to dream out his dream of a double home and a dear domestic friendship next door. The bubble has burst. Poor Mr. Kenyon ! He bears up, and talks philosophy about the 'luxuries of life'—but I see that it is a hard stroke—and what is more, I *feel* it must be. Still, what he says, is true,—that anything is better than to be a restraint consciously upon his brother and induce him to remain in England against his own secret wishes. Well! So dreams dissolve, you see! This is one of the thousand a minute.

He and I were talking yesterday of Miss Martineau's book which he admires, only not quite as much as I do. I told him that I differed with *you* about the letter-question,[1]—*you* approving of her mode of considering it: and my own words reminded me that I never told you why, or explained in what degree. My dearest Miss Mitford—and then Mr. Kenyon said – – that whether the view were right or wrong, it was a great inconsistency, after Miss Martineau's personalities in America, which she justified at the time upon principle—and I agreed with him, just as I disagree with her and you—I agreed with him consistantly; because I justify (as you know) both the personal memoirists and the printers of letters, . . always presupposing a discerning delicacy on delicate points. But the squeamishness of this Age, . . this Ostrich age . . which exposes its own eggs, and then hides its head in the sand, . . is really to me quite monstrous. The shrieks on all sides because Mr. such a person tells the astonished public that Mrs. such a person has a nose, could scarcely be louder if he had attacked her character in a public court. And as to the printing of letters, I never will believe (for all Miss Martineau may re-iterate) that a man or woman either, let them live ever so in perpetual presence of the grand possibilities of Posterity, would write restrained sentences to their very intimate friend; under the idea that after they are dead their letters will be printed by their executors. Tell me honestly my dearest friend, did such an idea ever restrain a thought of *yours*,—*you*, who must be perfectly aware that nobody worthy of your correspondence, would destroy your letters? Is not the natural thought when the time comes for thinking—'Let whatever is good in me of heart and intellect live as long as the world will let it, for the use and service of the world'? Is not *that* the natural and disinterested thought, with which we should look down from Heaven? Consider,—if everybody had acted as Miss Martineau says she has, . . what a mass of valuable literature would be swept away for ever from our eyes at this moment. Consider,—*you* – – who delight in personal memoir and record – – and never say again, oh never say again that you 'agree' with Miss Martineau in her view of the letter-question. For my part, just in proportion to my appreciation of Her, was my indignation at this view. As if, . . when we have passed from the world, . . we should be 'content to live in decencies' like these, any more! As if . . when we have seen God, we shall care for man seeing *us*! It is monstrous, I think. For Mrs. Hemans, with that conventional excess of delicacy which was the flaw in her fine genius, to exclaim, . . 'Do not let them print my letters', was only a characteristic circumstance and disappoints us in nothing. But for Miss Martineau with her clear and healthful discernment, and capability of generalizing, to do the like,—and what is more, to found the unwillingness upon a *rationale*, . . makes one absolutely angry, and doubtful of the consistency of mortal judgements.

Tell me if you do not, on reconsideration, move a little round to *me*! Do tell me! Think of the Sevignes, Deffands,[2] Cowpers, . . take all the unlike! At any rate, . . mind—you may talk,—but practically you will gain nothing by it. You never would or could invoke away from me the twelve volumes (to be moderate in my calculation) of letters, which people will be reading under the trees a hundred years hence. Oh—there are delicacies to be observed, of course! Let the delicacies have ample room and verge enough, and I make no single objection. But the observation of the most ample delicacies is compatible with a view directly opposite to this of Miss Martineau's. . .

[1] Harriet Martineau had decided that the preservation of letters for publication was an evil, since it inhibited spontaneity and veracity between correspondents. She refused to allow her own letters to be published and asked those to whom they were addressed to destroy them.

[2] Madame du Deffand (1697–1780), the blind aristocrat of the Convent of St.-Joseph, and the brilliant correspondent of Horace Walpole and Voltaire.

[50 Wimpole Street]
Monday morning [March or April 1844]

My beloved friend, let these words go to you, as a kiss through the air, until I can write more. I want to thank you a thousand times for your dear kindness in coming here and bringing Flush,—and I have scarcely spirits for *one* time. Crow left me the day after I saw you . . and suddenly to *me*, – – because they had kept the time of her going, concealed from me—and I have been shaken into sleepless nights and depressed days by it, . . the bow has lost its elasticity. Wait for a day or two,—and I will write. This word is just to prove me . . no monster of ingratitude towards you—I love you better and dearer and more gratefully, on the contrary, than ever. And although, to be sure, the Flushies did break our talk into bits, I cannot repent having seen your's. He is in my mind for evermore. I know him. I see him. His Idea is with me, faithful and complete from henceforward.

And then, May, May!—I look forward to May.

What was worse than the barking of dogs when you were here, was the aching of my head. *How* it ached, as if to put to shame the pleasure of the heart! And it has ached ever since, I think. Never was such a head.

But I have seen you—and I have seen Flush—and your goodness in coming I lay up on the top shelf of my precious thoughts and consecrated recollections.

May God bless you! Heroic person you were, to do so much, so resolvedly, that night!

Now, remember *May*. I shall chirp May into you, like a bird.

Your own
E B B.

Ah yes—your loss is more *bitter* than mine, . . from the manner of it—but mine is more affecting than yours, from my aspect towards it. My morbid dislike of strangers . . too natural under circumstances of confinement and total personal dependence, . . *you*, who are active and social, can scarcely imagine, perhaps. But the thing is to be borne—and complaints are *nought*. May God bless you, dearest friend.

[50 Wimpole Street]
Tuesday. May 7, 1844

. . . Crow has been very kind. She has come day after day, sometimes two or three days together, to dress me and arrange little things for me—shedding abundant tears when the time came for leaving me. She said, it was as great a deprivation to her as it could be to me,—she said *that* very kindly and earnestly. I earnestly hope she may be happy, poor thing,—and, so far, the business seems flourishing, and he is very attentive and apparently fond of her.[1] She goes to her mother's to be confined,—and *then*, will come the full loss to *me*!

Wilson, the new maid, is very willing, very anxious, . . almost too anxious!—very gentle, . . almost too gentle! a little failing in the vivacity and cheerfulness I like about me. I am afraid I shall never like her as well as Crow, – – altho' she appears to be amiable beyond any finding fault with, and desirous of pleasing. Is that ungrateful of me? Perhaps so. My sisters say I shall like it all better presently. Perhaps so. But what I miss is,—the affectionate, gentle (always respectful) controul which poor Crow used towards me, – – the sort of half-nursing,—and arranging of everything. She was with me when I was very ill and weak—and something of the gentle authority of nurse to patient, remained in her manner and ways. The 'you must *not* have the window open in an east wind',—and the like. Do you understand? I miss it all drearily. *Now*, I may have the window open all day, if it blows a hurricane,—unless my sisters come into the room and look that way! I may take double morphine draughts if I like! I may go to bed as late as I please,—and talk as long. It is a liberty I am not grown strong enough for,—and I feel the weight of it.

How querulous!

How childish! I am ashamed of myself almost, to write so to you. Only you do not despise me always, for even my foolishnesses.

Not time for a word more!

May God bless you, my beloved friend!

Ever your attached

E B B

You received my last letter surely?

---

[1] Crow had secretly married William Treherne, the handsome young butler at Wimpole Street. He set up in business as a baker in Camden Town.

. . . If I had not heard from you today, I should have written I think,—for I had arrived at the point of imagination, which always turns ill with me, and was beginning to select out of all possible evils the worst, for the cause of your silence. Well—I am delighted that it is my fault at last. *That* is the most satisfactory of catastrophes to me. Only I am not 'angry' at the change of plan about London,—'of all the birds in the air' I am not such a goose. Come when you will, it will be holiday time with me; and the sooner or later depends on my good or ill fortune. In the meantime I am delighted that you like your maid—although I cannot help thinking the deafness and ill-health serious drawbacks. Poor Wilson . . and I say 'poor Wilson', because I take her part against myself . . has really no obvious one,—except not being Crow, . . and wanting a little in vivacity. It amuses me too to see how she exerts herself to be talkative and cheerful, having heard that I like it—and I was rather touched yesterday when I started as she came into the room, and said, 'Really I thought it was Crow—' and she answered, . . 'ah no! I am afraid, it is nobody equal to Mrs. Crow.' There is great softness and kindness and humility in her, . . and I feel that I *shall* like her 'better and better', as my sisters say I shall. Crow has gone to Lincolnshire to her mother at last and will stay there until after her confinement,—and the going away (since it was to be) is well over for me. The whole business has been full of pain to me—more painful than perhaps it should be. There has been a mixture of feelings—and that she was associated with the most fatal time and deepest suffering of my life, had its full part in the grief of seeing her leave me. Also it seemed to take fresh measure of my prison and to count the locks upon the doors. But this is being too querulous— even to *you*, . . to whom I am apt to speak out my daily 'groans' as they occur. . .

The first volume is just done printing, and I have sent much more than half of it, together with a MS. preface far too long, to America, . . Mr. Matthews having the goodness to under- take to superintend the publication at New York.[1] Oh no—

my dearest friend,—you exaggerate about the *idol*-dom, which made me laugh—but that there is some kind feeling for me in America it would be ungrateful to doubt—and I am grateful, among others, to your Professor and to Mrs. Sigourney. Talking of kindnesses, Mr. Horne was so very kind the other day (having through Mrs. Orme an aggrandized report about my 'killing myself with a book') as to propose to do all the correction of the press for me, root and branch. Very kind— was it not? Only it could not be accepted,—because I re-write and re-correct down to the very edge of the revise—adding new, and changing old,—in which, in fact, lies the fatigue to me. . .

I heard the other day 'Sydney Smith's [2] last', which sounded to me horribly droll. He said *gravely*, that 'the strongest argument in favour of uninterrupted Apostolical succession which occurred to him, was the extraordinary family likeness between Bishop Philpott and Judas Iscariot'.

Mr. Kenyon has returned, . . having been to see South-ampton and Nelson's Victory, and Stonehenge, and Bath and Bristol, and the Wye, and Malvern and Oxford, and so coming home again. . . How I should like to wander for years on the continent—oh, *how* I should like it! How it would open a new spring of life—quicken the impulses of life; and drive up one's ideas like a fountain of life! I feel the pricking of a gad-fly every now and then,—just like Aeschylus's Io—and would fly . . fly . . fly . . along the surface of the earth! The traveller lives life twice over, be sure—that is, *I* am sure.

Yes, 'Jean Cavalier' has fine things in it,—but to my mind, is, as a work of genius, inferior to Mathilde and the Mysteries.[3] But then, I am not fond of the historical romance, *as a Genre*. Have you read much of Balzac? To my apprehension, Balzac is a writer of extraordinary power, and as a describer, . . take him from his descriptions of old houses, upwards, . . he is unrivalled. He has a Dutch hand, and an Italian soul—finishes, to the very down on the wing of a butterfly—yet comprehends wholeness and unity. You touch, taste, and handle everything he speaks to you of—yet he can write withal such eloquent sentiment and passion, as to have produced (in his 'Lily of the Valley') one of the most perfect of the 'Nouvelle Heloises' of the day. An eloquent, powerful book, that 'Lily' is,—

although it will not please you, perhaps, as it did me. Still there are other books of Balzac which *will* and *must*—and I must ask you to make way through them!

Poor Flushie misses Crow dreadfully—and you would smile to see the utter disdain with which he looks at Wilson when she desires him to do anything—as if to say . . 'Obey *you* indeed!' Arabel was obliged to tell him to 'go to his own place' at bedtime—otherwise I believe he would have sate up the whole night for the mere pleasure of resisting an unconstitutional law . . so considered. He would not even take his favorite cake from her hand—looking at *me*, that *I* might give it to him instead! She told me that when she saw Flush down stairs, he was 'very kind' to her,—and she could not make out how it should be otherwise in this room—'just as if he did not like to see me here'. Which I believe to be the simple truth.

May God bless you my dearest friend!

Pray dont have too much to say to write to me,—because *that* is an obstacle which will grow larger and larger everyday until at last it will be infinitely invincible. In true affection

Ever your

E B B.

¹ E B B had been preparing for some time the material for the two-volume edition of her *Poems*. Although the MS. had gone to press at the end of March, publication did not take place until the second week in August. On these volumes, E B B's reputation was finally established. They were also to form the basis of her introduction to Robert Browning.

² Sydney Smith (1771–1845), the noted wit, and Canon of St. Paul's. Author of *Peter Plymley's Letters on the subject of the Catholics* (1807), etc.

³ *Jean Cavalier* (1840), *Mathilde* (1841), *Les Mystères de Paris* (1842–43) were novels by Eugène Sue.

[*50 Wimpole Street*]
August 14, 1844

. . . Well, now—*do* let me have a word from you to say that you are better! I thirst for that word. Mr. Kenyon saw Mr. Rogers yesterday who was suffering just from your present malady, and feared being prevented from going down with Moxon on thursday, to see Wordsworth. 'After all though', said he 'this is not the pleasantest time of year for visiting Wordsworth. The god is on his pedestal, and the worshippers wont let him talk.' Then he (Mr. Rogers) spoke of a plan of getting to Paris later in the autumn. 'There is much variety of amusement there,—' he said to Mr. Kenyon, . . 'and it is very pleasant to be able to go to Orleans by the railroad in two hours, and *back again in the same morning*'!! There, is an untired energy for you, after eighty! Now hasn't such a man a right to make fifty young ladies in love with him, if he pleases? Surely, yes! I admire him more for his old age than for his 'Pleasures of Memory' . . infinitely. . .

[*50 Wimpole Street*]
Sept. 1, 1844

Ever dearest friend I began a letter to you last week and had not the heart to go on with it. You may well reproach me for silence, and say hard words of me in your secret thoughts. Appearances are against me,—and I am not sure, . . for all this love for you which rises up at the thought, . . I am not sure that I am altogether innocent. Still, as I do love you, and have not been turned away from writing to you by over-much pleasure, you will try to forgive me, . . and will understand perhaps how naturally I have sunk into a distaste for the opening of my heart to you, when I tell you at last that two of my brothers, Stormie and Henry, are at this moment on their way to *Ægypt*. Everybody, except myself, knew of the plan long and long ago. The *Statira* is Papa's own ship, and takes out coals, to bring back wool from Alexandria,—and the young men (particularly Stormie, who sang for joy to the last moment) were wild with desire to go out in her—and Papa gave way, . . and had every possible luxury of preparation, . . up to hermetically sealed cream and Champagne, . . provided for them. A few days before they went, they told me—and although I had strength to avoid any scene or weak demonstration, the arrangement has naturally given me many a fearful thought and heavy hour,—and I bitterly think, even now, that the advantage of being in Ægypt a month, at Gibraltar two days, and at Malta, two days, is disproportionate to the long anxiety of those left at home. The ship is considered a good and safe one,—and the Captain is experienced,—and the voyage will be as agreeable, I suppose, as a voyage can be, from the airiness and size of the cabins, and the comforts of all sorts, with which they were furnished. And then I try to think of the fine bright weather, and the favorable wind! Only once, when the sun shone brightest I was near my greatest woe—and, so, there is nothing but to trust God for it that He will be merciful and spare us to meet happily again. They are to be at home at Christmas or before—and the plan is, if possible, to get down to Thebes while the ship is being loaded at Alexandria. Oh, they were so delighted to go! Even the sight of my tears as they stooped down to kiss me, could not change their smiles for a moment. They smiled on, as if they could not help it,—and I am sure they couldn't. Dear things! It is some comfort to know they are so happy— and then it is weak and morbid, I *feel*, to have such thoughts as I have struggled bravely against. Do you know I once thought of escaping the anxiety by sharing the risk, and of going with them to Malta, there to wait for the spring, . . flying an English winter in the same act! But then, I thought again, if I went, and Papa consented to it, my sisters would wish to go and he would insist on it,—and *that* would be undoing his home for him, as I swore I never again would. No—it is better as it is! Besides I have not striven in vain. I am more cheerful than I expected to be,—and not presentimental. . .

And now I am going to tell you of *my* books. There is not much to say. I have had some very gratifying letters,— very—but there has scarcely been time to guess at what will be the ultimate judgement of impartial readers. The only review I have seen yet, is the Athenaeum's, which is most kind, and leaves me satisfied and grateful.[1] Did you not see it? It *began* a number,—and scarcely obliged you to the effort of page-cutting. Then, I hear of a review in the John Bull[2] of yesterday, which is said to cut me into gashes, on the ground of the vicious ambition of emulating Milton. I have sent for the paper, as I wish to know the head and front of the violence done to me—the praise or blame of that publication not being however of much importance, to my apprehension. Also, it is said to be more gracious to the minor poems. I have had kind letters from Carlyle, who told me that a person of my 'insight and veracity' ought to use 'speech' rather than 'song' in these days of crisis,—which would be too like Pope's advice to Wycherly to turn his poems into prose to be exceedingly gratifying, if he had not followed it by some cordial kindness. He had not read all the poems when he wrote,—had not read the 'Drama', nor the 'Vision',—and singled out 'Geraldine's Courtship' as his favorite so far. Well, then,—Wordsworth only 'looked forward with great pleasure' to having leisure to read,—this being 'his season' at the lakes. The same with Landor, who wrote before the parcel containing the books reached his hands. Leigh Hunt is from home. Mrs. Jameson used strong language of praise to Mr. Kenyon, and said that she meant to write to me—but she has not yet written. Miss Martineau promises a full and unreserved opinion 'for better or worse' when she has finished the reading,—but she has not yet written. Mr. Boyd is demonstrative to the highest degree in satisfaction with the 'Drama', but (except his Cyprus wine) has read nothing else. Among my private friends, you know how it must be—they show only the sunny sides of their thoughts. That I have made progress, and particularly improved in *clearness*, appear general admissions—and made not only by the Athenaeum. By the way I do not at all doubt that Mr. Chorley is the author of that criticism,—and I am sincerely grateful to him for it. It is a review of the minor poems,—with a reference to a purpose of taking the long poems into consideration on a future occasion.

There now! Have I not told you all? All that you will care to hear, I think. It would have been abominable of me to resist your request; and I have made my confession as well [as] I could. Would you like to see Carlyle's letters? You shall see and hear whatever you care to see and hear. Reserve to *you*, would be ingratitude in *me*.

After all, I have thought little of the book lately, as you may well believe. Let John Bull tear me up if he pleases. . .

And do you know anyone who, having a young child from four to ten years of age, wishes it to be taught French, English, Italian, and music, by a daily governess? Miss Haydon is anxious to undertake the teaching of such a child,—and her father has written to beg me to do what I can to meet her wishes.[3] *I* - - what can I do? But *you*, who know everybody

221

in the world, may know some evil disposed person in town, inclined to torture his or her poor child. . . May God bless you, ever dearest Miss Mitford!

Do not forget me all at once.

I am as always

Your most affectionate

E B B

¹ Miss Barrett's volumes, wrote the reviewer, 'ought to be sought for— respectfully by men, affectionately by women; as remarkable manifestations of female power'. (*Athenaeum*, August 24, 1844.)

² 'Simplicity is everywhere sacrificed to the superficial glitter of phrases . . . So Miss Barrett does not publish the poems before us, but "trusts them into the current of publication" . . . It is the more provoking to see one like Miss Barrett fluttering away in such gaudy tinsel, because she is evidently capable of better things, both from the impulses of her own genius and the advantages she possesses from a highly cultivated mind.' (*John Bull*, August 31, 1844.)

³ Eight years later, having 'learnt truth and goodness from her many trials', 'poor Miss Haydon' was 'teaching as a daily governess, at eight shillings a week'. (L'Estrange, Vol. III, p. 249.)

[50 Wimpole Street]
Saturday Sept. 28, 1844

. . . And now I will tell you what happened once to me (not long ago) with respect to Harriet Martineau. You know that she has written to me occasionally since last autumn, when she began the intercourse by the kindest note imaginable about my poetry. I answered it with a warm appreciation of a kindness and honour which had touched as well as surprised me from such a quarter,—and she wrote again at long intervals, I always answering her letters. Well,—at last, just as my books reached her, and before she had even cut the leaves, I had from her the most singular letter I ever received. She intimated in it that I had done myself harm with her by flattering her,— that I had flattered her more than was becoming to a Christian woman to flatter or be flattered,—that Miss Sedgewick had done the same, . . had persisted in doing it in the face of her remonstrances,—had in consequence been rejected from her correspondence, . . and that, thereupon, Miss Sedgewick

222

had 'changed her hand' and called bad names instead of good.
The infinite surprise with which I read this letter, – – the
humiliated surprise – – for there are charges which humiliate
nearly as much as if they were convictions, . . you will
understand without difficulty. With all my faults, I am not
accustomed to see myself reproached for this of falseness,—
and then I had been so utterly unconscious of 'flattering' Miss
Martineau, that I feel sensitively it would have been an act
of presumption in a stranger like myself and with an unestab-
lished reputation, to take the liberty of praising her to her
face, even according to my honest view of her powers and
gifts. I cannot believe that I did more than express in a
general manner my sense of what she was and my grateful
sense of her condescension to me—and if I expressed it
warmly, the warmth came from my heart certainly, and had
nothing in it of phosphoric falseness. I told her so in reply.
I thanked her for speaking to me of the impression, since she
entertained it—and I respected a virtue which I could not
however help feeling was, at that moment, somewhat austere
towards me. From the other emotion of humiliation, I did not
speak to you of it *then*. I really felt abashed. Can you understand? I thought everybody would think as even Papa did,
'*Why what can you have been saying*?' And really, really, I am
true! I write the truth (as it appears to me) even to strangers
who send me books, and perhaps expect nothing but thanks
and praise. I write the truth (as far as I can perceive it) even
to friends, whom I love dearest and most blindly. I seek the
truth myself, and seek it earnestly. I am not fond of using too
strong language, and of dealing in the common commerce of
compliment. And yet, you see! Well—I could not help
thinking it rather hard, and undeserved—but there was a
nobleness on her part, even in the hardness,—and her letter
about the books has overcome, in good measure, the painful
impression, and left me grateful for her sympathy. . .

As to the amendment in health, it may be as you say.
Lady Harriet Cocks, after a seclusion and suffering of years, . .
after wasting, wearing away like a snow-wreath, and becoming
at last unable to take food, except *turtle-broth* and grapes, . .
suddenly cried out for bread, eggs, meat! Such an appetite
never was heard of! She frightened the whole house with

eating. Lady Margaret told me that she could not be satisfied,—and it was dreadful to see, the manner in which the
insatiable appetite seemed to cry out within her. *That* was
supposed to be when the tumour receded and left an unaccus-
tomed vacancy in the stomach. Then she was delirious and
raved,—then, sank into a stupour, and lay insensible for
days. At the end of that time, she was *well*—the desease had
past—and she recovered steadily hour by hour. She is in
perfect health at this moment. . .

As for myself my dearest friend, if I could make a patch-
work of sunny summers, I believe I might live many years
under their canopy,—yes, and be strong to live. But I have
not your faith (having tried and known much of it too) in mere
country air—and I believe that much exertion in order to
get into it, would be full of risk to me. When I talked about
the Rhine,—*that* was a peculiar means. The *water* passage, I
could bear without effort,—knowing *that* by experience,—and
my dream (the mere dream of a dream . . thrown out as any
other dream might be!) was, that two or three summer months
of drifting on the water, and resting on its shores, might give
'me strength enough' to get over into the Rhone, and so to the
warmer south of France for the winter. A mere dream!—but
differing, as a dream, from your's, which includes more fatigue
and no escape (the most vital point) from a winter in
England. . . No, my dearest Miss Mitford!—I must take
courage and patience,—and in time I shall perhaps quietly
live back again to life and strength. Poor Dr. Scully told
me honestly that I never should be otherwise than an invalid, although I might hope to be better: but then I am
better than I ever hoped to be, and I think better of myself
unawares.

Papa is absent,—gone to Cornwall, to examine a quarry
in which he has or is about to have, shares,—and not likely to
be at home until the middle of next week. I inherit his
bedroom during his absence,—and my room is, by his desire,
being made so clean and perfect by the whole generation of
sweepers and cleaners, that it will not know itself again, they
say. Then, I am to have a green double door instead of the
cloth curtain, which will save me from the footsteps on the
staircase, and from Flushie's barking out the consequences

thereof. I am well pleased with the green double door. And I am going (perhaps) to have a blind for my open window, with green trees on it, which will be as rural as Mademoiselle de Scudery [1] in 'Pays tendre' . . .

I had a letter from a poor poet the other day . . who calls himself Owen Howell [2] and lives in Bartholomew Close, and has written poems called 'Westminster Abbey' and 'Life' dedicated to Rogers. He wrote to say that he was writing 'a similar poem to my Drama of Exile', and begged me to sub-scribe to it, – – which of course I did directly. But didn't it sound rather oddly of the noble Briton?

Yes,—but to leave out a line in a sonnet! *That* is as wrong as to put a weak one in, – – isn't it? Are you in earnest, . . do I understand you rightly, . . that you advise me to send my books to Madme Dudevant? I am half ashamed to confess how often I have thought of doing it, myself—but everytime I shrank back. *Could* I have courage? *Might* I have courage? Do you know that in general I have rather a dislike to sending about my books as a gift to persons whom I admire,—it is so like thinking them worth their acceptance,—and asking for praise in return. Except to Carlyle, I have sent to nobody, without a specific reason for it. I have not sent even to Joanna Baillie—to whom perhaps I *should* have done it. . .

Ah—you tempt me with George Sand! And Mr. Kenyon is going to Paris directly, early in October, and might take the books. Suppose you send her 'Belford Regis' or another work, and let me slip mine into the shade of it? Suppose we join *so* in expressing, as two English female writers, our sense of the genius of that distinguished woman?—if it did not strike you as presumption in me to put my name to yours as a writer, saying '*we*'. We are equally bold at any rate. Mr. Kenyon told me I was 'a daring person' for the introduction of those sonnets. [3] He had heard an able man say at his table a day or two before, that no modest woman would or *ought* to confess to an acquaintance with the works of George Sand. Well!—are you inclined to do it? Will you? Write and tell me. I would give anything to have a letter from her, though it smelt of cigar. And it would, of course! Answer me directly—for I have taken a fancy to the plan in writing of it. She would know *your* name! Think of it!

Once, I had a romantic scheme of writing my whole mind to her of her works. *That* was when I first read them,—and I lay awake all a night in a vision of letters anonymous and onymous—but it passed away,—and I considered how little good it could do.

May God bless you, my beloved friend!

I write you to death when I begin.

Ever your attached

E B B

Have you a particular meaning in saying, 'when we meet'? Delightful words! Do write me a sermon on that text—do, do! I long to see you beyond what I have any words delightful enough to say.

¹ Madeleine de Scudéry (1607–1701), the eminent blue-stocking of the 17th-century Parisian salons. Her novel *Clélie* (10 volumes, 1654–60) contains the famous 'Carte de Tendre', charting features of a sentimental Arcadia.

² An Owen Howell also wrote *Abel: written, but with great humility, in reply to Lord Byron's Cain* (1843).

³ E B B's *Poems*, published a month earlier, contained the sonnets *To George Sand: A Desire*, and *To George Sand: A Recognition*. The first begins:

'Thou large-brained woman and large-hearted man,
Self-called George Sand! whose soul, amid the lions
Of thy tumultuous senses, moans defiance
And answers roar for roar, as spirits can; . . .'

an unconscious echo, perhaps, of Jules Janin's 'an abominable creature . . . who goes howling like a lioness after the senses in which she is deficient': his description of *Lélia* in the *Athenaeum*, June 10, 1837).

[*50 Wimpole Street*]
Monday Oct 1, 1844

Ah my dearest friend,—it will never do, I fear. I know Mr. Kenyon's face so well, before I appeal to it, that I daren't do it! Besides, you see, what he might forgive, if done, he would never advise as a good thing to do,—*that* is sure and certain. As to Papa, why he knows nothing of Madame Dudevant,—and I dont feel inclined to explain her to him. Of course if I were to say . . 'she is a great genius, and no better than she should be, . . and I have read her books and want to write to her',—he would think I was mad and required his paternal restraint in all manner of ways. He has very strict ideas about women and about what they should read, (you would not think so now, from *me*!) and I heard him say once that he could not think highly of the modesty of any woman who could read Don Juan.!! He used to keep a canto of Don Juan locked up from wandering eyes,—and does the same at this time, with the Heloise—Don Juan and the Nouvelle Heloise being Hanah More and Wilberforce by the side of certain books that we wot of. At the same time, I fancy that he has a high opinion of my curiosity about books, and is content that I should be supposed to have read them, right and left, through a filter, without having done myself much harm. Only if I were to *ask* him for that copy of the Eloise locked up in the drawer, – – my dearest Miss Mitford,—he would as soon give me Prussic acid if I were thirsty!

For the rest, I think as you do, that the man-woman, called George Sand, is kind, generous, noble, . . and that she would meet *us* in a generous spirit, and *you*, in a grateful one. Well—shall we wait, and consider! You will be going to France yourself next year; and in any case, we shall have opportunities. There is no hurry about it, my dearest friend, . . and time to think, will do no harm. If we did it, need anybody know? I mean, need we subject ourselves to any stress of conventional opinion, which of course would go against us? You see, if Mr. Kenyon heard that we had done it, he is the very man to smile kindly and make the best excuses possible,—but if we put him into a chair, and asked his '*opinion*,' . . why then with all his fervour and generosity, he is the very man to have the fear of the London drawing rooms before his eyes, and to be thinking of what Mr. So and so would say in an epigram. Now isn't it so?—isn't it just so? Well—we can consider. As to Papa, if we *do* send, I wont tell him that the 'French authoress' who is to be the recipient, smokes cigars and is discontented with the decencies of life. I shall keep *that* among the 'Mysteries of Paris'.

The dangerous point in George Sand, appears to me to lie in the *irresistible* power she attributes to human passion. The *moral* of 'Jacques',—to apply such a term to the most immoral of lessons, . . is just that Love, . . guilty love, observe, . . cannot be resisted by the strongest will and most virtuous individuality. Then the disgusting tendency she has towards representing the passion of love under its physical aspect! I could not read *Lelia*, for all its eloquence. After all, however, she *is* great, and capable of noble elevations both intellectual and moral: and I should not be ashamed before the whole world, to confess my sense of this. If I had a reputation like her own, I would do it the next moment. As it is, the question is different—only I shall be always grateful to *you* my dearest indulgent friend for not being ashamed of 'going up' with me (as they say at school) and for being willing (even in a fancy) to carry my name close to yours into another country.[1] Every now and then I catch myself loving you better! . . .

[1] But cf. Miss Mitford to Mrs. Ouvry, April 7, 1852: 'So entirely do I join with you in condemning George Sand, that I point blank refused Mrs. Browning to send her my books with hers some years ago'. (*Letters of M R M*, ed. H. Chorley, Vol. II, p. 128. Bentley, 1872.)

[*50 Wimpole Street*]
Monday Dec. 14, 1844

. . . For the population doctrines, I am aware how things can be misconceived, and misrepresented. I am aware how men speak—and how women speak. The advocacy of a woman's rights, also, will at any time disprove the theory of the advocate, by a great cry of horrified women on all sides—and she has suffered from this, in addition to the other. Think of a female friend writing to me the other day from the country, . . a woman of intelligence and refinement . . 'I do not like Mrs. Jameson. She is uneasy *because women are not as wicked as men*.' Such are the thanks of our sex to such women as advocate what they call our rights—such understanding is given to their arguments—and from such observations comes my full conviction, that women have quite as many rights already, as they know how to use without wrongs. When I said lightly to Mr. Boyd one day that the difference between men and women aro[se] from the inferiority of the education of the latter, he asked me *why* the education was inferior, and so brought the argument to an end. I should not dare to write so to a common woman,—but *you*, who are a woman and man in one, will judge if it isn't a hard and difficult process for a woman to get forgiven for her strength by her grace. You who have accomplished this, know it is hard—and every woman of letters knows it is hard. Sometimes there is too much strength in proportion to the grace—and then . . O miserable woman! The abuse which even *I*, with my narrow notions of society, have heard lavished on that poor, noble Harriet Martineau, is beyond my repeating! [1] And the why! —the why! and surely we do owe, as women, our righteous indignation to such 'villanie', . . as old Chaucer would call it righteously. . .

[1] Nine letters from Harriet Martineau on the subject of her cure by mesmerism of an internal tumour appeared in the *Athenaeum* between November 23, 1844, and April 12, 1845. Earlier in her own letter, E B B had been discussing, at length (at very great length), H. M.'s 'courage in speaking the truth at the expense of the personal exposure'.

[50 Wimpole Street]
Dec 30, 1844

EVER DEAREST MISS MITFORD

Three times welcome, your letter is—and it will be delightful to me, I feel, to quarrel with you a little in return today. Because (to begin) Jules Janin's 'si non *le plus inspiré*' perfectly resumes my impressions of your Casimir.[1] I will admit him to the 'juste milieu' place, if you desire it, between Racine and Victor Hugo,—and also, if you like, according to your own phrase 'midway between the coldness of Racine and the extravagance of Victor Hugo'—but then it must be besides under a modification of mine,—viz *without the extenuating perfection of Racine's style, and without the redeeming glory of Victor Hugo's genius.* We have in him neither the perfect execution, nor the inspired conception—and the 'juste milieu' does therefore, to my mind, savour of mediocrity. . .

And then . . the '*Chimes*'! [2] I disagree with you quite in your measure of them. I think, that, with all drawbacks, . . such as the undeniable one on which you dwell, of a dislocated story and a want of artistic coherency, . . and with the still greater objection which I cannot waive in my own mind, in respect to its tendency to oppose class to class, . . it is a book full of beauty, and life, and sympathy, and true-heartedness.

I do think—I cannot help thinking *that* of it. To compare
Dickens to Balzac as a great artist would be impossible to me.
He is fathoms below *him* as an artist. Still, Dickens has that in
his writings 'which goodness bosoms ever', and which is the
dew on the amaranth,—and his genius, which is to my mind,
undeniable, puts out two warm human hands of sympathy,
(both very *clean*) to be clasped by men and women and children.
Oh—the Chimes, touched me very much! I thought it and
still think it, one of the most beautiful of his works ; and I do
not believe that *I* (whatever *you* may do) shall live to see Dickens
'put down' as a writer of genius. Now mind! I am not at
all disraught about Boz. I never sent to ask him for his
hair. I do not enter into the madness of his idolaters in any
degree—and my secret opinion has always been that he is of
that class of writers who arrive during their own lives at the
highest point of their popularity. For instance, when I think
of the most gifted men in England, I always think of Alfred
Tennyson long and long before I get down to Dickens. But
to deny his genius, as Mr. Reade does, and as you are more
than half inclined to do, my dearest friend,—*that*, I cannot if I
would! Of course, the French writers precede him in both
power and art—the Victor Hugos, and Balzacs, and George
Sands . . and peradventure the Eugene Sues : but to deny
his genius altogether and *per se*! No—I could not, and would
not.

David Sechard ends uncomfortably. You may be sure
that I did not like David's giving up his 'inventiveness' so
quietly, even for Eve's sake : and I disliked it, in fact, very
much. And then, what *is*, literally and plainly, the fate of
Lucien? Did the Spaniard adopt him in order to make a
mouchard of him—or what? It is obscure and uncomfortable.
Not that I care much for Lucien. The author teaches the
reader such contempt for him, poor 'femmelette', that the
interest fails.[3] But David, so great and noble! David, the
true man of genius of the book! *He* was worthy . . not to
prosper—(which genius does not often do in life) but to perse-
vere—which true genius does always do. When he settles
quietly among his cabbages, I feel as if I had a devil against 'le
grand Cointet', and could stab him. Also it is a fault, I think,
in the book. What do *you* think? Are not the calculations

right? Do you make them out to be wrong? In that case my
ignorance is bliss, and I have a high appreciation of it. . .

So you disbelieve the Duchess!⁴ Nay, but I do not understand why you should. Her mother was a beautiful woman,
and Napoleon, very young, and inclined evidently as his
subsequent choice proved, to admire *mature* beauty: I see no
reason to disbelieve her. Then, do you believe or disbelieve
in the tender attentions offered to her own self during his
consulship, as you read in the Memoires? Yes—when I hear
OConnell called a great man, I think Napoleon was. There
was in *him* the odour of greatness,—the poetry of it—and I
understand you when you intimate that you could have lived
or died for him. And Junot loved him—(it was one of the
qualities of his greatness that he could command love) Junot
loved him, however mad and extravagant he might have been
otherwise. The stain upon *her* was her temporising with the
Emperor of Russia and his allies when they were in Paris,—
and she *feels* it I fancy, while she writes. Have you read so
far, or not? It is a delightful book,—and surely she must have
been a fascinating woman in many ways—and I like her something the better I think, for her Greek origin. What you tell
me of the extravagance explains the poverty. Thank you.

No—I am afraid of Napoleon for a subject: and also it
would not I fancy, suit me. If I had a story of my own I
might be as wild as I liked, and I should have a chance besides
of interesting other people by it in a way I could not do with a
known story. And I dont want to have to do with masses of
men,—I should make dull work of it so. A few characters—a
simple story—and plenty of room for passion and thought—
that is what I want – – and am not likely to find easily . .
without your inspiration. . . And now tell me,—where is the
obstacle to making as interesting a story of a poem as of a
prose work—echo answers *where*. Conversations and events,
why may they not be given as rapidly and passionately and
lucidly in verse as in prose—echo answers *why*. You see
nobody is offended by my approach to the conventions of
vulgar life in 'Lady Geraldine'—and it gives me courage to
go on, and touch this real everyday life of our age, and hold
it with my two hands. I want to write a poem of a new class,
in a measure—a Don Juan, without the mockery and impurity,

. . under one aspect,—and having unity, as a work of art,—
and admitting of as much philosophical dreaming and digres-
sion (which is in fact a characteristic of the age) as I like to
use. Might it not be done, even if I could not do it?[5]—and I
think of trying at any rate. . .

Your most affectionate

E B B

[1] Casimir Delavigne (1793–1843), author of *Marino Faliero* (1829), *Louis XI*
(1832), *Enfants d'Édouard* (1833), etc.

[2] *The Chimes: A Goblin Story*, by Charles Dickens, was published as the
Christmas Book of 1844.

[3] Cf. Miss Mitford's impression of the young Robert Browning (p. xi)
with Balzac's description of Lucien de Rubempré :—

'Lucien was slender and of medium height. On seeing his feet, a man
might have been tempted to think him a girl in disguise, all the more so
in that, like many subtle, not to say crafty men, his hips were formed like
those of a woman. That indication, rarely misleading, was confirmed in
Lucien; the tendency of whose restless mind often led him, when
analyzing the actual condition of society, to the frontiers of that depravity
peculiar to diplomatists who believe that all means, however shameful,
are justified by success. . . . Lucien had read much and compared
much . . . [and] gifted with an enterprising, mobile spirit, had an
audacity which conflicted with the soft, almost feeble lines of a body
full of feminine graces.'

[4] Laure Permon (1783–1834), in childhood nicknamed '*Petite Peste*' by
Napoleon, later married one of his generals, Junot, who became the Duc
d'Abrantès. The *Mémoires de Madame La Duchesse d'Abrantès* appeared 1831–34;
and *Mémoires sur la restauration*, 1836–37.

[5] It could be done. It appeared in 1856. It was called *Aurora Leigh*, and
it went into twenty editions.

[50 Wimpole Street]
Jan. 15,[1] [?] 1845

Well, my dearest friend—it shall be Charles de Bernard's
soul instead, 'an it please you'. Indeed it remains doubtful
whether that Paul who is *not* the apostle,[2] has a soul of any
kind, even 'so much as to swear by' . . . Do you find him 'un
peu fort' as to nastiness—he who is nasty 'for fun', just as an
ill bred schoolboy is? Tell me. You know you bore him
wonderfully at first. You did not bear Balzac—you did not
bear George Sand—the 'taint' of both stank in your nostrils.
But Paul de Kock, you forgave, for his broad laughter,—you

thought him a capital fellow—you know you did !—you even
tried to get up a moral scheme for his grisettes, and thought he
might be translated (with a very little *trans*) into excellent
moral reading for 'prude Angleterre' . . . Paul is the writer
of farce, . . broad farce . . and for impulsive gaiety, he has
not his peer. I think the more of him just now, because they
sent me, a few days since, by a mistake for another work, from
the library, 'Mon ami Piffard', which is not his best work, and
yet set me laughing most cordially. It's a farce rolled out into
the narrative form,—neither more nor less. A little nasty of
course, to mark, not exactly the *hoof* of Paul, but his snout.
But what particularly struck me, in this, as in other works of
the same writer, was the impulse, the cant-help-myself joyous-
ness of the book—he does not smile in it, nor laugh in it—he
roars. And then, (tell me the reason, for I dont know) *I*, who
hate to hear the Irish Lever 'roar like a sucking dove' innocently, . . I, who get a headache with all that smell of punch
and rattling of glasses in Lever, can get through certain parts
of Paul who is not the apostle, most wonderfully well. After
all, he is less *jovial* than Lever and more *gay* – – or I fancy so.
I hope it isn't the indecency which I take to so kindly in him,—
although 'by your smiling, you may seem to say so'. I wish
you would tell me what you think— for really and truly I want
to know.

My dearest friend, of all confiding persons in the world
(and I have a theory, that confiding persons are less liable to
be deceived than all other persons) you are the most unhappy.[3]
Stony hearts must the people have, to be proof to your kindness
and trust, and repay you *so* ! This gardener ! And *you*, on the
point, you say, of coming, or thinking of coming, to London
for several weeks ! And we are all to suffer for this abominable
gardener—you, first, in your goods—*I* next and not least in
my joys ! . . .

Yes—indeed and indeed, I do think that you are severe on
poor Miss Martineau. She may have acted inexpediently and
imprudently,—but her high intentions in doing so, do appear
to me above these suspicions. She may love notoriety—I have
no personal means of knowing whether she loves it or not.
But I do not see the proof of such a love in this act, nor in any
previous act of her life which ever came to my knowledge.

Her *love of truth* is proverbial among her friends, and even among such as are averse from her present views. One friend says . . 'I always was of opinion that Harriet Martineau was at once the most veracious and the most credulous person of my acquaintance', . . and a chorus takes up the chaunt. . .

I mean to buy Delavigne—but as to ever thinking him equal as a lyric poet to Lamartine, I promise you I never will do it. Berenger I admire as much as you can—and Victor Hugo, more.

But . . for Mr. Chorley . . it was only an exchange of letters . . or scarcely more,[4]—and although I went so far as to say that I should always be glad to hear from him, I could not very well ask him for the comedy.[5] He will send it if he wishes me to see it—and if not, . . I do *not* like to ask for it.

And I have had two delightful letters from Mr. Browning— (did I tell you?) and I (you know) believe in Mr. Browning as a man of genius and an original poet, worth just fifty of the Delavignes.

Oh—I do like to teaze you a very little bit.

And I go on . . and on! I sometimes mean to write briefly to you and begin with somebody else, but I never can *end*, so as to *begin*. I have a multitude of things to say to you now—now after all this writing.

May God bless you, my dearest friend! For your two delightful letters, thanks upon thanks! My letters never can deserve them except by being *responsive*—and I abjure your 'soliloquies'.

Your ever affectionate

E B B

---

[1] The second figure is blurred : it is possible that this date is January 16.

[2] Paul de Kock (1794–1871), described by Jules Janin (*Athenaeum*, June 10, 1837) as 'one of those inexhaustible treasuries of invention which send out as many romances as the fall of Niagara flings up wreaths of foam'. *Mon Ami Piffard* appeared in 1844.

[3] Miss Mitford had been plundered by 'a thieving gardener'.

[4] At the end of 1844, anticipating Robert Browning in this respect, Chorley had written to E B B to thank her for her *Poems* which had 'restored to him the impulses of his youth', etc. She wrote to him again on January 3, 1845, and also on January 7. Three days later, on January 10, Robert Browning sent his first letter to Wimpole Street, followed by a second on January 13.

[5] Chorley's first play, *Old Love and New Fortune*, a comedy in blank verse, was 'produced successfully' at the Surrey Theatre on February 18, 1850.

[*50 Wimpole Street*]
Wednesday Feb. 1845

What I was going to say of men, or rather of a man,—was just this of Mr. Hunter. It might be amusing if it were not so vexatious, to hear him talk as he does – – talk *at* you (viz at me) as he does. Ever since my last book has brought me a little more before the public, I can do or say or wish to do and say, nothing right with him—and on, on, he talks epigrams about the sin and shame of those divine angels, called women, daring to tread in the dust of a multitude, when they ought to be minding their clouds. All this, not a bit in joke—but gravely and bitterly. Every new review he sees, there is a burst of indignation—and the League-motion, obliquely entertained as it was, wrapt me in a whirlwind.[1] You know . . and I tell him, . . the feeling is all to be analyzed into contempt of the sex. It is just that, and no less. For a woman to hang down her head like a lily through life, and 'die of a rose in aromatic pain' at her death, – – to sit or lounge as in a Book of beauty, and be 'defended' by the strong and mighty thinkers on all sides of her, – – this he thinks, is her destiny and glory. It is not the pudding-making and stocking-darning theory—it is more graceful and picturesque. But the *significance* is precisely the same,—and the absurdity a hundred times over, greater. Who makes my pudding, is useful to me,—but who looks languishing in a Book of Beauty, is good for nothing *so far*.

Angry as all this makes me, I am *not*, as you are perhaps aware, a very strong partizan of the Rights-of-woman-side of the argument—at least I have not been, since I was twelve years old. I believe that, considering men and women in the mass, there *is* an *inequality* of intellect, and that it is proved by the very state of things of which gifted women complain; and more than proved by the manner in which their complaint is received by their own sisterhood. At the same time, the argument used by men in this relation, should go no farther than the fact,—and it is cruel and odious to see the yearning they have, not to meet the weakness of women with their manly protection, but to exaggerate that weakness, in order to parade their protection. I know that women (many of them) encourage this tendency by parading their weakness—and it is detestable to my eyes, in an equal degree, on both sides of sex. . .

¹ E B B had been asked by a Leeds Committee to write a poem attacking the Corn Laws. The strong disapproval of her family forced her, much against her own inclination, to refuse.

[*50 Wimpole Street*]
March 5, 1845

Ever dearest friend   It is delightful to know (so far) that you have not paid the cost in your health on all the great, great pleasure you vouchsafed to me on monday.   I have seen nobody since, and have been thinking over and over the talk we had . ., which left so much to be said that I am provoked as usual.   But the cold!   It over-rides me—and not even your 'sweet influences' could set me free altogether from a sense of treason in the air which is very oppressive to the spirits.   When we are imparadised at Hyeres, it will be otherwise—wont it?   What a dream!   It is an agreement too (has been since last year) that when I go up the Rhine, Mr. Kenyon will go too—so that, I shall have patron saints the whole way of it.   And in the meantime, I am delighted that you got home safely, and had a bright welcome from Jane,¹—it is worth so much!—and that you consider yourself under a vow to come here for good and *something*, about April, . . if not earlier. Oh!—I assure you, I lean with emphasis on the '*if not*'.   And when you come we shall say all manner of things which were 'skipped' on the 'Blessed Monday', and fill up every possible hiatus.   That you did not materially suffer by your kindness, your dear kindness, of keeping faith with me through the rain and the headache, is a sort of omen for good in the future. Yet you shall not do so again.   I mean, my dear dearest Miss Mitford, you shall not *again* run such risks for me,—because you see if you *had* suffered, I might have been savage enough, in my disconsolation, to reproach you for the very kindness,— and to abuse it as a naughtiness and a foolishness.   So, recollect! —no vow is to hold for the future, between you and me, in the face of a headache.   Your health is a better thing in my eyes than your presence,—and I beg you to remember it loyally.

While I write, comes a note from dear Mr. Kenyon, and among other things in it, is a little bad news. I have no right I suppose to call it bad news—and perhaps as Mr. Hunter says, I am spoilt. But, repeats Mr. Kenyon from Moxon, . . '*The book has somewhat relented in sale, though six copies had been sold the day before*'. So now, suppose after all, Mr. Moxon was romancing when he talked of the second edition? I tell you the whole argument, you see,—and let you see that I am a little nervous about the 'relenting'. Well!—there's Balzac to go back to—and I am in the midst of 'La Femme Superieure'. The truth of this work and the subtlety and deepness of the *life* in it . . for I will not call it portraiture, . . are wonderful but certainly it justifies the attribute of heaviness and slowness we talked of the other day. Also your observation on the *details of dress*, came home to me with my own counter-thought in rebound—and it does appear to me more and more, that he does not stoop to these things from attaching too much importance to them, (bearded man as he may be!—) nor as a costume-writer with scenic intentions,—but from seeing in them, with that subtle power of apprehension and combination peculiar to him, the outward expression and sacramental sign of the inward man. Be sure, that for Balzac, a man's soul has a lineament in his gilet. As my Greeks read the will of their gods in the viscera of animals, so does he take the measure of a piece of human nature, 'all round his hat', and in the pantaloons. At any rate his treatment of these outsides comes to my mind with quite a different degree of significance, to the same thing in the hands of other writers,—of Scott, for instance —or lower down, of James,[2] who has vexed me twenty times with his costume-minuteness. Do you not think so? Is not the effect on the mind of the reader absolutely different?— which difference proves a peculiarity in the writer's intention. Now just look at the catalogue raisonné of the Rabourdin clerks—and grant the wonderfulness of the characteristic emphasis which comes in the dress. We do not so much see the men more for it—we *know* them better for it! Then I have the 'Ecole des Journalistes',[3] and shall have deep interest in it, I know. Oh, my dearest Miss Mitford, . . I go back in my thoughts from all this to *you*. I cannot help thinking of you! How great is your affectionateness—and how dear to me!

How unworthy I am of half of it, except by loving you!
May God bless you. It comes to that,—and silence.

Your ever attached

E B B—

¹ Jane was Miss Mitford's maid.
² G. P. R. James (1801–60), an industrious imitator of Scott, who wrote over a hundred novels.
³ *L'École des journalistes* (1839), a comedy by Madame de Girardin, *née* Delphine Gay (1804–55). On January 21, 1827, Goethe showed Eckermann 'a volume of New French poems, by Mademoiselle Gay, and spoke of them with great praise'. (*Conversations*, p. 185.)

[50 Wimpole Street]

March 18 1845

Ever dearest friend—How my love for you has been pulling at my sleeve these two days, to write . . and write! But I have been so low, and weary, and tired of life. It is as much as I can do to stand up against this bitter wind, without smoothing down my petticoats! Still—I am not ill in the strong sense . . mind! I am weak—my heart is disordered,— and I feel all day long as if I were lying on the edge of a fainting fit—do you know what *that* is? Yesterday, I went to bed at four oclock—and even the ninth volume of the 'Juif'¹ would not animate me as it should.

And now . . in à proposity be it spoken—your 'Ecole des Journalistes' disappointed me. That is—you did not praise it as a drama,—but it really was twenty times worse than I expected. Jules Janin may wind his compliments as he will and can, but there is nothing in that work to hold them—it is insufferably feeble and empty—a complete void. But the letters ² did interest me, although you know, I differ from you and take the Jules side of the argument, – – I think him right, and Mdme Girardin and her advocate wrong—and I think also that he is nobly right and that she is ignobly wrong. When she libels the journalistes she dishonours all the great writers, her contemporaries, who because they are not *journalistes only*, who because their genius is essentially of a nature to outgrow the temporary medium, have not the less on that account made use of it, and are not the less journalists *certainly*. In every profession there will be to a certain extent, a *populace*— but it is precisely the populace of it which does not fairly represent it. Altogether I have kept fast to Jules, and I commend him—except indeed where he proves himself mortal by his disrespect to Balzac. How is it possible that Jules Janin can in his secret soul depreciate Balzac,—can it be possible? If he had recognized the power, and then blamed him for the sin of Mdme de Girardin, I should have applauded still. You know that I *do* attribute to Balzac, great writer as he is, a want of patience and sympathy towards his brethren in letters,—and thus I could hear this attributed to him by another, without wincing. But to deny his genius in the production of the *Illusions perdues*, is past bearing, and beyond wondering at! What can Jules mean by it?

Do you know 'Le Macon' by Michel Raymond? [3] It is not as vivid as most of these books from France,—nor as passionate,—but it is interesting as a picture of the life of the people in Paris and I have read it with pleasure. Oh yes—to be sure the French conception of English manners is something marvellous. I think it is in a novel of Madme Bodin,[4] where the daughter of an English nobleman marries the butler of a neighbouring establishment, who having made up a little money 'at service' and inherited some land in Ireland, instantly becomes *Sir Ralph* as a matter of course, and is visited by the whole aristocracy. One laughs at first at these absurdities, but at last it grows to be too much idiocy for even laughing at.

Ah—Mr. Chorley. But you know, I cannot exchange him quite for Mr. Browning. Mr. Browning and I have grown to be devoted friends I assure you—and he writes me letters praying to be let in, quite heart-moving and irresistible. In the summer I must see him—and Mr. Chorley too. I shall like to see *both*. And then for Hyères and everybody!

You see what Mr. Chorley says of Paracelsus? You see it is not merely a dream of mine!—he is full of genius.

And then he writes letters to me with Attic contractions, saying he '*loves*' me. Who can resist *that*?

But do not talk of it if you please, although it is all in the uttermost innocence, . . as testifies the signature

of your most affectionate

E B B

---

[1] *Le Juif errant*, by Sue.
[2] *Lettres parisiennes de Mme É. de Girardin* (1843). Jules Janin, *Revue de Paris*,

Vol. 21, pp. 233-62 : an account, by Janin, of Mme de Girardin's reading aloud of her comedy to French authors and journalists, with letters, pro and con, inspired by the occasion.

³ *Le Maçon* (1828), by Michel Raymond, was written in collaboration by Raymond Bruker and Michel Masson.

⁴ *Scènes de la vie anglaise* (1836), by Mme Camille Bodin (Jenny Bastide) and Lord Ellis.

[*50 Wimpole Street*]
Monday—April. 1845

My dearest friend, I agree with you that 'Le Beau Pere' ¹ is not equal to the 'Homme serieux', which is admirable and the writer an artist. But this M. Charles Bernard, man or woman, (and I lean with you to the pantaloons) is a surface writer, a painter of manners,—and I class him far below George Sand and Balzac who go deeper. It is pure comedy as you say, but it is not full humanity. And then, if he is not gross in his tendencies, he is highly immoral to my mind all the same,—not so much on the ground of chastity as on other grounds. His men and women with whom he would most favorably impress you, lie and cheat all round, as if they did it in pure innocence. He is a very wordly writer, to my mind,—and really I like George Sand's wickedness better,—it is of a higher order. . .

And now I must beg you to order and read 'Le rouge et le noir' by a M. de Stendhal . . a 'nom de guerre' I fancy. I wish I knew the names of any other books written by him. This, which I should not dare to name to a person in the world except you, so dark and deep is the colouring, is very striking and powerful and full of deep significance. I beg you to read it as soon as possible. Balzac could scarcely put out a stronger hand. It is, as to simple power, a first-class book—according to my impression,—though painful and noxious in many ways. But it is a book for you to read at all risks—you must certainly read it for the power's sake. It has ridden me like an incubus for several days.

Yes, my dearest friend—we shall find no where on the earth, I believe, the climate of Paradise ; not even at Hyères. In Mdme Charles Reybaud's ² 'Deux á deux', which interested me more than any book of hers I have read since, . . (I withdraw my praise of her,—she is a weak commonplace writer, I think,) there was some good praise of Hyères and the orange trees. But the skies are fair in no place always, except in books—and muskitoes and simooms are disagreeable things. The truth of the matter lies in this nutshell, – – that a perfect climate is to be found nowhere—and a climate better than the English, everywhere! By the way, I have just heard of my uncle Hedley's having taken apartments in Paris for *four years* from this summer. But he comes to England in May or June with all his family for a few months, and is to set down the children at Brighton to be properly baked, while the elders of the house come to London or go elsewhere.

Oh, your pedlar poetess! [3]—*that* is a curious variety of the species, to be sure!—and '*as* your fellow-poetess'—oh the modesty of one's fellow-creatures! The asking for five shillings was nothing to the adjuration! Talking of poetesses I had the kindest of notes this morning from Mrs. Sigourney on the subject of my poems,—quite spontaneous and unexpected— and also a letter from Mr. Lowell of Massachusetts, the poet, who is married, he says, 'after a betrothal of five years' and is very sentimental in consequence. He seems to have married a supernatural woman without a fault in the world. As to Mr. Browning, I forgot to tell you when I wrote last, that I do not believe a word of the 'silver forkism' you attribute to him. He has too much genius for it. Men of high imagination never subject themselves to the conventions of society,—though men of high reason often do. He lives in the world, but loathes it, he says.[4] Then, with all his darknesses and charades of light, he is a very masculine writer and thinker, and as remote as possible from Balzac's type of the *femmelette*, Lucien de Rubempré. . .

Flush was washed (for the first time for months) the other day,—and ever since, he has been in a right reverend curl all over. Never was anything so pretty! I lose my hand in his neck when I lay it there—it looks as if a bishop or a judge had given him the wig of lordship, to make a tippet of. In fact, although people are impertinent enough to call him *fat*, he appears to me just now at his prime of fattness. Certainly I never saw him so pretty before. And that makes me sigh— because you are not here to see him.

But you *will* come. And I hope you received the oysters—and I am going to send you some shaddocks as a chaperon to Mr. Horne's little book. May God bless you always! Do write.

In true affection your

E B B.

¹ A novel by Charles de Bernard, published in 1845.

² Madame Charles Reybaud (1802–71). *Deux à deux* appeared in 1837.

³ 'I have had a wandering poetess here to-day', wrote Miss Mitford to E B B on April 10, 1845. 'She and her mother are driving about the land in a pony-chaise, selling for five shillings, books typographically worth about eightpence—poetically, good for nothing. The mamma asks one to patronize her daughter—one's "fellow-poetess"—and wont go till she has got the money.' (L'Estrange, Vol. III, p. 197.)

⁴ 'For me, I always hated it—have put up with it these six or seven years past, lest by foregoing it I should let some unknown good escape me, in the true time of it, and only discover my fault when too late; and now that I have done most of what is to be done, *any* lodge in a garden of cucumbers for me!' (*Love Letters*, March 12, 1845, Vol. I, p. 41.)

[50 Wimpole Street]
Friday May 2, 1845

. . . The best good news I have to tell you, is the safe arrival of my Ægyptian brothers,—Storm and Henry, . . who after a voyage of nearly four months, . . head winds all the way . . are now in Sandgate Creek, keeping quarantine for the plague. Very absurd,—is it not?—and especially, . . when they let the pilots go out and in as they please? My poor brothers are locked up in a hulk for three or four days of purification, in as ill a humour as possible. I fancy that Stormie has had enough of a ship-life, at last. They were sailing round and round in the Mediterranean between two and three months till they had eaten and drunken all their bread and water, and in a state of famine and drought put in at Carthagena for a little refreshment. Then again, came the spinning round and round towards home—they reached the forelands nearly, . . on Kent, . . and had to put back to Plymouth, at the risk of being driven again into the Atlantic. Adverse winds—*head* winds . . all the way, implacably. My gazelle (did I tell you that they were bringing me a gazelle?) broke its leg in the cabin, and so died! Resolute (did I tell

you that they took the great German dog with them?) bore
up well and faithfully, though he grew thin during the famine.
And Papa's cargo is not injured, to signify. Also they are in
good spirits and full of jests upon their misfortunes——it is only
the hulk that is *de trop*. The quarantine is the drop of overflow,
and throws them into a fit of misanthropy against that part of
human nature which enters into the constitution of Boards of
trade. . .

Monday [*May 26, 1845*]

. . . Ah—Mr. Haydon! His letter made me more than
smile. Isn't it excellent, the indignation at the 'great fact' of
a poet who has 'thoughts too deep for tears', condescending
to put on another man's 'inexpressibles'? [1] It quite tickled
my fancy . . to use the common phrase. Also, it was not
unamusing to know that He of the Lakes did really come plump
down on both his knees before our queen's fair majesty, and
that a lordling or two were found ready to pick him up. I
never heard that particular. And now only fancy what harm
Mr. Haydon does himself by talking after this fashion at
Mr. Serjt. Talfourd's and elsewhere—think how he *kills* himself
by it! And after all, it isn't consistent doctrine for a man who
talks of the 'divine right' by the hour—now, is it?

I am writing to you in a pre-occupied mood today, my very
dear friend,—for my aunt Hedley is to be here tomorrow or
the next day,—and I *dread it through all my being. I shall see
everything over again,—and feel it.* I love her,—but would give . .
oh, so much! - - to be able to defer this meeting. I am a
coward, you see—and rankly[?] so. I have a dread of mental
pain, which grows and grows in me, to my own consciousness—
and really I fancy sometimes that I could be content to be
separated from all life and its emotions, so as to avoid the pang
of all. This is morbid—but then, I am morbid altogether—
and this east wind has shaken me, and 'jangled' my nerves—
and this expectation about the Hedleys, which has been on the
hinge for several weeks now, creaks at the least breath. Oh—I
shall be better after I have seen her, you know! It is nonsense
—foolishness . . weakness, at best.

Mr. Kenyon has not returned yet,—but will, I suppose, at the end of this week, or the beginning of next – – and oh!—did I tell you in my last letter that I had seen lately (*now I beseech you to keep my counsel and not tell Mr. Horne—and not tell Mr. Chorley*!) Mr. Browning? He said in his courtesy more, in the way of request, than the thing was worth,—and so I received him here one morning, and liked him much. Younger looking than I had expected—looking younger than he *is*, of course— with natural and not ungraceful manners,—and full of his art, which he is destined, I believe, so worthily to sustain. He is kind enough to promise to read my new Prometheus [2] for me,—and we shall be good friends I hope. You and I differ about his genius,—and also on the dignities of pen and inkishness in general—but a poet is something after all, ... *even if* (to quote from Mr. Haydon's idea of the profoundest degradation) in another man's inexpressibles! Alfred Tennyson is in London, or has been lately,—and likes it beyond all places, I understand—his soul rejoicing in Polka and Cellarius—and in going home to smoke,—and otherwise professing an intention of writing no more, because he has written all he has to say. Do you like *that*? No—no—no!—*I* do not like it for one—I even like it so little, do you know, that I feel quite sorry to have told you.

Thank you, thank you, for letting me see the pencilled lines by poor Clare! [3] How strangely melancholy, that combination is—of mental gifts and mental privations! Poor Clare! . . .

Well—I must end here! I love and think of you my dear, dear friend!

Pray for your

ever affectionate

E B B.

You know as to seeing Mr. Horne an older friend, why he has never asked—since he 'had no time'. Dont tell anybody.

[1] Wordsworth attended the Queen's ball on April 25, 1845. The new Laureate 'went to court in Rogers's clothes, buckles and stockings, and wore Davy's sword. Moxon had hard work to make the dress fit. It was a squeeze, but by pulling and hauling they got him in.' (*Life of B. R. Haydon*, ed. Tom Taylor, Vol. III, pp. 305-6. Longmans, 1853.)

[2] *Prometheus Bound*, in EBB's translation, was first published in 1833. The new version appeared with *Poems* of 1850.

³ John Clare (1793–1864), a 'Northamptonshire Peasant'; so labelled in his first publication, *Poems descriptive of Rural Life and Scenery* (1820). Granted an annuity of forty-five pounds a year, he was periodically invited to dine in the servants' hall of some eminent patron's house. After 1835, when *The Rural Muse* appeared, his mind gave way, and he spent his last years in an asylum for the insane at Northamptonshire.

[*50 Wimpole Street*]
Wednesday [*June 4, 1845*]

EVER DEAREST MISS MITFORD,

. . . I had heard nothing of the Tennyson marriage, and if he has found a princess dowered with 'fine gold', under 'a silken coverlid', . . why so much the better,—at least so I hope! ¹ She must condescend to the smoke,—and perhaps to the polka—but the smoke is said to be so essentially Tennysonian that he couldn't be supposed to rhyme without it. As to my friend Mr. Browning, you made me smile a little at your anxiety about the influence of this cloud-compelling Jupiter among my clouds. You seem to think that, between us, reasonable people have no chance of ever seeing the sun! Well—I will take care, as you tell me! And then you know I have other faults *besides* the fault of obscurity – – (and Mrs. Jameson had the boldness to tell me to my face the other day that she did not think me obscure!!) and Mr. Browning may show me how to correct *these* . . seeing that I recognise him for a master in art, 'after his kind', however to your astonishment. And for my 'Prometheus', if my former attempt was anything but a disgrace, as a poetical rendering of Aeschylus, and if my present one is not in some degree worthier, . . (for I do not praise it, mind) then, I am ignorant of Aeschylus, and of myself, and of the first elements of poetry as an art, . . and 'grope as the blind' . . .

Yes—I did not suppose Mr. Browning to be younger,— and only observed that he did not look older, if so old as I expected—which comes, as you say, of the slightness of form and figure. You are a little wrong, I believe, in fancying that his personal friends only hold him in estimation as a poet. His poems pay their way . . which is something in these beggarly days ²—and my brother hears him talked of among the lawyers . . far on the outside of Mr. Serjt. Talfourd—and then,

I really must remind you, dear friend of mine, that Pippa Passes made an impression on yourself. As to Mr. Horne he has never seen nor thought of asking to see MS from my hand. He is too much occupied for such misdoings. Have you heard from him?—and has a note from the viola accosted the ear of your Hayward Grace? [3] I expect him to go down in a flash of lightning one of these days, with a heart ready blown to offer in his right hand, and the left hand extended for your mediation.

You will see that I am not so depressed, without my saying it—and indeed the meeting with Mrs. Hedley is over, . . and I was able to cry well and be quiet afterwards, . . and now I shall enjoy her presence and society. The worst of me is, just now, that I have left off sleeping, 'for the nonce' . . and without Frederic Soulié's expedient of sowing up my eyelids, I really cant *see* where it's to end.[4] Oh—but *that* is jest—and you are not to mind it! I have not murdered sleep . . and shall be in a deep doze before long. There's no need for doubting. And in other ways I am growing better and stronger as the sun shines, and walked into Papa's room yesterday, and shall try to get out in the carriage perhaps before the century ends, . . and people begin to say that I look better. From Mr. Kenyon I heard the other day, and he returns about the sixth. And the Hedleys are at St. James's Hotel for three weeks or a month,—so that I talk of my 'visitors'. No— Lizzie is a Barrett, the daughter of a cousin of Papa's—and as her father is in the West Indies and her mother, insane, . . poor little creature, she is next to an orphan, . . and we are not likely to lose her.

That dreadful, dreadful event at Raggetts's—did you read of it? [5] It was brought near to us by the body of the unhappy Mrs. Round being carried to her sister's house, Mrs. Green Wilkinson's . . our opposite neighbour, – – in a shell three days ago—just the poor, charred, mutilation of a woman, . . they say . . 'very little of her', . . to quote the ghastly naked phrase, . . and the hands not to be known from that black mummied hand three thousand years old, which my brothers brought from the sepulchre of Ægyptian queens, and which I refused to look at a fortnight since! Yet on the evening of the morning when the shell brought these poor 'remains' to the door opposite, a box remained engaged at the Opera in her name! What an antithises, altogether! And isn't it dreadful to consider what the poor daughter must feel now, – – she in her distraction, having actually left her mother on the stairs—mad through terror, I suppose—but what a memory to have to live with!—that desertion! Better that she had died, a thousand times, than live with such a recollection!

Not a word more. Love me my beloved friend! And write and say if I can do anything, supply you with anything gowns . . collars, etc.—now do! Am I not your own affectionate

Ba?

1 Alfred Tennyson's engagement to Emily Sellwood, recognized by her family in 1838, was broken off, on the grounds of Alfred's financial instability, in 1840. The marriage did not take place until June 13, 1850.

2 *Strafford* excluded, the cost of publication of all Robert Browning's work, from *Paracelsus* to the final 'Bells and Pomegranates', No. VIII, was borne by his father.

3 R. H. Horne had been travelling in Germany with Abraham Hayward and his daughter. Hayward (1801–84) was the translator of Goethe's *Faust*.

4 Robert Browning wrote his 'intemperate' letter, containing a proposal of marriage on May 23, 1845. After receiving it, E B B later confessed, 'I could not sleep night after night,—could not,—and my fear was at nights, lest the feverishness should make me talk deliriously and tell the secret aloud'. (*Love Letters*, Vol. II, p. 164.)

5 On May 27, 1845, Raggett's Hotel in Dover Street was burnt down. The fire started in the room of a guest who had left it to get 'iced liquorice water'. It was discovered by a police constable, who sprang his rattle : but through the inefficiency of the man in charge of the escape ladders, four people lost their lives. Mrs. Round was the wife of the hon. member for Essex.

[50 Wimpole Street]
Saturday morning [June 21, 1845]

It makes my heart leap my beloved friend to think of you as coming so soon. Would it be quite the same thing if you were to come instead on *thursday*—by the way? Answer freely—only *at once*.1 And, to keep you in countenance, here am I going to speak out freely in a matter for which perhaps you will reprehend me. But I appeal to your known goodness and indulgence my dear dear friend, and open my heart to you, and entreat you (taking courage from the imagination of your smile) to *forgive me if I do not see Mr. Chorley*—though of course *you* shall see him, and he is as welcome as the air to this house. Now here is my case. I am weak and morbid—be it so!—I confess fully . . if you give me your absolution afterwards and leave me to the free enjoyment of my favorite sins. But it is not all weakness and morbidness—and to prove it—listen to me!

Here is the summer, and for the last fortnight or longer (except for the want of sleep) I have been growing and growing just like the trees—it is miraculous, the feeling of sprouting life in me and out of me—and now I begin to sleep again and to look altogether like another person. But to get on and make progress such as I hope to make this summer, I *must* be quiet—and if you did but know the effect of seeing one person, or of talking to people I am accustomed to see, on the whole night's rest after, you would say as all my medical advisers have always said—that '*repose was my life*'. Well then—just now is the turning point of the summer,—and besides I am in the most peculiar circumstances you can fancy . . and persecuted on all sides, beyond your fancy, by letters and messages, and entreaties in each and all, of people who want to come in 'for one moment'. As a statistical fact I will just mention to you that *forty* of our relatives are at this time in London,—everyone of them with an especial claim in his or her right hand—and male cousins (to boot) constantly in this house, and never seeing me! Add to these my friends—infinitely more zealous, to do them justice—and the whole flock of sighing Aramintas! *Now a line must be drawn*—or my sepulchre must be prepared—do you not see the necessity? I confided to you *as a secret and in my trust in you*—that I had indeed . . after a struggle . . seen Mr. Browning—but then, writing about poetry and criticism, in a correspondence we had, had made us personal friends, in a manner, before he came—and I honour his genius and could not refuse a request he thought it worth while to press so kindly on me . . when the circumstance of his *living seven miles out of London* made him exceptional, in itself,—and when he promised, in all faith, that the fact of his having seen me should never escape his lips. Mr. Kenyon too, whose friend he is, will not betray it—and *you* will not I know—but, you know, it would be too ludicrous to administer such qualifying oaths of secrecy to one's visitors all round,—and

I neither could nor would do such a thing. I see the ridiculous side of it too quickly—if there were nothing else. No. And thus, altogether, you will take pity on me and let me draw my line just now as I feel myself forced!—and my dear friend, I must confide to you besides that a peculiar reason why, just now, I object to receiving Mr. Chorley, (whom, for the rest, I honour for many reasons and to whose acquaintance I look forward with hope for another brighter day,) is, . . that if Mr. Horne were ever to know of my having given a welcome to his critic before I had done so to *him*, he would think it (not unnaturally) a mark of extreme unkindness on my part. You know I am grateful with reason to Mr. Horne—he is my friend . . and I owe him my regard. Well—I *could not*, comfortably to my own consciousness, receive Mr. Chorley without receiving him—and really and really I am not equal to receiving all these men (if I quite liked it otherwise) in this room, on this sofa—the penalty being, after every interview, that I never can sleep in the night. Think a little of all this— and smooth those massive brows of yours my dear indulgent friend—and remember besides (what is truth) that to have room and strength for all the joy you bring me for so many hours of the day, it is a physical necessity for me to see *only* *you* that day . . unless it should be Mr. Kenyon who is at once nobody and everybody. And now be kind, and get me off just for the present with your Mr. Chorley . . will you . . dear dearest friend? . . .

I shall send off this letter . . that you may receive it as early as possible. May God bless you—and do let me hear on monday morning, whether you can come on *thursday* next. Praise me for not falling into wailing and gnashing of teeth because you come for 'a few hours' instead of abiding by the bond. But I was half prepared for a temporary disappointment of the kind—and you wont let it be a final one—and then I cannot bear to teaze you when your goodness brings you to me at all.

Ever dearest Miss Mitford's
gratefully affectionate
E B B

Poor Catiline is dead of sudden illness. The bloodhound you remember. It makes us all melancholy.

[1] EBB to RB, June 24: 'Miss Mitford talked of spending Wednesday with me—and I have put it off to Thursday :—and if you should hear from Mr. Chorley that he is coming to see *her and me together on any day*, do understand that it was entirely her proposition and not mine . . .' (*Love Letters*, Vol. I, p. 107.)

[50 Wimpole Street]
Thursday [July 10, 1845]

EVER DEAREST KINDEST MISS MITFORD,

I write to throw at your feet a burden of thanks and praises from many whom you made happy and grateful yesterday. My brother Alfred said to me expressively . . 'Miss Mitford won every heart of us' – – and *that's* true—for he does not often fall or rise into enthusiasms. How kind of you,—how good of you—how I thank you! Only all picnics are spoilt to the general mind in comparison, from this time forth for ever—nothing after Whiteknights and your garden, being found commonly dreamable. Everybody came home in a sort of 'tipsy jollity' and a full bloom of recollection—and *you* were in each—your name, and that of your cottage and your colossal strawberries in proportion to the joys. And to show that it wasn't all a dream, here are only the flowers!

Will you ask your gardener, by the way, to look in the garden for a pin of one of my brothers, . . a coral pin, I think . . which, planted there, is not likely to sprout up into a coral grove. And also will you understand that as soon as we can get an order for the post, we will send you our debt about the tickets. Acquit us in the meantime of dishonesty prepense— just as I do your lady of the Browning traditions, of intentional exaggeration—though . . while I receive part of the gossip into belief, I assuredly, like a second Jove, 'dispense the rest in empty air'. Do you think that a man can want money, who is travelling . . now to the east, now to Russia [1] . . spending four years in Italy—(for if it is true that he was an attaché when under age, *that* was years ago) since from 1836 to 40, he was abroad, and again last year, and would be in the east now, he says, except for his anxiety about his mother's health.[2] Also he reproaches other poets for that very thing of which his friend accuses him—a want of masculine resolve to work like common men, when they want money like them.

'How can work do dishonor to any man?' he has said—'and what is there in poetry to disqualify one from ordinary duties.' So that the charge is altogether unlike and contrary to the nature of the man, which is eminently masculine and down-right—strikingly so I think! Not an inch of gold lace or broidery in what Chaucer would call the 'full yerde long'. So I quite, quite disbelieve. You know my dearest candid friend, its quite possible to be a 'visitor and family friend', without knowing very accurately, and without *talking* very accurately. His family may regret perhaps that he does not, by means of his talents, climb the woolsack rather than Parnassus Hill—*that* sort of regret is possible enough!—but I feel quite confident that if his position had required him to work, he is the last man under sun to shrink from it—I would throw down my silken gauntlet to maintain that point. That your informant *can* be wrong, the tradition about the *age* proves—for here's a fact—Paracelsus was published in 1835—and *not* the first work of its author. Now it was well understood that Paracelsus was the production of a young man several years above twenty. No—you were more right at first, be sure. And in fact, if Paracelsus was produced at twenty, with all that curious learning and profound thinking, it is the most wonderful work produced by man—*that*, I should say. But no—he was young—only not quite so young as that, I believe—in fact, I am con-fident. And I remember facts enough to justify much con-fidence. It is true that Mr. Browning senior, is full of refine-ment, book-refinement,—without the son's genius. He (the father) was at school with Mr. Kenyon. The sister is con-siderably younger than her brother,—'by many years', he has told me ³—and I hear that *she* is something more than a girl. So you see! Mind you dont talk of my mysteries of Eleusis before Mr. Horne when he comes—or indeed before *any other person*—for, if you do, my beloved friend, you will bring me to bane. Also I *trust to you*—heart to heart . . and gossip to gossip. . .

I have been talking, and *am* so tired that I begin to feel for *you*! Write to me—will you?

I am your ever affectionate

Ba—

Shall it be?

251

Talking of Eleusinian mysteries, did you understand that the escapade yesterday was unknown to the High priest here?—to Papa, I mean? Very wrong! Yes—*that* is true. *You must not mention it*! A little over-strictness sometimes *drives* into temptation.

¹ Browning was in Russia with Chevalier George de Benkhausen, the Russian consul general, for about three months, in the spring of 1834.

² Browning paid his first visit to Italy in the summer of 1838: he did not go abroad again until the late summer of 1844.

³ Sarianna Browning, born January 7, 1814, was one year and eight months younger than her brother, who was born on May 7, 1812.

[50 Wimpole Street]
Friday [July 1845]

I send you the order at last ever dearest Miss Mitford, and my parcel must be for another day. Your letter was three times welcome and four times kind—and it is delightful to me to know that your indulgence is so great towards me and mine as to allow you to forgive the character of an *escapade* which with your true and just notions of the filial tie and its duties, must have struck you (if only your instincts worked) as something so blameable and wrong altogether. I told them all what you were likely to think of them!—but *you* are better than my traditions of you, were—and really,—I, for one, feel just as grateful as if I belonged to the criminal body belonging to me. Yes—there is an excess of strictness. Too much is found objectionable. And the result is that everything that *can* be done in an aside, *is* done, without too much consideration perhaps of the right and the wrong. Not that there is the least inclination to an over-wildness—*I* see nothing of such a thing—nothing! But dear Papa's wishes would be consulted more tenderly, if his commands were less straight and absolute. We are all dealt with alike, you know—and *I* do not pretend to more virtue than my peers. Nevertheless I could not, I think, have let that pleasure pay for the pain . . the anxiety and fear . . of the day at White-Knights, . . as they did: and as it was, I was in a complete terror the whole hours of their absence, I do admit to you, . . and in an agony, when our grand Signor's step sounded on the stair just ten minutes before Arabel appeared in my room. It did however all pass

off serenely here—and nobody seems to suffer much from
remorse in consequence of these mysterious pleasures by the
side of the Lodden. 'The lady in the pink bonnet', I understand to be Mrs. Roberts . . who was the wife—the widow . .
of Papa's brother—and who re-married some four or five years
ago, after a two years' wearing of weeds. She is no great
favorite of mine—though I understand that it is ungrateful of
me to say so—and in fact, she has certainly taken one or two
unmistakeable steps towards a sentimental friendship with me,
for which in her relation, I feel myself perfectly unfitted. I
love my uncle's memory too dearly and tenderly for it—and
then she has pretensions, which are not quite claims, to poetry
and German philosophy, and talks of the union of souls as she
ties her ribbands. . . Mr. Roberts I do not know personally—
but he is said to be scientific, and unrefined, as those scientific
men are apt to be—only very much in love still, and fond of
his wife and her baby. . .

Just at present my aunt Mrs. Hedley is staying in the
house with us, and between my two little cousins Ibbit and
Lizzie I am living as among guardian angels. They both of
them choose to love me with a passion—and I tell them that
they will end by making me the vainest person in Christendom.
Such pretty little girls, both of them—and Ibbit, who is only
ten years old, the most enchanting, carressing little creature
under the sun—full of fancy and joy,—and with an overflow
of life which really seems to flow in an electric current down
to the very shining ends of her long golden ringlets. Lizzie
you know, is quietness itself—serene and meek—with a still
deep passive sensibility which rather absorbs than expresses.
Ibbit on the contrary, cant be still a moment, any more than
she can move without grace—her very hair all alive, as I
said, . . and the sense of life kindling and breathing from her
eyes and lips—and the sense of life the same thing with the
sense of *love*,—so passionate she is! It is a picture to see those
children together—and they have nearly kissed my cheeks
and fingers away this morning, dear things!—with their
'dearest Ba's' said one against another. On saturday Ibbit
goes to Brighton with her mother—for a time at least.

I continue to gain strength very much, and surprise people
who see me only at intervals—and if no winter were coming I

should half begin to take courage again. I was in the carriage the other day and got as far into Regent's Park as the bridge, without fainting absolutely—and I can walk about as well as a child of two years old—that is, . . without faltering and tottering too much. Asses milk has done some of the good, and the sun the rest and most of it—and your goodness and affectionateness make me talk of myself in this shameful way!— for I assure you *I never* do it to people in general. . .

Ever dearest Miss Mitford's attached

E B B

[50 Wimpole Street]
Saturday [August 1845]

. . . You are kind too in wishing to see me in my chair— although you made a mistake in fancying before, that I never changed my position from a reclining one. You saw me lying down because I could bear most, talk most, and forget myself easiest in the posture of least exertion,—but I have been in the habit of siting up everyday since I have ceased to be very ill and confined to my bed, you know. Also . . it was a mistake (rather) of yours, when you lamented to Arabel that I liked to shut my windows and live in the dark. But do you know what it is to live in what dear Mr. Kenyon calls 'an empyrean, up two pair of stairs' . . nay, up *three* . . where the windows show nothing but white sky? . . .

And for Eliza Cook [1] . . the shyness as to manners may be remarkable—only it does not, in her case, express any modesty of self-appreciation, or she would not address the public as she has done—and for her position as governess in Alderman Harmer's family . . I am *told* that her position in his family is of a far tenderer, if of a less moral and didactic a character. *That* is the scandal – – *a* scandal, perhaps! I will not answer for it or against it—and you have it as a piece of 'telling', just as it came to me. . .

[1] Eliza Cook (1818–89), popular poetess. Author of *Lays of a Wild Harp* (1835), *Melai, and Other Poems* (1838), etc.; and editor of *Eliza Cook's Journal* (1849–54). Many of her early poems, notably *The Old Arm Chair*, appeared in the *Weekly Dispatch*, a paper of advanced political and religious views, owned by Alderman Harmer, of Ingress Abbey, in Kent.

[*50 Wimpole Street*]
September 1845]

Ever dearest Miss Mitford if I have not written the details
you desire to know, instantly, it has been because really I am
scarcely in possession of them yet, it being undecided between
this next week and the week after, on which day I am likely
to sail. I will tell you however what I can . . and if it is not
much, blame the stars who are shining so doubtfully just now
'tra si e no'.[1]

For the last two or three years I have been so much better
and stronger in the summer and thrown back so hardly in the
winter, that the wisdom and necessity of getting nearer the
sun if I ever meant to live again, in the sense of ordinary life,
was quite obvious to me. Last autumn when my brothers
went to Ægypt, I was on the verge of desiring to go with them.
But in this present summer, better and fitter for travelling
than I ever found myself, and exhorted besides by my aunt
Hedley who saw with her eyes how the change came with the
sun, and how, from a feeble colourless invalid, I strengthened
and brightened as the season advanced . . she, seeing it day
by day ! . . I took the courage necessary for contemplating a
winter passed in the south somewhere—and Malta, I thought
of first. Well, then, Papa wished me to see Chambers and have
his advice—and I sent for him, and was examined with that
dreadful stethescope, and received his command to go without
fail to *Pisa by sea*. He said that it was the obvious thing to do—
and that he not merely advised but enjoined it—that there
was nothing for me but *warm air* . . no other possible remedy.
He thought me comparatively well in certain respects—and
that the malady on the lung was very slight and likely to be
without results if the right precautions were taken—although
I should be careful, as relapse was too possible. The weakness,
he said, came from the action of the cold on the muscular
system covering the lungs, and on the vascular system of the
lungs, which were both very weak and sensitive to changes of
temperature—and he also observed that the general nervous
system was shattered and impaired. You see there is nothing
for me in England during the winter, but to be shut up as I
have been :—and the cold kills me and the seclusion exhausts

me . . and there is no possible alternative here. Also, the cold cannot be shut out so effectually as not to operate injuriously, *for*, said Dr. Chambers, 'you are not to think this, merely nervous weakness—though you are very nervous!—it is in great part from the muscles covering the lungs being affected by the cold air . . and nothing but warm air is a remedy to it'. He left me in great spirits about myself and about what Pisa is to do for me—and I have since heard nothing but good of the place and climate. The sea is to do good too, I understand . . and I am not fearing it in any way. At the same time I am in very doubtful spirits—very agitated and full of sad thoughts . . from many causes on which I cannot enter now. You shall hear from me my ever dearest Miss Mitford, before I leave England—and over the Alps, my letters shall fly by as many a drove as shall be reasonable on considerations of postage. Dr. Chambers named *May* as the earliest time on which he could allow me to think of leaving Pisa—and in the meantime, all who have any kind regret to lose me, must consider that they lose only the sight of my bodily weakness and exhaustion—the sight of me stretched out on that sofa . . and what is *that* worth, to the kindest? Whereas during my absence, I shall be perhaps out of doors every day in an Italian sun . . every day that it does not rain . . and able to think of my friends with gladder if not with fonder thoughts. So do not regret me my very dear kind friend—do not. And (but for the parting and my nervousness now) I should have liked you to have seen me once so as to be able to think of me 'after my own likeness' a little, and not as you have been used to see me lately. Mr. Kenyon has just been persuading me that he never saw me looking so well in his life before!—which if not precisely true, means at least that I am looking much better and more like what I used to be, . . though still tottering and trembling about the room, and growing white with an exertion. And I cannot take the usual means of growing strong, you see—and Chambers persists in desiring that I should live chiefly on milk and vegetables, and eschew the 'strong meats and drinks' of the strong . . which proves that he has some fear of me in the face of his hopes.

I will write dear Mr. Kenyon's address on the flyleaf of my letter—but he is in town only for a day, and you are not likely to find him immediately. This is his time for 'flitting' you know! His goodness and kindness to me have been inexpressible as they are past speaking of,—I cannot *try* to speak of them . . in reference to this Pisa-business. I can only be grateful all the days of my life to him—be the life shorter or longer!

And now, no more. Only you shall hear again. Oh no, no—your affection for me *should not* draw you into such a toil . . even if it were possible for you to go to Italy, which I know it is not. Besides I shall be 'back again in a moment' you know. Ah—but to write lightly when my spirits are as they are . . you do not guess how!

May God bless you—Your E B B.

It is all uncertain about my companions. I hope for too many brothers and sisters perhaps and it is all unsettled. You shall hear.

¹ Although E B B first mentions on July 18, 1845, a plan of sending her to Alexandria or Malta for the winter, it is not until August 30 that there is a discussion of 'the Pisa affair'. By September 3, Dr. Chambers has given his full approval to Pisa: on September 8, there is a discussion of steamers, and first, ominous mention of 'this dead silence of Papa's'. On September 17, E B B writes, 'it is all over with Pisa'. On September 25: 'I have spoken again, and the result is that we are in precisely the same position'. By September 29, cabins and berths have been taken in the Malta steamer for both the 3rd and the 20th of October. On October 14, the whole plan is finally abandoned.

[50 Wimpole Street]
Saturday [September 1845]

Ever dearest Miss Mitford, how I thank you for this pretty *translation* of your thoughts of me—for so I like to consider it. It is the prettiest pen wiper I ever saw. How kind, and how I thank you!

Will you give the five shillings to your gardener—(I enclose the order) and thank him for finding my brother's pin?

And more I would say, but am very much in anxiety and tribulation about Pisa. It is all uncertain whether I shall go or not—and in the meantime I am vexed out of patience.

You see the winter is stooping through the wet and damp

to come nearer to us. But you do not suffer the rheumatic pains, I hope and trust.

Mr. Kenyon's address is 40 York Place, Regent's Park—but you will not find him there, as he has left town for an indefinite time. He has been most kindly anxious about me . . I mean, about sending me off as soon as possible—seeing the wisdom and the propriety—but even such a god could not cut the knot . . which is tightly knotted . . too tightly : and it seems a hard thing to have one's life in one's hand for the best uses of it, and to be forced to drop it again. Well! Write to me of Balzac. If I do not go, I shall be nearer you. I wish I had the least news to tell you in the world, but none comes near me—except that I heard of the digging of the foundations of Miss Martineau's cottage the other day, and of her descanting on Magnetism without any foundations at all.[1] For the rest, she is said to be quite well . . and 'looking quite handsome' to boot. She does not write to me.

Believe in the true affection

of your

E B B

[1] On September 16, 1845, Mrs. Wordsworth wrote to Crabb Robinson that 'yesterday week my husband and I as we passed the 'Descenting [*sic*] Shop' saw your friend as we thought behind that building staking out the foundation for her house, on our return yesterday to our surprize the walls had risen roof high—Surely she must have mesmerized her workmen. . .' (Morley, Vol. II, pp. 608-9.)

[*50 Wimpole Street
Monday October 1845*]

I upbraid myself for not writing to you my ever dearest Miss Mitford—but I have had no heart to write . . no heart . . it is just the word!—for mine has been tossed up and down by sadder thoughts than the mere non-recovery of health could bring me. Let us leave the subject—I cannot talk of it. *I should have gone infallibly*, if it had not been for the apprehension of involving others with me in a series of difficulties . . which (as to *them*), would have constituted my condemnation in my own eyes. As for the good to be desired, I see it as you see it—and perhaps every-one else sees the

same. It is not the *sight* which is awry—not the power of
seeing. I want only the sun—I faint here for lack of the sun :
and it is proved to me that I should be in as good health as
the rest of the world, if I could have the two things together,
warmth and air. But this shutting up you see, which is necessary to prevent the tendency to organic disease of the lungs,
shatters the nervous system—and the alternative of either evil
is inevitable while I live in this climate. I feel like a bird in a
cage . . inclined to dash myself against the bars of my prison—
but God is good, and counter-motives have been given to me
in moments of the greatest bitterness, sufficient for encourage-
ment. So I live on—'bide my time'—only without the slightest
expectation, my loved friend, of the results you speak of from
the quarter you look to—no! In fact, nothing could ever
induce me to appeal again, on any personal ground whatever,
to that quarter. It is from no want of frankness . . this
reticence to you . . and you will be the first to understand
the respect of my silence. So let us leave the subject for what
is pleasant—for I shall see you . . shall I not? Any day, this
week even, I shall be delighted to see you—any day after
tomorrow, tuesday. Begin from wednesday, and go on. Only
it is too bad to think of bringing you so far through the cold—
but I let your kindness have its way. Only again, I suddenly
think that you may be retained by prudential motives—
because one of my brothers has been ill with fever of a typhoid
character (not absolutely typhus) and though now convalescent,
and able to leave his bed and take soups and strengthening
things I know what a sound typhus must have [in] your ears.
Yet the medical men have been of opinion throughout that no
harm was to be apprehended for visitors at the house—and
my other brothers who sate up, night after night, with the
poor invalid, have been and are perfectly well—I tell you in
any case : judge for yourself . . and in the case of the least
fear, do not come. You will find me (if you do) still off the
sofa, and able to walk about—only not looking quite as
flourishing as I really did in the summer—a little fagged (as
must needs be) with all the heart-bruising! And I shall
struggle not to sink this winter,—and if it is a mild winter . .
ah, well!—all this is with God. And the *wound* is apart from
it, . . apart from the mere *health*, and to be unaffected by it.

259

May God help me!—my reeds have run into me from all sides almost . . yet still I cling!

Everyday for a week I have reproached Wilson at set of sun for forgetting to send you oysters—but what with illness in the house and change of servants, her memory has really been overburdened. You shall have them today or tomorrow.

Balzac's 'Paysans' in its one volume, (for *I* have seen only that one volume) is another proof of the purpose of the times towards sympathies with the people. And a new work by George Sand 'Le Meunier d'Angibault' goes the same way, but with diminished power certainly. Her hand grows cold when she extends it from the chair. And *he* – – why he is Balzac still in 'Les Paysans'—but story there is none, and so no interest—and no unity, as far as that first volume indicates : and I found it rather hard reading, . . despite the human character, and the scenic effects. As to 'Le Juif' I have done with him, and am not sorry to have done. The last volumes fall off step by step. Now is it not true that when people determine professedly to be didactic, immediately they grow dull as school-masters? it seems so to me. V Hugo is a true poet.

Mr. Horne is busy, it appears,—but I had a few lines from him the other day.

Well—you will write in any case.

And I am ever your affectionate

E B B

[*50 Wimpole Street*]
Friday [*November 21, 1845*]

Day by day I have had my heart *almost* in my pen to write to you, ever dearest Miss Mitford, and the sun sets somewhere behind the fog without my doing it. The obstacle has been the thought of the 'list of books' which was to be wrung from my reluctant memory—but write I *must* today let the memoirs be ever so un-come-at-able . . and I write. Have you seen (to make amends) a work of Balzac, 'late St. Aubin' says the title page, called 'L'Israelite'? It is not *new* of course—and I have nothing good or bad to say of it, but it is just sent to me

from the library, and 'my heart leaps up' . . as hearts of
the innocent do at the rainbow, you know . . .

Have you read Pomfret? [1] . . . I hold it to be the most
successful work of imagination produced by Mr. Chorley, . .
only *not* precisely a *strong* book. He wants sustaining and
developing power. But it is a good true and natural book—
and I like the noiseless unassuming acting out of the 'private
judgement', without any rustling of silks and stamping of
cothurns. . .

The amateur comedy was crowned with success—the
theatre, crowded, and every seat, equally in boxes and gallery,
went for a guinea—and Mr. Foster [*sic*] and Dickens were
admirable, the cry is on all sides.[2] There is to be another
performance . . of the Alchymist it is supposed, . . for the
benefit of Miss Kelly. You know that 'Every man in his
humour' was played this last time and the time before. Yes—
and the next news is, that Boz the universal is on the threshold
of an immense undertaking . . no less a one than the editing of
a newspaper, a daily newspaper, to represent ultra politics at
the *right end* . . anti-corn law interests and the like.[3] It is
said that some twentyfive thousand pounds have been sub-
scribed to the speculation by great capitalists, and that seven
first rate reporters have been engaged for three years at the
rate of seven guineas a week : also that the newspaper is to
combine literature with politics as in the French journals.
What do you think of this ? Is Dickens fit for it ?

My next news is that Mrs. Butler arrived in England some
ten days ago with the intention of assisting her father in the
readings by which he is making sixty guineas a week,—but
was followed so closely by a letter . . from her *husband*, the
conjecture goes,—some letter of influence . . that she changed
her mind and is about to go back straight to the land of stripes
(according to the scandal) and stars undramatic ! [4]

Then Mrs. Jameson is said to be in London after her
wanderings in Germany and Italy. I have not seen her yet.

How much news (for *me* !) I have sent you today. Methinks
I deserve a letter back again. Mr. Browning has published a
new 'Bell and Pomegranate' . . a new number, . . full of
power and various and original faculty, . . on which Landor
has addressed him in some beautiful verses, worthy, I think, of

the praised and the praiser.[5] Though you are an unbeliever
I shall write them down for you underneath. See.

'There is delight in singing, though none hear
Beside the singer; and there is delight
In praising though the praiser sit alone
And see the praised far off him, far above.
Shakespeare is not our poet but the *world's*,
Therefore on him no speech, and short for thee
Browning!—Since Chaucer was alive and hale
No man hath walked along our roads with step
So active, so inquiring eye, or tongue
So varied in discourse. But warmer climes
Give brighter plumage, stronger wing: the breeze
Of Alpine heights thou playest with, borne on
Beyond Sorrento and Amalfi, where
The Siren waits thee, singing song for song.'

W. S. Landor

After which I say goodbye. Your ever affectionate E B B.

[1] *Pomfret: or Public Opinion and Private Judgement*, a novel by H. F. Chorley,
was published in 1845.

[2] On September 20, 1845, Charles Dickens, with his friends Forster,
Cruikshank, Cattermole, Jerrold, Lemon, etc., put on Ben Jonson's comedy,
Every Man in His Humour, at Miss Kelly's theatre, the Royalty. On November 15 the performance was repeated in aid of Dr. Southwood Smith's nursing
home in Devonshire Terrace.

[3] This was the *Daily News*, the first number of which appeared on January
21, 1846.

[4] Fanny Kemble, daughter of Charles Kemble, married an American
planter, Pierce Butler, in 1834. There was a divorce in 1848.

[5] *Dramatic Romances and Lyrics*, 'Bells and Pomegranates', No. VII, was
published on November 6, 1845. The verses which Landor had sent to
Browning were forwarded by Browning to Moxon soon after he received
them. A copy was in EBB's hands on November 20. On November 22
they were printed in the *Morning Chronicle*. 'The *Chronicle* was through Moxon,
I believe', Browning wrote to EBB on November 23. (*Love Letters*, Vol. I,
p. 298.)

[*50 Wimpole Street*
January or February 1846]

MY EVER DEAREST MISS MITFORD,

I want to hear how you are, and feel immodest in asking,
seeing that I ought to have written to you some days ago.

This weather which makes me safe from all reverses, is trying, people say, to the majority . . and you in your kindness and goodness are over-active for others and forgetful of precaution for yourself. Tell me how you are—and how your patient is. Just *that* system was tried upon me . . precisely *that* . . with the exception of the talking part of the process . . every attempt at talking aloud being followed by cough and spitting of blood with me, so that I was scolded everytime I opened my lips. But the rest was tried and failed . . in fact, did me infinite harm. My poor cousin died under it at Cheltenham. [Word illegible] there is a difference of constitutions, and with some patients the success has been very decided. May the restoration of your friend justify it to the uttermost in the present case!

And not a word of coming to London? Shall I not see you soon . . really? You surprised me by speaking of the bazaar as passed—I fancied it would not take place till the spring. And you wrote no story? Tell me, dear friend. Tell me too if you have seen the Daily News and if you abuse it as I do . . I who expected the laying down of broad principles, and found nothing but a wedge-face set against the falling Corn Law. Vexed and disappointed I was. Corn law is a favorite abuse just now—but there are other abuses, I fear, scarcely less stringent . . and there is a deep root under all. Mr. Kenyon calls me 'impracticable' . . or *did* before he went to Dover a few days ago . . but, impracticable or not, I see no objection to being philosophical and reasonable—do *you*? He was in the House during Sir Robert's recantation, and called it 'the finest thing he ever heard'.[1] There was very evident emotion, repressed just enough . . and a predominant appearance of conviction and resolution to be true to perceived principles, which was grand of its kind and very effective. D'Israeli's was a mere baying of the moon in comparison, with all his talent.

And now I want to ask you. Have you ever seen Madame Laffarge's memoires?[2]—and will you read them and let me have your impression of her guilt or innocence. They have made a very painful impression on me . . very—and I cannot believe her, having read all, to be a guilty woman—I cannot. Do read them. The look into the state of French society, especially in the provinces, will repay you, if you get no better result. I would give much to know what life that wretched woman is made to lead in the correctional prison, of which there is no account. I think the pillory and the marking were remitted penalties. But an accomplished woman accustomed to the luxuries of life, brought so low, . . and the case so dreadfully doubtful! Also these volumes will illustrate by a terrible light your great doctrine concerning the marriage of convenience . . which I, for my part, consider *legal* prostitution, —just that and no more—not *moral* prostitution, by any means. . .

May God bless you, dearest friend! Be well and happy— and say if I have a chance of seeing you?

Your ever affectionate

E B B

¹ Queen Victoria, on January 23, 1846, wrote to congratulate Peel on 'his beautiful and indeed *unanswerable* speech of last night'. (*Letters of Queen Victoria*, Vol. II, p. 86.)

² *Mémoires de Marie Cappelle, veuve Lafarge: par elle-même* (1841–42). In August 1839, Lafarge, a widower, married, despite great reluctance on her part, a young orphan, Marie Cappelle. Some months later Marie was brought to trial, accused of administering arsenic to her husband. She was found 'guilty with extenuating circumstances', and sentenced to hard labour for life.

[50 Wimpole Street
February 1846]

. . . Madme Laffarge's case does not, I admit, fulfil your conditions of the mariage de convenance—there was no 'esteem'—no personal knowledge whatever. Still, if you retreat no farther than to 'esteem', I differ with you by the width of the whole world. Esteem and affection are conditions of friendship—but place marriage with its full significance, in the conditions of friendship . . and the position becomes hideous, revolting—for Madme Laffarge could scarcely have been better off, if she had 'esteemed' to the uttermost. Oh surely you see! At any moment of my past life I would have deliberately preferred a leap down a precipice to a marriage with the best and greatest of mankind whom I did not love in the sense of *love*. *Marriage in the abstract*, has always seemed to me the most profoundly indecent of all ideas—and I never could make out how women, mothers and daughters, could talk of it as of setting up in trade, . . as of a thing to be done. That life may go on smoothly upon a marriage of convenience, simply proves to my mind that there is a defect in the sensibility and the delicacy, and an incapacity for the higher happiness of God's sanctifying. Now think and see if this is not near the truth. I have always been called romantic for this way of seeing, but never repented that it was *my* way, nor shall. . .

[*50 Wimpole Street*]
Tuesday [*May 12, 1846*]

My dearest Miss Mitford I must pray to hear a little more of you, besides what you have written. How are you?—and how are you managing about your maid? Has she left you— and have you the prospect of another? and do you think at all *about coming to London*? I have been expecting day by day to hear from you, and, now that the letter comes, here is not a word of you except as to your connection with Dumas, which is too distant to please me, let him have ever so much, as you say, of other merit. For the rest, I am glad that you are at work—but I do not like *Amaury* . . it is dreadfully heavy, it appears to me. Of Dumas generally, I do not think particularly lowly. He has a great deal of talent and writes most amusing books—I like him in his way, very much. His 'Guerre des femmes', a late work of his on the Ligue wars, made me weep like a thunder cloud—but I dont think I have cried over another of his books. Do not set me down as a despiser of Dumas. And do you select the decent ones?—or what is the test? [1] Do you venture to leave out passages? Answer or do not answer those questions . . I leave them to your generosity—but *do* say how you are—because the knowledge of *that* is a matter of necessity with me.

For me, I have been out once or twice or thrice in the carriage—and yesterday was tempted to get out and feel the grass under my feet in the Regent's Park. It was a pure and strange feeling of pleasure. Very well I am of course, with the sun and nearing summer. I put on my summer looks, you know, as people do the fashions.

And I am glad that Mr. Buckingham has gone, since he was to go—for you seemed to me nervous and fearful over-much.[2] When *I* go, my very dear friend, it shall not be to America—I am faithful to the Mediterranean. Only, while the summer lasts England satisfies me. Even the Regent's Park where I was yesterday, looked to me like a region of Arcady, . . the trees and the grass, saturated with their green sunlight! I put both my feet on the grass—I gathered it with my hands—I laid it against my lips. Such a strange pleasure, it was. And so beautiful as a scene! You blaspheme against our London-country, through not knowing what manner of country we have.

Today Mrs. Jameson has been here. I like her increasingly, —and she is quite affectionate in her goodness to me. Now, she has two books in the press . . her work on Art, of which, extracts appeared in the Athenaeum, and a volume of miscellaneous essays.[3] Dear Mr. Kenyon has gone away in haste and sorrow to Portsmouth, on account of the dangerous illness of his friend Commodore Jones.

Is there news? No. Yet I hear distantly that Mr. Dilke is about to take the ruin of the 'Daily News', and set it up again at $2^{d\frac{1}{2}}$ . . on the Parisian plan. I hear too that Tennyson is in London, standing godfather to Dickens's child—who is christened *Alfred D'Orsay Tennyson*, so as to be half a poet and half a . . '*paletot*'! Do you approve?

Ever your affectionate E B B

[1] Miss Mitford was editing a volume for children of selections from the works of Alexandre Dumas.

[2] Miss Mitford's friend, Mr. Buckingham, had been 'ordered by his medical adviser' to 'spend four or five successive months on the sea'.

[3] Thirteen extracts from Mrs. Jameson's *Sacred and Legendary Art* appeared in the *Athenaeum* between January 11 and December 20, 1845. Her *Memoirs and Essays* was reviewed in the *Athenaeum* on June 27, 1846.

[50 Wimpole Street]
Thursday [June 1846]

I am delighted to have your letter, ever dearest Miss Mitford,—for my patience was gasping for breath, and certainly if I had not received it *just then*, you would have been dunned for it forthwith. On the whole, too, it is a good pleasant letter, and satisfies me about your maid—though, I, who am ambitious for you, should have liked a more *accomplished* person than you describe—still, good temper, good principle and simplicity are excellent things in their way. . .

Why, Mr. Buckingham has lingered indeed! I am glad he is off at last, and hopeful that you may have good news of him when he has lived long enough on the sea. As for me, I am flourishing more and more, and really am as well as possible when I keep quiet and do not overwork myself. This is my time for *living*, you know, . . this summer-time—and none of your roses (may they pardon the profane comparison!) bud and blow faster than I do. You see, the miracle of last winter kept me from my annual descent—and so, I rise now from last year's level. I was told yesterday by somebody who had not seen me since my illness, that I look rather better than I did *then* . . *before it*! . . which sounds 'un peu fort'—but the truth is that I am surprisingly well. Every morning, if I do not go in a carriage, I walk out . . to the bookseller's at the corner of the street, there to rest and turn—and I have been in the carriage to Hampstead without suffering. Still, you know, I do not set up for *strength*, exactly—and I am forced to take precautions and cultivate myself rigidly . . i.e. with more care than I am worth—for a sharp winter would undo me again . . of that, I am aware perfectly. Ah well,—let the winters go! Who would talk of winter, with the summer round them? Such an exquisite summer too! I feel it in my soul, do you know. I have had a heavy life, so far . . but perhaps God means to give me a little compensation even in this world. You, in the meanwhile, lament about the heat, and I will grant to you that *during three days*, when the thermometer stood in this room at *eighty*, I did call for the winds and the dews and every modification of impossible coolness. Only, however, during those three days. On every day beside, I was glad, and grateful . . I hope . . it is an exquisite summer. You who have the trees to fan you, . . how can you be too hot? But *being* too hot, how good of you and dear of you, to be glad of the heat for *me*? I thank you, dearest kindest friend!

Mr. Horne was only a week in London and left it without

writing more to me than the little note announcing his arrival.
Mr. Dilke has the Daily News, and Mr. Horne serves under his
government—which surprises me considerably. Mr. Went-
worth Dilke, the son, takes the Athenaeum, which grows
duller and duller, fainter and fainter, it seems to me. Dickens
is in Switzerland . . for a year. Mrs. Jameson goes to Italy
in the autumn. The Countess Hahn Hahn[1] is in London.
Our other visitor Ibrahim,[2] was dissuaded, I hear, with the
whole power and might of the French language, from risking
his delicate health in our 'horrible climate' :—this, at Paris—
he comes, and finds our thermometers at eighty. Instead of
being chilled to death, he is nearly broiled. Which is too
intense a surprise to be quite a pleasant one, perhaps.

Your Dumas, I hope you know, has been writing a more
than usually amusing book in his Comte de Monte Cristo. It
kept me afloat through the three hot days, and, though as
improbable as possible, I owe it none the less thankfulness for
some hours of dreamy amusement. He is an excellent story-
teller—and if I were a Sultana, as Sultanas used [?] to be, I
would give him a corner of the divan and a golden cup, and
never think of cutting his head off. As to the difference between
good and evil, he does not know it—but he knows his right
hand from his left . . he is a clever fellow. Nearer, he is,
upon the whole, to Alexander the Great, than to Alexander the
coppersmith—so vive Alexander! Mind you read Monte
Cristo—particularly, if you are too hot. I recommend Monte
Cristo . . taken between glasses of lemonade.

And now, I suppose, you begin to hold your drawing rooms
and levees—the strawberry beds do not ripen in vain for all
the neighbourhood round. Yet let nobody tire you, dearest
Miss Mitford—keep from your superfluities of hospitality . . I
am afraid for you, almost. For our part, we are going to have
a whole army of aunts, uncles, cousins and cousinets, down
upon us from Paris and other places—and almost I am
frightened at the prospect. A cousin of mine, Mrs. Hedley's
eldest daughter, is going to be married to Mr. Bevan, a younger
brother of the great Brewer—and there is to be anticipated a
press in ipimus, of the pressissimust, as they all come to England
for the nonce.

Write to me . . do . . and tell me all of yourself. It is

wise of you, of course, not to *tempt* the heat, since you suffer from it. Love me, in the meanwhile, not *coolly*.

Your affectionate as ever

E B B

¹ Gräfin Ida Hahn-Hahn, the one-eyed author of *The Countess Faustina* (1844), *Letters from the Orient* (1845), etc., arrived in England in the company of a male friend, one Oberst Bystram—'the ugliest pair of adulterers', according to Samuel Rogers, that 'he had ever had in his house'. (*Monckton Milnes*, Pope-Hennessy, p. 224.)

² Ibrahim Pasha, son of Mahomet Ali, arrived in London on June 6, 1846. 'Lord Aberdeen has taken the principal suites of rooms at Mivarts Hotel, Brook Street, for Ibrahim Pasha and his followers . . . Already the prudery of our Englishwomen has taken alarm at the possibility of his harem, or any portion of it accompanying the Prince. Declarations have been made that not all the persuasions of Lord Aberdeen will induce the matron of a certain hotel to receive beneath her roof any of these Eastern beauties.' (*Daily News*, June 6, 1846.) On July 16, after a strenuous programme, taking aboard with him a new set of false teeth and some domestic fowls, His Highness left for Alexandria 'greatly delighted with the *beau monde* and the attention he had received during his stay. The English of distinction disposed to visit Egypt may, he has repeatedly said, count on a kind reception from him.' (*Daily News*, July 16, 1846.)

[50 Wimpole Street]
Monday [July 6, 1846]

How I thank you my very dear kindest of friends, for writing me out the verses by Mr. Horne.¹ And they are nobly true, and touchingly true—I felt them deeply :—and now tell me if any other but a generous and feeling man could have written that poem as it stands!—(*let* it be fair in me to turn on yourself the weapon with which your own hand has furnished me) They are good and deep words, in truth, and a worthy testimony of an artistic nature on such a subject—oh, it affected me very much.

And poor, poor Haydon! Mr. Kenyon came here yesterday to tell me that he has left a paper which it will not be *advisable* to publish on this point of the subscription, a very curious paper, entering into the motives of his last deed,—with a profession of faith in christian doctrine—a very curious paper. And he says in it among other things, that he leaves to *me* all his private papers, with a desire that they should pass from my hands into Longman's. Mr. Forster ² asked Mr.

269

Kenyon to make this communication to me. Naturally I could only be touched by such an apparent proof of confidence, where he might have selected some personal friend of more experience and ability—but, on consideration, I do think, and said to Mr. Kenyon so, that he probably referred only to the fact of their being in my hands, these papers,—pointed to me as the actual holder of them.[3] Only it must of course depend on the wording of the paper which I have not seen yet. I am not any wise a competant editor of what I understand to be twenty six volumes of memoirs. I know nothing of the times treated of—of the persons referred to—and that province of Art is not one with which I am familiar at all. Can it be that with so many friends full of experience . . competant to the uttermost, . . he should have meant to give *me* such work to do?—for, observe, that not merely an *editor* is wanted, but a laborious and skilful editor. Now I have not even seen his pictures . . except in such sketches as he has sent me—and he could have chosen, surely, some one artistically competent, and for the rest, nearer his age, and mixed up with his times. Then a friend of mine suggests that, just *because I am ignorant* and, so, unprejudiced, he may have selected me. Uneasy I am you may suppose. Tell me what you think of all this.

But first, first, do believe of me that I am grateful beyond words for your dear goodness in coming to give me all the pleasure I had from your visit—so good you are, so kind![4] You gave me some happy hours, and if I forgot half of what I wanted to say to you, it was rather leapt over than stept aside from . . leapt over with some other thing said or listened to in a gladness as great. How kind of you to drop into my lap such a heap of golden hours! That you did not suffer . . did not grow poor by having given them to me . . doubles their price to me. Thank you my dear dear friend.

Since you went I seem to have been tossed about from aunt to cousin, from cousin to aunt, like Sancho Panza in his blanket. The bones of my spirits (oh happy metaphor!) ache a good deal already. Also the Hedleys arrive on thursday, and there is to be a great marriage festival at the end of July or beginning of august, which shall shake the foundations of the earth. Long I have fancied that they were not fixed altogether securely,—and now—. What nonsense one gets to write. . .

My aunt who has spent three successive winters in Paris, knows less of it than we two do. The English live in their English quarter in the manner of the Jews at Rome, knowing nothing, seeing nothing, answering nothing. All that roaring literature goes off in their ears, as a minute gun near a deaf man. How singular it seems to me! Better it is (of the twain) to live in England and read Balzac. Tell me of your Dumas as soon as ever you have news.

Dearest friend, here is an end today to my letter! I will take care of the basket, and let you have it when I can find something to put into it.

As for the jam . . you should let me exercise my faith. Perhaps at last I may learn to believe that you really did make it . . with the help of a preserving angel.

Your ever affectionate and grateful

E B B

¹ B. R. Haydon committed suicide on June 22, 1846. Verses entitled *To the Memory of B. R. Haydon By the Author of 'Orion'* appeared in the *Daily News* on June 29, 1846.

² John Forster (1812–76), biographer of Goldsmith, Landor, and Dickens, whose pompous and officious manner caused Thornton Hunt to nickname him 'The Beadle of the Universe', and Dickens to portray him as Mr. Podsnap in *Our Mutual Friend*.

³ At the end of June 1843, Haydon had asked E B B to store for him at Wimpole Street several boxes containing personal papers and manuscripts.

⁴ Cf. E B B's remark to Browning on July 1, 1846. 'Well!—and to-morrow morning Miss Mitford comes to spend the day like the dear kind friend she is; and I, not the least in the world glad to see her!' (*Love Letters*, Vol. II, p. 288.)

[50 Wimpole Street]
Monday morning [September 14, 1846]

My dearest friend, With many wishes rushing on to reach [?] you, I could not write as you desired directly, to fix about wednesday. A sudden command to be ready to leave this house for six weeks or two months, while it is being cleaned and painted, rendered it quite uncertain whether we should be here *today even*—or tuesday or wednesday therefore, of course.¹ We now pause, simply because of a difficulty as to lodginghouses,—a difficulty which seems to bend or break,—Tunbridge Wells offering what are considered suitable resources.

Under the circumstances . . and under *others*, influenced by them, . . of which I will speak to you, dearest Miss Mitford, in a short time, . . I write with pain to ask you to defer the visit. It seems best. My heart is full when I think of seeing you, after I have made room for you (if I could contrive it) on the sunniest half of one of these uncertain days. I have a great deal to tell you, to entreat your sympathy for—your indulgence even, perhaps.

In the meanwhile do, do write and let me hear what you mean when you seem to refer to something painful. May I not hear? As *you* shall, at length, presently. Do try to love me always, and let me be in every case and place, as in this haste,

Your affectionate and grateful

E B B

¹ On Wednesday night, September 9, 1846, EBB wrote in haste to inform Browning of the decision of Mr. Moulton Barrett to send his family out of town as soon as possible, while number fifty was cleaned and repainted. As a result of this emergency Elizabeth Barrett and Robert Browning were secretly married on the following Saturday, September 12, 1846.

[50 Wimpole Street]
Friday [September 18, 1846]

My dearest friend   I have your letter, and your prophesy,— and the latter meets the event like a sword ringing into its scabbard. My dear dearest friend I would sit down by your feet and kiss your hands with many tears, and beseech you to think gently of me, and love me always, an⬤ ave faith in me that I have struggled to do the right and the generous and not the selfish thing,—though when you read this letter I shall have given to one of the most gifted and admirable of men, a wife unworthy of him. I shall be the wife of Robert Browning. Against *you*,—in allowing you no confidence . . I have not certainly sinned, I think—so do not look at me with those reproachful eyes. I have made no confidence to any . . not even to my and his beloved friend Mr. Kenyon—and this advisedly, and in order to spare him the anxiety and the responsibility. It would have been a wrong against him and against you to have told either of you—we are in peculiar circumstances—and to have made you a party, would have exposed you to the whole dreary rain—without the shelter *we* had. If I had loved you less—dearest Miss Mitford, I could have told you sooner.

And now . . oh, will you be hard on me?—will you say . . 'This is not well'?

I tell you solemnly that nothing your thoughts can suggest against this act of mine, has been unsuggested by *me* to *him*. He has loved me for nearly two years, and said so at the begining. I would not listen. I could not believe even. And he has said since, that almost he began to despair of making me believe in the force and stedfastness of his attachment. Certainly I conceived it to be a mere poet's fancy . . an illusion of a confusion between the woman and the poetry. I have seen a little of the way of men in such respects, and I could not see beyond that with my weary, weeping eyes, for long.

How can I tell you on this paper, even if my hands did not tremble as the writing shows, how he persisted and overcame me with such letters, and such words, that you might tread on me like a stone if I had not given myself to him, heart and soul. When I bade him see that I was bruised and broken . . unfit for active duties, incapable of common pleasures . . that I had lost even the usual advantages of youth and good spirits— his answer was, 'that with himself also the early freshness of youth had gone by, and that, throughout his season of youth, he had loved no woman at all, nor had believed himself made for any such affection—that he loved now once and forever—he, knowing himself. That, for my health, . . he had understood, on first seeing me, that I suffered from an accident on the spine of an incurable nature, and that he never could hope to have me stand up before him. He bade me tell him, what, if that imagination had been true, what there was in that truth, calculated to suppress any pure attachment, such as he professed for me? For his part, the wish of his heart had been *then*—that by consenting to be his wife even so, I would admit him to the single priviledge of sitting by my side two hours a day, as a brother would : he deliberately preferred the realisation of *that dream* to the brightest, excluding me, in this world or any other.'

My dear friend, feel for me. It is to your woman's nature that I repeat these words, that they may commend themselves to you and teach you how *I* must have felt in hearing them—*I* who loved Flush for not hating to be near me . . I, who by a long sorrowfulness and solitude, had sunk into the very ashes of selfhumiliation. Think how I must have felt to have listened to such words from such a man. A man of genius and of miraculous attainments . . and of a heart and spirit beyond them all!

He overcame me at last. Whether it was that an unusual alikeness of mind or (the high and the low may be alike in the general features) . . a singular closeness of sympathy on a thousand subjects, . . drew him fast to me—or whether it was *love simple* . . which after all is *love proper* . . an unreasonable instinct, accident . . 'falling', as the idiom says . . the truth became obvious that he would be happier with me than apart from me—and I . . why I am only as any other woman in the world, with a heart belonging to her. He is best, noblest. If you knew him, *you* should be the praiser.

I have seen him only and openly in this house, observe—*never elsewhere*, except in the parish church before the two necessary witnesses. We go to Italy . . to Pisa—cross to Havre from Southampton . . pass quickly along the Seine, and through Paris to Orleans—till we are out of hearing of the dreadful sounds behind. An escape from the winter will keep me well and still strengthen me—and in the summer we come back . . if any one in the world will receive us. We go to live a quiet, simple, natural life—to do work 'after the pattern in the Mount' which we both see . . to write poems and read books, and try to live not in vain and not for vanities.

In the meanwhile, it is in anguish of heart that I think of leaving this house *so*. Oh—a little thread might have bound my hands, from ever working at my own happiness. But all the love came from *that side*!—on the other – – too still it was— not with intention . . I do not say so—yet too still. I was a woman and shall be a wife when you read this letter. It is finished, the struggle is.

As to marriage . . it never was high up in my ideal, even before my illness brought myself so far down. A happy marriage was the happiest condition, I believed vaguely—but *where were the happy marriages*? I, for my part, never could have married a common man—and never did any one man whom I have had the honour of hearing talk love, as men talk, lead me to think a quarter of a minute of the possibility of being married by such an one. Then I thought always that a man whom *I* could love, would never stoop to love me. That was my way of thinking, years ago, in my best days, as a woman's days are counted—and often and often have I been gently upbraided for such romantic fancies—for expecting the grass underfoot to be sky blue, and for not taking Mr. A or B or C for the 'best possible' whatever might be.

We shall not be rich—but we shall have enough to live out our views of life—and fly from the winters in Italy.

I write on calmly to you. How little this paper represents what is working within in the intervals of a sort of *stupour*.

Feel for me if not with me my dear dear friend. *He* says that we shall justify in our lives this act,—which may and must appear to many . . as *I* say . . wilful and rash. People will say that he is mad, and I, *bad*—with my long traditions and associations with all manner of sickness. Yet God judges, who sees the root of things. And I believe that no woman with a heart, could have done otherwise . . much otherwise. You do not know *him*.

May God bless you—I must end. Try to think of me gently—and if you can bear to write to me, let me hear . . at Orleans—Poste Restante.

Here is the truth—I *could not* meet you and part with you now, face to face.

Tell me of Mr. Buckingham—I shall be as faithful as ever to anything you will tell me. Why that man must be a wretched villainous [?] man—after your [word illegible] goodness to him ! [Two words illegible.]

May God bless you my dear dear kind friend—

Your most affectionate

E B B

Wilson goes with me of course. And the [word illegible] with the last commission [?] She has Rolandi for you. God bless you

INDEX